The Becoming of Age

The Becoming of Age

*Cinematic Visions of Mind,
Body and Identity in Later Life*

PAMELA H. GRAVAGNE

McFarland & Company, Inc., Publishers
Jefferson, North Carolina, and London

LIBRARY OF CONGRESS CATALOGUING-IN-PUBLICATION DATA

Gravagne, Pamela H., 1946–
    The becoming of age : cinematic visions of mind, body and identity in later life / Pamela H. Gravagne.
    p.   cm.
    Includes bibliographical references and index.
    Includes filmography

    ISBN 978-0-7864-7260-4
    softcover : acid free paper ∞

    1. Aging in motion pictures.   I. Title.
PN1995.9.A433G83 2013
791.43084'6—dc23   2013012820

BRITISH LIBRARY CATALOGUING DATA ARE AVAILABLE

© 2013 Pamela H. Gravagne. All rights reserved

No part of this book may be reproduced or transmitted in any form or by any means, electronic or mechanical, including photocopying or recording, or by any information storage and retrieval system, without permission in writing from the publisher.

On the cover: Clint Eastwood in *Gran Torino*, 2008 (Warner Bros./Photofest); background image © 2013 Shutterstock

Manufactured in the United States of America

McFarland & Company, Inc., Publishers
  Box 611, Jefferson, North Carolina 28640
  www.mcfarlandpub.com

For Rob

Table of Contents

Preface 1
Introduction 3

1. Understanding and Theorizing Aging and Old Age 11
2. Masculinities and the Narrative of Decline 37
3. The Silence and Invisibility of Older Women 65
4. Intimacy and Desire in Later Life 94
5. The Cultural Work of Alzheimer's 131
6. Age as Becoming 158

Chapter Notes 187
Bibliography 193
Index 201

Preface

The ideas I present in this book have developed from one basic premise: that the pictures we paint of growing older and the stories we tell about aging and old age matter. They matter not only in the sense that they influence the way we think about our lives, but also in the sense that they shape the very material stuff of our bodies and their relationship to the rest of the material world. Rather than reflecting some essential "truth" about aging and old age that exists independently from the ways we represent it, I argue that these pictures and stories matter because they actually constitute both our understanding and our lived experience of what it means to grow older — our becoming of age.

The intellectual and experiential implications of this premise are profound, affecting everything from the structure of our social, political, and economic institutions to the organization of our personal lives. To take them into account requires a significant shift in the way we think about, measure, and attribute meaning to growing older. In order to foster this shift in thinking, in this book I promote a critical engagement with the pictures and stories of aging and old age we see and hear in contemporary popular film that will make transparent the power of these representations to shape the trajectory and quality of our lives. By offering a systematic yet flexible way to evaluate to what extent a film participates in the portrayal of aging, from a predictable and homogenous experience to a more ambiguous and intangible process of becoming, I hope to open up the ways we depict and describe the aging experience to conscious critique and revision.

By consciously and deliberately examining the pictures we draw and the tales we tell about growing older, and by seeing them in their historical and philosophical context, we can expose the largely negative physical, psychological, social, cultural, and material effects our present constructions of aging and old age have on our lives. And by taking responsibility

Preface

for how our constructions of aging and old age work to constrain the lives of the old, lives that often already exceed the model, we can begin to imagine, picture, and tell about other ways to age. Ultimately, this shift in thinking may lead us to use the power of popular film to actively and creatively draw pictures and tell stories about aging and old age that will reintegrate this time of life into the becoming that characterizes life at any age.

I wish to thank Jake Kosek for first encouraging me to take the study of aging seriously; Peg Cruikshank, Leni Marshall, Erin Lamb, Aagje Swinnen, and many other friends for keeping me going on what at times seemed like an impossible task; Vera Norwood for her patience and support while I worked through many of the ideas contained in this book; and especially my family, Rob, Ian, Amy, Stephen, and Anthony, who, along with me, have learned to see the world through an age-tinted glass.

Introduction

As I think back on what inspired me to write this book, my Grandma Alice always comes to mind. Although she was a rather diminutive woman when seen next to her 6' 4" husband and her forest of long-legged children and grandchildren, no one ever called her small. Even when my grandfather died suddenly in his late 60's from an infection he contracted while at the hospital, her very presence was the model of large and solid, of propriety, of always knowing how to behave and what to do. She was one of my rocks, a model for how life was supposed to unroll, which in my mind at the time, probably conformed fairly closely to the narrative of aging as decline. That is, until Ralph reentered the picture.

Ralph, an older single man, longtime friend of the family, and former business partner in my grandpa's glove factory, came to visit one day a few years after my grandfather's death. Gallantly offering my Grandma Alice his hand, he asked her to walk with him, openly admiring her still shapely legs as she stood and smoothed her dress. The look of resistance, embarrassment, and pleasure — of not quite knowing how to behave and what to do — that crossed her face as she stepped outside and closed the door has remained with me to this day. With only that wordless glance, my grandma, then not much older than I am now, managed to create a connection between us that made me understand that old age and youth are entangled with each other in ways that continually frustrate either's attempt to frame a place that is safe from what the other may seem to represent. By openly and unselfconsciously defying any expectations I might have harbored concerning the proper "doing" of age, Grandma Alice quite neatly exposed the arbitrary nature of the narratives and performatives that bind the old to fictional aged identities.

Because I was caught unaware, without time to marshal my age-related defenses, I began, in my own way, to question the essence of old — not the facts of physical or cognitive change, or the reality of death, but

Introduction

the idea that there is a natural old body and a predetermined story that goes along with its appearance. Seeing the way Grandma Alice and Ralph courted that summer, the girlish way she smiled and flirted, and the way she winked at me whenever Ralph came round, made me realize that all of life is full of endings that are also beginnings, a realization that continues to play a part in the way I approach both my own aging and the way I study age. Although I certainly didn't know it at the time, that picture I carry of my grandma as she closed the door and stepped out with Ralph into a new and uncertain world, was also the first step in the formulation of the questions that drive most of my scholarship: "What is age?" and "What kinds of difference does age really make anyway?"

The first chapter of this book, "Understanding and Theorizing Aging and Old Age," presents a way of thinking about aging and old age that attempts to take into account the ambiguity and intangibility of age I saw that summer; a way of thinking that wants to make visible the idea that age, rather than an independently existing entity, is in some way constituted by the very act of its measurement; a way of thinking that interrogates and challenges the meanings we attribute to the measurements we make concerning age; and a way of thinking that exposes the profound physical, psychological, social, cultural, and material effects these acts of measurement and the meanings we give them have on our lives. Since so much of the information we use to measure and give meaning to age comes from the visual, this chapter also presents a way of thinking about age that examines the entangled character of the virtual pictures of ourselves and others we carry in our heads and the actual pictures to which we are exposed daily in popular film in order to uncover the deeply complicit nature of reality and its so-called representation.

In order to better evaluate not only how any particular film portrays aging or older characters, but how it tells the larger story of aging itself, chapter 1 also presents a framework with which we can assess what shared meanings, discourses, narratives, or myths a movie relies on to convey the meaning of the tale it tells. This framework consists of four basic philosophical views through which we construct knowledge of the world and of our existence within it: essentialism, a view of growing older that ties it to the appearance of certain inevitable, usually negative, characteristics and behaviors, most easily seen today in a story such as the narrative of aging as decline with no possibility of gain; social construction, a perspective on aging that maintains our knowledge about age is historically and culturally constructed, a view taken by the current practice of critical

Introduction

gerontology that sees the aging process as heterogeneous and indeterminate; a combination of essentialism and social construction, a concept that says what is essential about aging only appears so due to its earlier social construction and, thus, is really subject to change through processes such as the looping effect which takes into account the exchange between ideas about old people and old people's ideas about themselves; and the collapse of the distinction between essentialism and social construction, an approach that theorizes the natural and the social together, and argues that our knowledge about aging and old age, along with our knowledge about other areas such as the quantum world, is actually materialized through our practices of knowing.

Despite the paradoxical nature of devising a categorical system with which to critique the systematic categorization of the old, a contradiction of whose potential for unintended consequences and exclusions I am acutely aware, the use of this framework as a way of looking at films with older characters, and movies about the experience of or problems occurring with growing older, can help make clear how deeply popular film is implicated in the cultural struggle over the way that old age is discursively and materially constructed. Its use can also reveal how crucial a role popular film plays in making literally visible alternate ways to view and live into old age — in doing what age scholar Stephen Katz would call undisciplining old age, and what the rest of us might see as freeing old age from the attitudinal, cultural, and material constraints that hobble its exuberant expression.

Chapter 2, "Masculinities and the Narrative of Decline," utilizes the critical framework discussed in the first chapter to explore the ways in which the movies *Gran Torino* and *Up* simultaneously rely on essentialist, ageist, masculine stereotypes to render their protagonists intelligible, and defy these same stereotypes by allowing Walt and Carl, their main characters, to create counterstories by engaging in the social construction of old age. In these counterstories, they reinvent themselves by letting go of imprisoning pasts and entering into new relationships that enable them, at least partially, to redefine the basis of their sense of self and masculinity in a way that expands it beyond notions of value related to productivity and brute strength to include the value of reciprocal friendships and caring. Looked at critically, these movies make visible the connection between the largely depoliticized idea of the stages of life with the very political project of social control through the use of life stages to characterize retirement as lack of productivity, and to

Introduction

routinely deny access to progress stories and modes of socially relevant creativity to the old.

Yet, despite the way these films let us see and hear the violence of ageism, experience and identify with the existential despair the narrative of decline can foster, and then allow us a glimpse of what a life lived in resistance to these debilitating forces can look like, they shrink from the task of creating a new narrative of aging. When Walt decides that death is the best way to save his new friends and "family," and when Carl comes home from his amazing adventures to be cast in the role of grandfather to his new friend, these movies reinsert both men into culturally acceptable positions by re-equating old age with illness and death, and with sacrifice for and service to the younger generation. They ultimately fail to provide viable and lasting alternatives to the stereotypes and narratives that circumscribe old age that would take into account the possibility of living a full life despite disability, illness, or loss.

"The Silence and Invisibility of Older Women," chapter 3, looks at the films *Saving Grace* and *Calendar Girls* to mount a critique not only of the cultural devaluation that older women face due to their changing bodies, but of the continuing invisibility of the structural and institutional policies that lead to the economic and social inequalities restricting their lives. The stories these movies tell follow a trajectory similar to that of *Gran Torino* and *Up*: the protagonists are initially presented as leading conventional, stereotypical lives constrained by both gendered and age-related expectations, when due to unanticipated circumstances they undergo a life-changing transformation that leads them to take a stance in opposition to these constraints— to invent a counterstory. Yet they end up, to a large extent, reinfolded within hegemonic patriarchal and ageist structures. Nevertheless, a critical viewing of these films will show that they, like *Gran Torino* and *Up* do for their male protagonists, bring to light both some of the basic problems that characterize older women's lives and the ways in which these difficulties are often attributed to some essential deficiency in older women themselves even though they are neither natural nor inevitable.

Fortunately, *Saving Grace* allows Grace, its protagonist, to successfully, and frequently hilariously, imagine and inhabit an almost utopian world in which an older woman can defy the status quo, provide for herself, maintain good although not always law-abiding relations with her community, and enjoy the entire process. *Calendar Girls*, in turn, shows how its protagonist Chris, whose actions are modeled on a true story,

Introduction

manages to mount a well-received challenge both to the uglification industry's manufacture of dissatisfaction with the older female body and to gerontology's enduring reliance on an initially distorted view of female aging that regularly and unreflexively conflates it with diminishing social currency. But again, despite the success of Grace and Chris's efforts to expose the socially-constructed stamp of women's aging, these movies ultimately fail to explore the ramifications of older female empowerment and resort to fairy-tale-like endings to reintroduce, through the devices of rescue by a prince charming and guilt for engaging in selfish behavior, both women into androcentric and patriarchal institutions.

Chapter 4, "Intimacy and Desire in Later Life," examines the films *Something's Gotta Give*, *The Mother*, *Beginners*, and *The Best Exotic Marigold Hotel* to see how well their portrayal of love, romance, sexuality, and desire in later years both challenges ageist social conventions that construe the elderly as predominantly, and rightly, asexual, and reflects the experiences and concerns expressed by the older women in the documentary, *Still Doing It*. Ranging from a romantic, often comedic, look at the way falling in love can upend the settled trajectory of an older person's life as much as that of a life at any age, to a more serious, often confrontational, examination of images and actions that practically compel us to face our own unconscious ageism concerning love, romance, desire, and sexuality, these movies bear witness to both the pain and anguish caused by ageist attitudes that assume a lonely and loveless existence for the old, and the determination of older people to create and maintain the ties of intimacy throughout all of life.

By juxtaposing the sometimes contradictory bodily anxieties and the enduring desire for personal and sexual intimacy the women in *Still Doing It* convey with the way that similar bodily fears and desires, for both older men and women, are presented on the screen, this chapter opens up a space of productive tension between habitual, unexamined expectations about aging and the more unconventional depictions of aging presented cinematically that reveals the usual frame of aging to be an artifact of youth bias rather than a reflection of any innate physiological and psychological process. Thus, by changing the way aging is framed, by presenting the possibility that older bodies may be both desired and desirable, these films bring to our attention not only the vast diversity of later-life relationships, but the active resistance of the old to romantic and sexual marginalization along with their resolve to make the now of the last days of life into a fully alive reality.

Introduction

The evolving way in which the cognitive changes associated with Alzheimer's disease are made comprehensible in the movies *The Forgetting, Iris, Away from Her,* and *Wellkamm to Verona* is the subject of chapter 5, "The Cultural Work of Alzheimer's." Dealing with the current so-called "epidemic" of Alzheimer's and drawing on deep reservoirs of cultural and historical anxiety about the dependency, decline, and debility associated with growing older, movies such as *The Forgetting* and *Iris* collapse the person suffering from dementia into the disease by both erasing the personhood of the sufferer and by circling the wagons more tightly around the inherent ambiguity of the way we construct self and memory. The stories that these two movies tell largely ignore both the uneven and often highly contested evolution of what we now call Alzheimer's disease, as well as the changing historical relationship between memory and the construction of self. For example, the brain scans that are used to make the difference between normal and abnormal visible in *The Forgetting* and *Iris* cover over the unproven critical assumption that brain function itself *can* be measurable and knowable. And the conceit that loss of memory equals loss of self leaves unexamined the ways in which the self is relational rather than autonomous, is composed of more than its memories, and continues to exist and evolve outside of language and cognition in the body itself.

Conversely, a film such as *Away from Her* does admit to the possibility of continuing personhood and growth despite serious cognitive losses, and urges us to see as culturally and contextually contingent the line drawn between us and them. *Wellkamm to Verona* moves the line even farther by taking the perspective of those institutionalized due to dementia, giving meaning to the "inmates'" version of reality by uniting the existence of self to the cohesive intention of a narrative rather than to its external "truth." By relying on person-centered care to validate rather than contest an altered perception of the world, movies like this nudge us out of the realm of pure essentialism or social construction into an arena where the very meaning of rationality and the existence of the independent self may begin to be questioned. They can lead us to both reevaluate the way we envision Alzheimer's disease and to recalculate the way we value those who live with and die from it.

Perhaps the most enjoyable movies to critique are those that openly embrace the ambiguity, unpredictability, and vulnerability of aging by allowing the ongoing becoming of the old to take center stage. Films such as *Strangers in Good Company, The Straight Story, The World's Fastest Indian,* and *Howl's Moving Castle,* analyzed in chapter 6, "Age as Becom-

Introduction

ing," highlight the continuing dreams and desires of the old, implicitly challenging a straightforward narrative of aging as decline, and offering up images of old age as a creative and still competent involvement in life that draw us in rather than repel us. Such images also challenge traditional film theory's positioning of cinema as a representation of reality, bringing out the ability of film to *shape* our world and our selves rather than to simply *represent* it. By portraying older characters as people whose identity is in a constant process of formation rather than as individuals who are caught in the final stages of a unidirectional, abstract, and predictable journey of life, films like *Strangers in Good Company* enjoin us to consider an alternate concept of time, one in which time, rather than being linear and absolute, is actually produced by the ways we choose to entwine mind as virtual memories of the past with matter as the actual material of the present.

In the same vein, movies like *The Straight Story* and *The World's Fastest Indian* bring out the ability of life, even the so-called diminished life of the old, to expand itself by rendering prosthetic the material in order to successfully meet not only the physical challenges that old age may cause, but the far more serious social and economic challenges that our negative perception of old age may present. These two ideas, one calling into question the linear and abstract nature of time, the other destabilizing the static and unyielding nature of matter and its supposed separation from life, come together in the movie *Howl's Moving Castle*, a film that literally animates the nonlinearity of mind and time, and the malleability of matter and space. The protagonist Sophie, whose apparent old age is as subject to sudden shifts as is her material world, exemplifies the inherent openness of life to the dynamism of time and of matter to the dynamism of life. Her performance of age as a fluctuating experience marked by intra-action with others and with her environment reveal both time and space to be historical and cultural configurations, or chronotypes, that represent a particular worldview, and that are no less influential in the "reality" of our everyday lives than in the "imaginary" world of cinema.

Many of the films discussed in this book ally themselves with emerging critical theories of aging that consistently exhort us to take note of all the ways the lives of the aging and the old overflow the boundaries we have set for them. They ask us to deconstruct the often rigid binaries that separate youth from age, and to question the social and cultural construction of time and space that underlie the Western life course and that are

Introduction

used to justify its persistently negative attitudes towards growing older. They make us notice how much of what we call old age is performative, the result of coercive age relations, rather than expressive of some interior essence of old. They call on us to recognize the relational nature of consciousness, self, and memory, a recognition that should lead us to question our reliance on the autonomous individual as a measure of who should receive the rights and privileges of personhood. Ultimately, films like these tell us to pay closer attention to the actual lives of the old among us, to see and hear them differently, and to take responsibility for the manner in which our construction of the life course, of impairment and disability, and of the predictability and uniformity of old age works to place unnecessary and nonessential obstacles in the way of the continued becoming of the old and of their necessary entanglement with the world.

If a critical engagement with film can make us more aware of cinema as a crucial site of struggle over the meanings we give to aging and old age, and therefore, over the shape and texture of our lives, then perhaps Robert Butler's 1982 prediction that the unleashing of "the unimagined resources of people growing older all over the world ... is the next step in society's evolution" just might come true. Then maybe the questions I asked at the beginning of this book, "What is age?" and "What kinds of difference does age make?" will neither be asked in search of justification for inequalities and exclusions based on age, nor in an attempt to argue against the discriminatory and oppressive nature of these practices. Instead, they will turn into polite inquiries into the quality and character of our becoming, simple requests for information about our ever-changing lives and selves at any age, like, "How is the courtship between Grandma Alice and Ralph going?"

1

Understanding and Theorizing Aging and Old Age

> People look curiously at us as we file into the Riviere Rouge for lunch ... for we look to them just like seven old women.... One day, after three oafish, unshaven men in checked shirts and muddy boots have been too engrossed in staring even to drink their beer, Winnie says wryly, "I wanted to say to them, 'What are you staring at? Haven't you ever seen film stars before?'" The three men didn't know that we were film stars disguised as old women; they didn't have the magic power to penetrate our disguise....
> — Mary Miegs, *In the Company of Strangers*

What is age? Is it a position that we achieve such as legal age, a stage of life that we enter as in middle age, or a process that is simultaneously within and beyond our control as in aging? How do we experience age? As linear and chronological as with birthdays, as cyclical as in the concept of generations, or as of longer or shorter duration depending on the nature of our experience? In relation to what do we measure age? Does the act of measuring age in some way constitute what it is or does age exist independently from any act of measurement?

The first entry in the American Heritage Dictionary defines age as "the period of time during which someone or something exists" while period is defined as "any of various arbitrary temporal units." As a noun, age is a being, an existence which in geology can be tens of thousands of years, whereas in quantum mechanics it can be less than a femtosecond (a billionth of a microsecond). But age is also a verb, "to cause to grow older or more mature," a doing or a process that never can be precisely pinned down. The reality of a concept as intangible as age may be that it is inherently ambiguous, that it is all these things and none of them at once. Whether or not we manage to accurately capture its essence or describe its behavior, the ways in which we define age and the meanings we attribute to it have very real physical, psychological, and material effects on our lives.

Ways of thinking about age "reflect enormously powerful cultural forces" that structure "the life course ... in the sense of making distinctions and imposing roles and expectations upon individuals within ... created categories" (Bytheway 1995, 43). Thus, thinking about age, whether a personal exercise in reflection or an academic exercise in theory-making that reifies or contests present practice, is a way of explaining and understanding what has happened and anticipating what is to come. It is a road map for our becoming, for both becoming in the sense of constantly changing as we age (a verb), and for becoming in the sense of turning into what we have learned to expect that we will become as we age (a noun). And it is a barrier to our becoming as well, in the sense that it may set up roadblocks in front of roads less taken. Therefore, the becoming of age encompasses a lifetime of change, a constantly becoming different. It is only when we try to be certain about the changes that come with age, to calculate them, arrange them, give them a positive or negative value, and institutionalize and fix them as knowable difference, that thinking about age can become a problem.

This book is a way of thinking about age, specifically about the ideas around aging and old age as they are understood, problematized, and represented in contemporary popular film. In looking at films that are about aging, old age, or the "problems" commonly associated with growing older, I will ask: What discourses about aging and old age do these films employ? Do these discourses explore the intersections of old age with gender, class, race and ethnicity? To what extent do these discourses reinforce the dominant narrative of decline — a linear and chronological biological, psychological, and social process of deterioration — and/or reimagine and provide alternatives to it? I will also investigate how these films use chronological age as a category to justify divisions and inequality, and if and how they incorporate emerging scientific evidence of life as a continuous and entangled process of becoming involving agency, growth, connection, and the remaking of the self at any age into their stories. By looking at contemporary popular film through the lens of a variety of wider social theories, such as feminism, postmodernism, and critical and narrative gerontology, I hope to establish new theoretical frameworks for understanding, interpreting,

1. Understanding and Theorizing Aging and Old Age

and problematizing aging and old age that will allow us collectively as a culture to think differently about the differences that old age makes and that will enable those of us who are aging and old to see ourselves individually as inhabiting a place unconstrained by the narrative of decline.

Yet, a critical evaluation of film involves much more than just thinking about age. It also involves developing an understanding of how meanings are made and shared in a particular culture, how meanings become discourses that organize our personal, political, and economic lives, and how discourses eventually turn into narratives or myths by which we structure our day-to-day existence. At an even deeper level, critically viewing film involves understanding the philosophical positions and assumptions on which our culture rests and that make the existence of shared meanings, discourses, and narratives possible. Therefore, before analyzing specific films about aging and old age in depth, I want to touch on the often contradictory stories some of these films tell in order to examine how shared meanings become narratives and how various philosophical positions and their assumptions about the fundamental nature of the world and existence lead us to see aging and old age in particular ways and may prevent us from imagining other ways to age.

From Shared Meaning to Narrative

At the end of *Gran Torino*, Walt intentionally gets himself killed, but at the end of a similar story told in *Up*, Carl embraces a new life as a surrogate grandparent. *Saving Grace* ends with Grace made safe through remarriage, while in *Calendar Girls*, Chris's life is judged incomplete without the permanence of love. Love arrives as an unexpected surprise in *Something's Gotta Give*, while it is deliberately and joyfully pursued in *Beginners*. Yet in *Strangers in Good Company*, the lost women find they are sufficient unto themselves. In *Iris*, dementia empties out and erases a person, whereas in *Away from Her*, dementia allows for moments of growth and grace. But in *Wellkamm to Verona*, those with Alzheimer's continue to communicate, love, and live to the end. *The Straight Story* shows that creativity and frailty can coexist, while *The World's Fastest Indian* highlights the persistent power of dreams. However, in *Howl's Moving Castle*, the very relationship between chronological and biological age, expectation and experience is questioned.

Ultimately, it is this questioning that leads to the realization that ambiguity is central to both the aging experience and our understanding of it. Any field in which we think about aging and old age, whether gerontology, philosophy, science, politics, or the arts, needs to embrace aging and old age as both determined and malleable, both lived and represented. By embracing the ambiguity of experience and representation, we can begin to see how what we know about "age" is the result of a dialectical relationship between the cultural environment, in this case movies, and our own attitudes and behavior, our reaction to them. And that knowledge, a merging of what feminists would call the personal and the political, is the first step towards change, in ourselves and in the field.

Shared Meanings

Each of the above films tells an individual story about aging and old age, but also a collective story about the political, economic, and social reality of growing older in a particular place and time, about the ways in which aging intersects with other social categories, about how to act, what is expected, and how to relate to other people, and, perhaps most importantly, about how to think of ourselves and our changing place in society as we grow older. So although each film tells an individual story, it never stands alone because it is made intelligible through the shared cultural construction of common meanings, activities, and purposes, or through what Stuart Hall calls the constant creation of categories through which our lives are represented and lived. Since all culture is concerned with the production and exchange of meanings among its members, these shared meanings allow people within a particular culture to make sense of the world in roughly the same way and, therefore, to engage in "'logics' [of] public debate which create limiting social realities about the way the world works" (Makus 1990, 495).

Although we experience the shared meanings of the stories these films tell as if they emanated "freely and spontaneously from within us" (Hall 1985, 109) and as if they were natural aspects of things in themselves, we are actually spoken by them. From the moment of our birth, or before, we are "already expected, named, positioned in advance" (109) by shared meanings that structure not only the way we use language, the manner in which we produce images and their associated emotions, and the ways we classify objects and people along with the value we place on the resultant classifications, but that give us a sense of our own identity as well. By producing the very categories of identity that we take to be natural, shared meanings function as "the background noise of our lives ... [that] you can't

1. Understanding and Theorizing Aging and Old Age

recall ... consciously, but ... might even adopt ... as your own experience" (Basting 2009, 25). They, therefore, enable culture to play a hidden yet powerful role in shaping both our selves and our social relations, and in defining what we take to be natural and normal ways of being.

The shared meanings of stories thus constitute a normalizing "system ... through which cultural practices [are] organized and by which ... people represent and understand their world, including who they are and how they relate to others" (Scott, J. 2003, 379). Judith Butler argues that it is through this system that our social existence becomes possible, that we are both recognized and made recognizable, and that we are put in our place. Butler's theory of gender performativity, which explains "the way in which social agents *constitute* social reality through language, gesture, and all manner of symbolic social sign" (Butler, J. 2003, 413) gives us one way of understanding how a stylized repetition of acts can institute the illusion of an essential aging or aged self. By arguing that an act is a shared experience, as it would be in the performance of a play that "requires individual actors in order to be actualized and reproduced as reality" (421), Butler shows how social action is an individual performance of a collective story whose purpose is to continuously render social laws explicit. If gender (age) is performative rather than expressive, then it is not performed to express or disguise an interior self but to produce a recognizable self in the interests of "a social policy of regulation and control" (423). This kind of act or performance both makes us intelligible and gives us our existence and place within the recognizable categories of human beings in society.

Yet, the same meaning-making system that gives us our existence may also threaten it. Since "the terms that facilitate recognition are themselves ... the effects and instruments of a social ritual that decide[s], often through exclusion" (Butler, J. 1997, 5) who is within the circuit of recognition, these terms also decide who is outside it. To the extent that an historical and naturalized knowledge of age operates as a "preemptive ... circumscription of reality" (Butler, J. 1999, xxiii), it also establishes the boundaries of a category within which a particular body may be given expression. To be outside of the system, then, is to be not only derogated or demeaned, but also to "suffer a loss of context" (4), a loss of the possibility of recognition, and a loss of place within the community of shared meanings. It is to suffer a kind of categorical violence that, although not bodily visible, can produce symptoms parallel to those of physical injury.

Martha Nussbaum refers to this kind of injury when she says

that living in a system of shared meanings in which an age hierarchy biased toward youth structures the world "leaves deep marks on the human spirit" (Nussbaum 2010, 30). Over time, there is a sedimentation of these marks that produces "a set of corporeal styles which, in reified form, appear as the natural configuration of bodies" (Butler, J. 2003, 419–420) into age categories. Bordieu calls this configuration, these marks, the habitus. The habitus refers to embodied everyday performances through which a culture sustains belief in its own naturalness and by which it produces certain binding social relations. Many of these social relations are organized by age, a master status through which "societies proscribe appropriate behaviors and obligations" (Calasanti and Slevin 2006, 4) and generate "*dispositions* which 'incline' the social subject to act in relative conformity with the ostensibly objective demands of the field" (Butler, J. 1997, 155). This sedimentation or habitus, thus, works towards the expression, or performance, of consent of the subordinated to their situation and against the expression, or performance, of alternatives.

Yet, whenever the behavior and characteristics incorporated into the category old are referenced to argue that an older person should be excluded by nature from certain opportunities or, due to age, should lose her place within the community where those opportunities reside, the fact that age relations of domination produced through performance, sedimentation of marks, and habitus have shaped not only the opportunities available to this person but her desires and emotional habits as well, is usually ignored. Therefore, if this person subsequently attributes the categorical characteristics of "old" to herself and displays a new deference toward the "young," these actions are not indicative of the immutable nature of "old," but rather are indicative of both the violence of a normalizing system and her desire to remain within the circuit of recognition by taking on or internalizing and performing the only identity available to her, by occupying the only place where she will be recognized and recognizable.

According to Nussbaum, the insight that the actions and preferences of the old are often performative rather than expressive, as Butler would say, "has enormous consequences for theories of social development and measurements of 'quality of life'" (Nussbaum 2010, 30). Whenever preferences and desires are formed by systems of shared meanings that posit only certain roles and activities as normative for the old, any theory or practice based on the satisfaction of these desires will "always be an unwitting accomplice of an unjust status quo" (30). Thus, reliance on preference-based theories to measure social welfare will inevitably end up reproducing, rather than bringing to light and challenging, the inequalities inherent in the age relations already present in any system of shared meanings.

Discourse

Over time, these shared meanings and ways of being can congeal into systems of knowledge that not only structure our thoughts, emotions, and actions, but provide the context within which we build our theoretical, political, and institutional life. Michel Foucault calls these systems discourses and bases their power on the historically contingent development of fields of disciplinary knowledge. Yet, disciplinary knowledge, rather than transparently reflecting already existing categories, also "'produces' what it claims merely to represent" (Butler, J. 1999, 5). Categories of identity are thus "formed, defined, and reproduced in accordance with the requirements of [disciplinary] structures" (4) which base their authority on the assumption of the pre-existing ontological integrity of the very categories they produce. The identity of someone within a category is, therefore, not necessarily logical or coherent, but becomes intelligible only in relation to socially constructed norms that pass themselves off as expressive of naturalized stories, meanings, and discourses.

Stuart Hall ascribes the seeming coherence or unity of objects and actions within a discourse to a process that he calls articulation. According to Hall, articulation functions as "a connection between different elements that have no necessary relationship among themselves or to the events they represent" (Makus 1990, 503). By invoking a chain of connotations within a discursive field, articulation can have a "widereaching effect on a culture's understanding of a situation and the array of meanings and possible courses of action which may be taken" (504). Due to articulation, disparate ideas don't function as individual entities, but are linked within sets of rules or networks that allow certain objects and actions to appear commonsensical while excluding others.

The evolution of the modern discourse of senescence provides a good example of the way articulation works. The nineteenth-century medicalization of the aged body connected into a whole disparate ideas about the body as a system of signification, a constantly dying entity, and a kind of body that was separate from other bodies. By representing the aged body as a visible map where disease could literally be seen, by conflating the signs of age with the symptoms of a progressive disease, and by interpreting that disease as many small deaths within life, the discourse of senescence redefined the aging body as an object specifically degenerative and different from other bodies. No matter how healthy and alive, no matter how functional and creative, the aged body was seen at one and the same time as pathological, since changes attributed to age were read as due to disease, and normal, since these changes were to be expected (Katz 1996). Thus, articulation allowed two states that are generally oppositional to exist simultaneously in one discourse about the aging body. Although, over time, within this discourse of senescence many words have acquired new definitions, multiple terms have been redefined, and various meanings have been "coupled with and uncoupled from signs" (Makus, 1990, 504), the images, proverbs, social myths, and stories spawned by this discourse continue to circumscribe the field.

Narrative

Like the discourse of senescence, the most appealing and tenacious stories often become myth-like narratives that make their way into our "private dreams, our public wishes, and our life storytelling starting in childhood" (Gullette 2009, 21), persisting across generations. Such narratives or myths "are permeated by the preexisting inventions of culture" (Gullette 2004, 21) and send implicit messages about the course and quality of our lives. These narratives, like all myths, are "based more on tradition or convenience than on fact," and express a "recurring theme, or character type that appeals to the consciousness of a people by embodying its cultural ideals or by giving expression to deep, commonly felt emotions" (*The American Heritage Dictionary of the English Language*, s. v. "myth"). They, therefore, work in tandem with the background noise of shared cultural meanings and the theoretical, institutional, and political constraints founded on the discursive "truths" of disciplinary knowledge to present an ideal model of ourselves to which we may strive to conform despite the existence of structural obstacles or personal failures. More crucially, they work to limit our ability to imagine other ways of being.

Although all societies have some kind of life-course narrative and use age to differentiate groups and to distribute social status, the institutionalization of age throughout the life-course in Western societies since the nineteenth century has resulted in an idealized model of the Western concept of personhood that neglects many of the realities and much of the diversity of old age. "In such models a logic of sequence (or narrative) organizes the stages of life into a universal and progressive arrangement.

1. Understanding and Theorizing Aging and Old Age

A logic of association correlates with each stage a set of specific behavioral attributes, conflicts, and opportunities.... Old age, ... the conclusion to the narrative of life, is identified with those anticipated behaviors appropriate to its place in the sequence" (Katz 1996, 60).

Before the 1800's, when most people lived in "families and communities regulated by religious and social principles of hierarchy, dependency, and reciprocal obligation" (Cole 1993, 230), it was culturally acceptable to acknowledge the infirmities of age. Physical decline required dependence on God who, although He did not take away the suffering, gave it spiritual and social meaning. But with the rise of Victorian morality in the 1900s, the infirmities of age and the aging body itself became both symbols of the old patriarchal order and communalism, and ever-present reminders of the reality of dependence, disease, and failure. Victorian morality with its commitment to material and personal progress marked the end of "American culture's ability to hold opposites in creative tension, to accept the ... unmanageability of human life" (231). This kind of progress-oriented thinking split old age and rationalized its experience in order to control it, resulting in a dualism of decline, dependency, and sin on one hand, and health, autonomy, and virtue on the other. Only by labeling the old body a failure due to "individual ignorance or lack of will, not from human limitation or divine providence" (110) or structural limitations, could the vicissitudes of old age be squared with the ideology of rationalized progress and self-reliance.

This dualism regarding old age instituted in Victorian times persists to this day, embodied in ideas such as intergenerational war, generational equity, the social redundancy of the elderly, and personal responsibility for the way we age. In producing a narrative of progress associated with constant accumulation of health and wealth, and with increasing control of the self as individual property, Victorian thinking exposed the dark side of progress as well as its optimism. As a result, old age, as a distinct stage of life, became stereotyped as an impediment to progress rather than an integral part of life. And the image of the life course, rather than climbing towards heaven and ultimate transcendence as it had before the nineteenth century, became a rising and falling curve or staircase in which progress was followed by inevitable decline (Cole 1993). Thus, in the attempt to cope with and control anxieties created by the complexity and uncertainty of life and the world, negative stereotypes about old age became embedded in the narratives and myths that are used "to infuse experience with shared meaning and coherence" (Cole 1993, 230).

The Becoming of Age

Nevertheless, the lives, experiences, and dreams of those who find themselves restrained by the walls of stories, discourses, narratives, and myths inevitably "overflow their sanctioned boundaries; ... defy theoretical stasis; wander unpredictably between metaphor, myth, and fact; and default on their assigned places" (Katz 2005, 16). In so doing, these lives embody an attitude that Foucault calls critical curiosity, an attitude that finds what surrounds us as strange and that is ready to disrespect traditional hierarchies and categories in order "to look at the same things in a different way" (Foucault 1997b, 325). They demonstrate that "at whatever biological, cognitive, or social register one studies the life course, one finds more diversity than unity, more paradox than consistency, more ambiguity than certainty" (Katz 2005, 189).

Nowhere is the power of narrative to shape our lives or the power of our lives to resist narrative more obvious than in old age. Despite the existence of an overarching narrative of decline that presents aging and old age as a process of inevitable and unidirectional physical and mental deterioration, as loss with no possibility of gain, and that structures age relations in such a way that older people are categorically disadvantaged and denied opportunities for growth and development, many of those within the category consistently subvert any disciplinary claim to know them. And despite the fact that the aging and the old are given a false homogeneity by being medicalized, stereotyped, portrayed as frightening, classified as subordinate and dependent, and stripped of difference due to gender, class, race, and ethnicity (Cruikshank 2003), many continually develop "new identities and ways to *be* older in body, mind, and spirit" (Katz 2005, 14).

Keeping in mind the constant interaction between personal and collective meanings, after we watch films that tell stories about aging and old age, after we cry or cheer or contest the ending, we should also look at how each film uses the narrative of aging as decline to help us make sense of its story. Does it use the shared meanings, discourses, and myths contained in the narrative of decline to reinforce or to reimagine it? to corral the lives of the old back into the fold or to allow their diversity to roam free? to argue that they've had their chance and should move out of the way for the next generation or to point out the social, economic, and political obstacles that structurally work to prevent them from reaching their potential? to hold them collectively responsible for threatening the viability and security of our social systems or to expose the ways in which each individual older person is entangled in a web of negative and culturally sanctioned discourses about aging that is largely beyond her control? to

1. Understanding and Theorizing Aging and Old Age

represent the life course as a "singular, industrialized experience based on prescribed developmental social roles terminating in old age" or to depict aging "as a more indeterminate process with several beginning, overlapping, and end points ... transitions" (Katz 2005, 14) and roles?

Unfortunately, many of the differences attributed to aging and old age, both in narrative and in everyday life, unrelentingly work to place older people in a category that portrays them as essentially "distinct from ordinary human beings" (Bytheway 2005, 362), often as less than fully human. If we wish to understand or contest the characterizations and material consequences of the narrative of decline, we need to understand more than the evolution of meaning to narrative, we also need to comprehend how various philosophical positions make possible and encourage or discourage the existence of such a narrative in the first place.

Philosophical Positions Underlying the Narrative of Decline

There are four basic philosophical views on the nature of the world and on what kind of knowledge can lead to the truth about existence. For the purpose of constructing a framework for evaluating discourses on aging and old age, I will call them essentialism, social construction, a combination of essentialism and social construction, and the collapse of the distinction between essentialism and social construction. Since each view leads to particular kinds of epistemological and ontological theories about what it means to be human and, therefore, to particular kinds of practices of classification or the transformation of people into types, of division or the separation and normalization of people, and of self-subjectification or the construction of a subject who "is rendered meaningful through relations of power and subordination" (Katz 1996, 12), which theory a culture or an individual subscribes to matters to the way aging and old age are imagined. Following a description of each philosophical position, I will, therefore, provide examples of specific theories that can be derived from each of the four positions along with an example of how these theories can affect the lives of the older people whom they attempt to describe.

Essentialism

A philosophical position is essentialist, or subscribes to the idea that rigorous objective and rational practices can discover how things are in themselves, whenever the category old implicitly refers to the attribution of an essence to older people. In this case, essence can be defined as a character of being that is assumed to be given, universal, natural, and not shared by people of other ages. Elizabeth Grosz describes the practice of essentializing as entailing a belief in "the existence of fixed characteristics, given attributes, and ahistorical functions that limit the possibilities of change and thus of social reorganization" (Grosz 1994, 84). Essentialism thus works as a conservative social force that rationalizes any prevailing hierarchical organization of social roles by assuming they are the best or the only possibilities given the essential nature of existing groups. Although Grosz wrote this passage in reference to the essentialization of characteristics having to do with sexual difference, her definition of essentialism and its various forms—biologism in which "social and cultural factors are [seen as] the effects of biologically given causes" (84), naturalism, a type of biologism in which a fixed nature can be "asserted on theological or ontological ... grounds" (85), and universalism in which "the commonness of all women [read old] at all times and in all social contexts" (85) is emphasized—and her evaluation of their uses can readily be used to recognize arguments that justify policies and practices that work to categorically differentiate the old.

Essentialist arguments that fit this definition are not new, having been put forth ever since Plato argued that all things, including man, must be measured by universal, unchanging, and abstract truths which he called forms. According to Plato, these forms structured a universe with an order of truth and value all the way from inanimate physical things to the ultimate idea of the good. Though separated from the actually existent thing, these forms also determined the essence of any particular kind of matter. Aristotle later criticized Plato's theory of forms, yet his criticism centered not on their significance but concerned their separation from the actual thing. For Aristotle, the form of a thing was always immanent in it and was common to all other things of its type. His universe thus consisted of individual types and species, each embodying its eternal form as matter, and each developing from potentiality to actuality in an ordered path determined by its form. Although Plato and Aristotle disagreed as to the location of an essence, neither denied its existence nor its influence on the nature of a thing or a person.

Therefore, when we consider Aristotle's characterization of the old in the *Rhetoric* as people who have become cynical, distrustful, small-minded, ungenerous, mired in lives ruled by memory rather than hope,

1. Understanding and Theorizing Aging and Old Age

and exhibiting an ineluctable decline in moral character, we should remember that he is describing not just surface behavior but what he believes to be the essential nature of the old. His characterization leaves room neither for consideration of diminished moral responsibility as being a consequence of depleted capabilities nor for recognition of external material and cultural pressures that might impinge on self-perception and choice of action as much as any internal change (Small 2007, 66). It is consummately essentialist in that it rests on both biological and ontological ground and is assumed to be universally true, any exception only proving the rule.

It's not difficult to recognize that, for many in today's culture, Aristotle's characterization of the old still rings true. For instance, the biomedical model of aging, a model that makes "certain assumptions about the ways in which people with outward signs of aging are likely to think and behave" (Powell 2006, 30), tends to homogenize all older people, subjecting them to medico-technical solutions to their "problems." This model both naturalizes ageist social practices and reinforces the notion that decline is synonymous with the process of aging itself. The biomedical view also influenced functionalist theories of aging, dominant in the post–World War II years, that viewed aging as a social problem in need of a solution. One solution was disengagement theory, which saw the "mutual withdrawal of the individual and society from each other with advancing age" (48) as natural and normal, even socially advantageous in that it minimized the social disruption caused by death. Another was activity theory, which, although it still maintained that old age was "a uniform process and a uniformly problematic and depressing state" (49), stressed the development of new roles and activities as the older person's only chance for contentment.

Margaret Gullette calls our contemporary version of essentialism the narrative of decline, a linear and chronological process of biological, psychological, and social deterioration that makes "human aging entirely bodily, predictable, and inescapably awful" (Gullette 2004, 8). This narrative erases the vast differences among older people, at once discounting their creative potential for useful work and categorically separating them from and subordinating them to the rest of society, while ignoring the structural problems that impede older people's continued development and growth.

One result of such categorical subordination of the old can be seen with the 2000 case of Kimel vs. Florida Board of Regents in which several plaintiffs sued under the Age Discrimination in Employment Act of 1967. When the case was heard by the Supreme Court, the majority found that "laws which classify on the basis of age need only pass the Court's 'rational basis review' test" rather than the legal classifications accorded race and gender where a "history of purposeful unequal treatment" exists (Kimel 2008, 2). When explaining the rational basis review, the majority stated that "a State may rely on age as a proxy for other qualities, abilities, or characteristics that are relevant to the State's legitimate interests ... That age proves to be an inaccurate proxy in any individual case is irrelevant. [W]here rationality is the test, a State does not violate the Equal Protection Clause merely because the classifications made by its laws are imperfect" (3).

A second Supreme Court decision in June of 2009 reversed a long-standing precedent allowing age to be only one of the factors in a layoff or demotion. Declaring age discrimination to be categorically different from discrimination based on race, sex, religion, or national origin, the court ruled that a worker must prove that age was the sole reason behind the employer's action. This decision not only makes age discrimination radically more difficult to prove, but further separates older people from the standards to which the rest of society must adhere, rationalizing, as Elizabeth Grosz's definition of essentialism says, the prevailing hierarchical organization of social roles, and reinforcing the age relations or the "system of inequality, based on age, that privileges the not-old at the expense of the old" (Calasanti and Slevin 2006, 1).

Social Construction

In contrast to essentialists, social constructionists argue that truth and values are never purely descriptive of an objective reality that exists out there or resides within things and people, but are materially and conceptually produced in a particular historical context, epistemology, and culture. Like essentialism, social construction is not new, dating back at least to Protagoras who, contrary to Plato, argued that man is the measure of all things rather than how things are in themselves. A more contemporary version of the essentialist-social constructionist debate took place between Noam Chomsky and Michel Foucault in the 1970's. Chomsky, taking an essentialist position, argued that human nature is characterized by unchanging and "innate organizing principles which guide our social and individual behavior" (Chomsky and Foucault 2006, 4) in the form of

1. Understanding and Theorizing Aging and Old Age

structures and initial limitations on the kinds of knowledge we are able to amass. Foucault, taking a position aligned with social construction, disagreed, arguing that the "relation of the subject to the truth [is] just an effect of knowledge" (17) because the system of regularity and constraint which makes knowledge possible lies outside of the human mind in ever changing social forms. This anti-metaphysical stance can also be seen in doctrines common to philosophers such as Heidegger, Nietzsche, and Derrida, but Foucault's work on the effects of discourse, discipline, and relations of power expresses it particularly well.

Foucault posits that discourses, or bodies of knowledge, are never purely descriptive of a deeper reality or structure that underlies the world, but are produced in historically specific institutions, practices, and meetings between things and people. For him, disciplinary knowledge, or the sum total of methods, procedures, concepts, and theories that are used to divide, classify, regulate, and govern groups or categories of ideas and people within a certain discourse, materially produces rather than reflects the very categories it attempts to describe. Through the imposition of disciplinary norms upon a group, individual difference or abnormality is also produced, difference which then must be controlled or erased through the implementation of policies and relations of power which attempt to achieve acceptance of the norms and worldview espoused by the very discipline that produced the difference. "We are judged, condemned ... destined to live and die in certain ways by discourses that are true, and which bring with them specific power-effects" (Foucault 1997a, 25). Yet, embedded within the construction of what Foucault calls disciplinary, normalizing discourses of truth and power lies the possibility of resistance, transgression, revolt — of freedom beyond disciplinary power. Thus, Foucault's ideas on discourse are about the historical specificity of claims to truth — about how things could have been and may be otherwise — and are intimately connected to the formation of human subjects, the normalization of the marginal or the other, and the changeable and discontinuous character of knowledge.

In *Disciplining Old Age*, Stephen Katz uses Foucault's ideas on discourse and discipline to explore how gerontology emerged as a "knowledge-formation ... linked to the disciplining of old age and the construction of specific subjects of power and knowledge" (Katz 1996, 1). Katz argues that the production of gerontological knowledge has led to the problematization of old age, to often coercive strategies of control and regulation of those who fall within the category, and to the erasure of alternative ways of understanding the aging process and its place in society. By engaging in historical aging studies that "critique the assumptions and images that pass for the timeless, scientific truth about aging" (27) Katz reveals the ways in which modern gerontological knowledge has shed its social and cultural moorings in order to depict itself as the only truth about aging and old age.

Yet, as Katz clearly shows, this objective truth has not always been true. Premodern thinkers envisioned old age as part of a larger cosmic context that by medieval times was understood as a dialectical relationship between the physical and the spiritual. In this relationship, old age was characterized not only by a decline in the body but by opportunities for spiritual transcendence and redemption. Death and dying, at any age, was a public, spiritual process that bridged the worldly and eternal realms, and worked against affixing subjectivity to the body. Even by the seventeenth and eighteenth centuries, when the natural and the cultural began to drift apart, old age was still not separated from youth in a way that its problems constituted an identifiable pathological state that required specific medical intervention.

With the Enlightenment, however, medicine reinterpreted signs thought to connect the spiritual and the physical in terms of disease and disorder. As these signs were mapped on a grid of normality and pathology, old age was redefined as a time of life distinct from other ages, one characterized by inevitable physical decline as well as moral and behavioral ills. Once these boundaries between youth and age were established, it was a relatively short step to cast the old as a homogenous, needy, and dependent group, and to use them as the basis of a disciplinary knowledge created in the interest of social control. Thus, the problematization of old age both legitimized new knowledge formations and transformed an inevitable part of human existence into a crisis of thought that required an array of practical responses and interventions from the carceral to the caring.

Katz therefore calls for the practice of critical gerontology, a genre that works to "resignify the aging process as heterogeneous and indeterminate" (Katz 1996, 4) rather than essentialist and biologically deterministic, a call that is taken up by Christine Overall in her article on the social construction of old age and disability. Overall not only argues that identities such as elderly and disabled are social constructs, but also refutes the assertion that there is an underlying "biological 'foundation' or 'substratum' on which the social identity rests" (Overall 2006, 126). In the case of age, she posits that there are two ways in which the social construction of age occurs: through the designation of a particular chronological age at which certain characteristics of the aging person are recognized as liabilities or defects rather than, for example, reserves of wisdom or normal human variation, and through the material manifestation of social factors such as poverty, inadequate health care, or environmental degradation. In "Ageism and Age Categorization," Bill Bytheway further argues that chronological age itself is a social construct, instituted in the eighteenth and nineteenth centuries by lawyers, bureaucrats, and legislators who, in the interest of quantification, required specific numerical ages for the assignation of certain duties and rights (Bytheway 2005). Both Overall and Bytheway agree that once the institutionally inspired linear imagery of the life course is accepted, ideas of sameness and difference are fostered, leading to the construction of age boundaries and categories, the incorporation of a number into a person's internal identity, and the rationalization of categorical subordination and marginalization.

Thus recognition of the social construction of the category old facilitated the production of theories such as the political economy of old age, a precursor of critical gerontology that focused on "how the state and its resources and institutions positioned the experiences and life-chances of older people in capitalist Western society" (Powell 2006, 50), and critical gerontology, a perspective that, although still concerned with structural inequalities, also works to incorporate the experiences of the old into gerontological knowledge. Looked at from these theoretical perspectives, old age begins to appear both as a site where supposedly essential traits become manifest and as a site where these traits and their meanings are socially constructed.

Combining Essentialism and Social Construction

In *The Social Construction of What?*, Ian Hacking takes the position that something can be simultaneously essential, or what he calls real, and socially constructed. He illustrates his point by taking the case of an illness that may be real or "a certain [identifiable] biological pathology" and yet may also be socially constructed or "evolving and changing" as the person who has it changes behavior in response to having been classified as having the disease (Hacking 1999, 119). Loosely following the subjectivism of Descartes, who separated a person's self-aware consciousness and thoughts from the physical world of nature, Hacking maintains a distinction between interactive kinds, or the kinds of social science such as a person or the idea of a person, that can change in response to the classification itself and knowledge about it due to self awareness, and indifferent kinds, or the kinds of natural science such as a microbe that causes an illness, that may interact with us and force our knowledge to change but "not because they become aware of what we know and act accordingly" (105).

Yet he also argues that, although essentialism and social construction are differing philosophical views about the nature of reality, their differences are largely semantic and it just doesn't matter that much which view is used by scientists or politicians to construct tools for accomplishing useful work. He characterizes essentialism as "an especially strong form of background assumption" (Hacking 1999,16), one that is taken for granted as common sense and, therefore, appears to be inevitable. Arguing that the claim of inevitability only makes sense if there truly is an unchanging intrinsic structure of reality given to humans by some outside force or higher power, such as Plato's forms, he concludes that essentialism is not really essential but only appears inevitable in a particular social and historical context. Recognition of the lack of inevitability, or contingency, of traits that are deemed essential is, for Hacking, the beginning of arguments in favor of social construction, or the development of an attitude that is critical of the inevitability and stability of the status quo.

Thus, for Hacking, social construction is not opposed to essentialism; rather the social construction of a category cannot proceed without some degree of essentialism, or strong background assumption, having occurred in the first place. In the case of old people, their presumed essential nature fuses with the construction of a category to contain it, resulting in the making up of a certain kind of human being that may not have existed before but, due to present social conditions, appears inevitable. Hacking further argues that what is really constructed is not an old person but the idea of an old person, "the classification itself, and the matrix" or social and cultural environment "within which the classification works" (Hacking 1999, 11).

Hacking continues to argue that the idea (of old) and the (old) person as an object in the world are often confused because "once we have the phrase, the label, we get the notion that there is a definite kind of person ... [and] this kind of person becomes reified" (Hacking 1999, 27). Furthermore, since the person is aware of what is categorically said and done to her, and of what is thought of her, there is an interaction between the idea and the person that may change how she feels, acts, and ultimately

1. Understanding and Theorizing Aging and Old Age

experiences herself. These changes can have consequences for the characterization of the very category invoked. "What was known about people of a kind may become false because people of that kind have changed in virtue of what they believe about themselves" (34), or a false characterization may become true due to the social and material way people are treated as part of that category. Therefore, when we talk about the social construction of any category, we are talking about the idea which is based on some degree of essentialism, the people described by that idea, the interaction between the idea and those people, and the social context in which the interactions occur. Hacking calls this circular process in which "ways of classifying human beings interact with the human beings who are classified" (31) "the looping effect of human kinds" (34).

The looping effect between the idea of old people and old people's idea of themselves can be illustrated by tracing changes in perception of both the category and the person since the enactment of Social Security. In a society that values individualism and self-sufficiency, passage of the Social Security Act was a ground breaking public and compassionate response to the massive unemployment and impoverishment of older people during the Great Depression. By characterizing the old as poor, frail, dependent, but most of all deserving, its passage not only provided benefits to a majority of older Americans, but also "politically legitimated the status of older persons as a major governmental concern" (Binstock 2005, 265) and voting bloc. Thus, its passage also created a category of people who, in part by internalizing the adjective deserving, gained not only material security but enough power to work together to construct a piecemeal old-age state that included Social Security, Medicare, and the Older Americans Act.

Yet, partially due to the success of these very old age policies, by the late 1970's, compassion for the elderly as a group was on the wane and the category began to be portrayed as greedy, rich, and burdensome. Subsequent political attacks on Social Security and Medicare not only threatened the material welfare of the old, but often changed their perception of themselves from deserving and influential to despised and marginalized as well. When these negative images are mutely accepted, they not only lead to feelings of worthlessness but can have serious health consequences. A study published by Becca Levy in 2002 found that older people who had a positive view of aging did better on memory and balance tests and lived an average of 7.5 years longer than those exposed to negative depictions of old age.[1] Margaret Cruikshank calls this looping process learning to be old, and notes that "we learn to be old partly in response to the ways we are treated" (Cruikshank 2003, 2). Thus, "classifications, ... when known by people or by those around them, and put to work in institutions, change the ways in which individuals experience themselves—and may even lead people to evolve their feelings and behavior in part because they are so classified" (Hacking 1999, 104).

Therefore, positions that fall somewhere between essentialism and social construction can provide resources to help the old "challenge the gaze of others and ... 'be for themselves'" (Powell 2006, 85). By allowing the old body to move between subject and object, these positions dismantle the fixed grand narratives of modernity to reveal alternative postmodern cultural processes for constructing more flexible epistemological and ontological narratives of aging. They also allow socially constructed meanings of old age to exist in tandem with the physical realities of age-related bodily changes, offering an opportunity to minimize the importance of changes in appearance due to age. Yet some of the ideas currently circulating as challenges to the biomedical or disease model of aging still overlook the role that class, gender, race, and ethnicity may play "in determining not only how healthy we are in old age but even whether we get to be old" (Cruikshank 2003, 2).

"Successful aging," for one, stresses later life potential but still measures success by competitive business standards that may not be applicable to all older people's pursuits or social situations. By continuing to value activity and accumulation over other pursuits, "successful" retired workers may temporarily avoid "the risk of aging itself by not succumbing to negative attitudes or behavioral traits that could be interpreted as 'old'" (Katz 2005, 149). Yet, such a stance can rarely be maintained and often diverts attention from our common vulnerability and thus delays collective solutions to problems of late-life agency and structure. "Productive aging" also leaves room for later-life growth, but places too much emphasis on the role of individual effort in achieving these goals. An emphasis on staying productive in a capitalist sense creates a societal attitude that is hostile to both the emergence of alternative empowering older identities and to anything but a positive answer to the question of whether a "busy life is truly satisfying or simply conforms to social expectation" (Cruikshank 2003, 163). By disguising structural problems as personal failures, "productive aging" also aligns itself with the goals of a governmental rationality that maximizes individual responsibility in the service of meeting the political goals of minimizing dependency and universal entitlements (Rose 1999).

1. Understanding and Theorizing Aging and Old Age

Both "successful" and "productive aging" also ignore the diverse experiences and life circumstances of the old, and the way in which "advantages acquired and disadvantages experienced earlier in life compound over time" (Calasanti and Slevin 2006, 191). When the cumulative advantage/disadvantage approach (CAD) is linked to the study of aging, it becomes clear that the inequalities of old age are due not only to individual and generation-related experience but to intersections with gender, class, race, and ethnicity as well.[2] Recognizing that our position as we age both shapes and is shaped by inequities that are cumulative in nature and that interlock with other power relations can expand the ability of positions such as "successful" and "productive aging" to offer more nondeterministic ways to view aging that allow specific cultural and individual differences to surface.

Collapsing Essentialism and Social Construction

Following in the footsteps of British empiricists such as David Hume, who argued that since knowledge could only be obtained through sense perception we could never know the nature of ultimate reality, Karen Barad, in *Meeting the Universe Halfway*, goes even farther towards erasing the distinction between essentialism and social construction. Unlike Hacking, who continues to make a distinction between social (interactive) kinds and natural (indifferent) kinds, Barad theorizes the natural and the social together. Drawing on the ideas of quantum nonlocality and entanglement, she posits that it is the essential nature of objects to be socially and materially entangled with each other because once they have interacted "their fates are linked however far apart they become" (Al-Khalili 2004, 97)[3]. In her theory of agential realism, she argues that the human is entangled in the very becoming of the world and in the way it is materialized through practices of knowing. Therefore, by looking at the body as a part of the world we seek to understand and as constituted by the material/discursive practices through which we seek this understanding, we can see that materiality (the natural or the essential) and intelligibility (the social or the constructed) are not unalterable dimensions of the world but are shifting performances or dialogues with a world in which we are responsible for what is said and who is included or excluded.

According to agential realism, materiality and intelligibility are never fixed aspects of the world but are agential performances in which apparatuses, or material and discursive arrangements through which concepts and objects are given definition and boundaries, produce, rather than discover, the phenomena that make up reality. Phenomena are differential patterns of mattering formed by intra-actions (not interactions since the term presupposes already separate entities) among multiple practices and apparatuses of bodily production — combinations of the human, the non-human, the technological, and the ideational — that allow part of the world to make itself differentially intelligible to another part. In order to become intelligible, these apparatuses must effect agential cuts in the world that actually materialize discrete entities for the purposes of measurement and description. Thus, subject and object, exterior and interior, cause and effect, as measured by concepts materially embodied in apparatuses, produce phenomena filled with separate entities where there were none before. "Objects are not already there, they emerge through specific practices" (Barad 2007, 157).

Barad bases her account of agential realism on Niels Bohr's philosophy-physics and his ideas about indeterminacy in quantum physics. Bohr argues that the wave/particle duality paradox caused by the inability to measure both the position and the momentum of a particle at the same time is due not to the nature of physical reality but to the cut enacted by the instruments of measurement. For him the cut, by which a wave with an ontologically indeterminate state becomes a mixture of particles with determinate characteristics, produces a separation of observer from observed and cause from effect, creating a perception of exteriority within a phenomenon, but does not and cannot either describe or destroy the radical entanglement of being in the world. Since a different cut will produce different boundaries and cause different differences to matter, bodily boundaries are inherently ambiguous and only come into being through intra-action with and as part of the world.

Biologist Donna Haraway illustrates indeterminacy by showing that the human is an intraspecies relationship that entangles the natural and the social, a reciprocal "becoming with" whose consequences are written in the flesh (Haraway 2008, 17). According to Haraway, only about 10% of the cells that occupy that space called a human body have human genomes; "the other 90% of the cells are filled with the genomes of bacteria, fungi, protists, and such" (4). "I," Haraway asserts, "am vastly outnumbered by my tiny companions" (4) and cannot become one without simultaneously becoming many. More complex life forms "are the continual result of ever more intricate and multidirectional acts of association of and with other life forms" and "the co-opting of strangers ... the infolding of others" (31).

1. Understanding and Theorizing Aging and Old Age

According to philosopher Alva Noe, even consciousness is not something that happens in us or to us but is "something that we achieve or ... do through our ... interaction with the world around us" (Noe 2009b, 29). Rather than picture the human condition as a private, rational, interior world impinged upon by outside forces, Noe, like Barad, sees humans as "ourselves dependent on and distributed over and ... made up out of the world and processes around us" (Noe 2009c, 8), including social processes. He views humans as entangled with each other across categories delineating species and kinds so that the environment and other people, even our desires and needs, are an essential part of who we are. Meaning is, therefore, not intrinsic but relational, "something that is achieved in [a] dynamic of interaction" (Noe 2009b, 29) and that is never achieved once and for all.

Barad, Haraway, and Noe all argue that in this entangled web of becoming there is no inherent independence because the body is engaged in a continuous and self-modifying intra-action with the world; there is no real autonomy from the other because the very integrity of what we call our body is dependent on our permeability to the life of the other; there is no disembodied rationality because thinking can never be divorced from the body within which it occurs. If there is no ontological distinction between the natural and the social, then there is no way to distinguish an essence from a construction or to attribute the injustice and inequality that may result from making up objects and categories to anything but ourselves.

So when we talk about aging as a narrative of bodily decline and deterioration, as an inevitable process of othering and exclusion due to a progressive loss of independence, autonomy, and rationality, and we see and treat the old as occupying a category separate from the rest of humanity, according to Barad it is because we fail to take into account strong physical, biological and philosophical evidence that the boundaries between self and other, human and non-human, are marked by symbiosis and inconstancy and are never clear. It is also because we fail to remember that "experimenting and theorizing are dynamic practices that play a constitutive role in the production of objects and subjects and matter and meaning" (Barad 2007, 56), not by intervening from outside but by intra-acting from within and as part of what is produced. Thus, whenever we conflate an older person with the characteristics of the category "old," an agential realist account of the world calls on us to question the givenness of differential categories and their exclusions, to examine the practices through which differential boundaries are stabilized and destabilized, and to take responsibility for our part in the ongoing configuration of the world.

Looking at aging and old age through the lens of Barad's theory of agential realism, a picture very different from the one drawn by the narrative of decline emerges. In this new picture, the boundaries around old age are more ambiguous, affording more chances for both subjectivity and creativity in later life. Rather than depicting old age as a time of predictably increasing rigidity and decreasing ability, this picture shows aging to be "a site upon which power is distributed and 'power/knowledge' relations are played out" (Powell 2006, 139). Margarette Gullete makes this point well in her description of a 2000 Paris art show called "Un Siècle" that starts with a photo of an eight-week old and continues around the gallery with photographs of one hundred different faces, each one older than the last. Although the artist uses chronology, he avoids telling a simple narrative of decline by allowing individual differences and personal contexts to dominate the photos. "A woman at ... 83 might look younger than another person at 66.... At any given age, 'What next?' was not a foregone conclusion" (Gullette 2004, 9).

In "Age as Adventure," a chapter in Betty Friedan's *The Fountain of Age*, she reinforces this idea of non-chronology in her interviews with elders who are intent on living every minute until they die. Acknowledging that "the age mystique, and the circling of the economic and social wagons around it" (Friedan 1993, 614) work to deny the old new possibilities, Friedan also believes, as Robert Butler said in the first United Nations World Assembly on Aging in 1982, that "to unleash the unimagined resources of people growing older all over the world ... is the next step in society's evolution" (574). Stephen Katz calls this evolution the undisciplining of age, a process "where knowledge relations disassemble and disrupt dominant truth-making practices" (Katz 1996, 136) in both individual lives and in gerontological theory and practice. He further argues that undisciplining old age involves not only emphasizing heterogeneity and diversity, but separating chronological linear time from lived subjective time, fracturing traditional environments of aging, and allowing the contradictory and ambiguous relationship of the old to the dominant culture to surface.

Both feminist gerontology — research and theorizing on gender differences, diversity, and age relations in aging and old age — and narrative gerontology — research that fosters an understanding of age from the perspective of the old through interviews, life reviews, and attention to the writing of older people themselves — are positions that undiscipline traditional gerontology and merge the natural and the social. Feminist and narrative gerontologists also feel "an ethical responsibility to function as social-change agents, broadening and deepening public perception and providing alternative images and conceptions of aging and old age" (Ray 2008, xi). According to Ruth Ray, these countercultural stories celebrate "the unexpected and the inexplicable," promote "the critical self-reflection ... needed to work through our own age anxieties" (xi), and ultimately create theory that juxtaposes the personal with the scholarly in "an open exchange between fields of thought, practice, and imagination" (Katz 2005, 98). Ray calls this kind of research, writing, and theorizing passionate scholarship.

Ironically, recognition that the old are just as much entangled as anyone in the becoming of the world can itself work to problematize the elderly. Although the association of activity with well-being in old age seems indisputable, when activity is "formulated as an instrument to administer, calculate, and codify everyday conduct in institutional and recreation environments" (Katz 2005, 122), as in the standardized framework of the Activities of Daily Living (ADL), it often construes as abnormal those who prefer idleness, thought, or reflection to busyness.[4] As Foucault explains in *Discipline and Punish*, when disciplinary power is employed to "intensify the use of the slightest moment" (Foucault 1995, 154) since "nothing must remain idle or useless" (152) in the interest of constant improvement and progress, then a picture of normative old age is produced in which anyone who isn't constantly engaged in an activity is marginalized and pathologized.

Moreover, constant activity can promote a preoccupation with the body that can position older people as targets for the marketing of agelessness. In a neoliberal consumer society where the distinction between the mundane and the eternal, the mortal and the immortal, is effaced in order to emphasize simultaneity rather than linearity, "images of aging that foster a more timeless and ageless experience of growing older" (Katz 2005, 193) often mask the reality of disease and create a standard of fitness that many may not be able to, financially or physically, or want to attain. For instance, the marketing of sexual dysfunction medications and the conflation of sexual functionality with healthy aging not only can aid in the expression of sexuality in old age, but may intensify "the sense in which performing gender becomes a lifelong project" (Calasanti and Slevin 2006, 91), reintroducing the restrictions of heterosexual normativity that might have been loosened by age. Thus, greater social equality and diversity may be rejected in the very expectation of "growing older unburdened by the limitations of aging" (Katz 2005, 193).

Whenever we watch a film that tells us something about aging and old age, we need to critically examine how the category "old" is materially and discursively constituted in order to expose the reifications that tacitly serve as substantial age cores or identities. Such an examination can allow us to denaturalize age, to uproot the pervasive assumptions about what is natural for certain ages and to see how these presumptions often violently limit both our illusions about age and its lived experience. Therefore, in addition to finding out to what extent each film uses the narrative of decline as a meaning-making device that reinforces or reimagines aging and old age, we need to investigate what philosophical and theoretical positions support the ability of a film to convey a particular meaning. Does a film present old age as an essential, natural, and universal condition that erases difference and homogenizes the behavior, attitudes, and desires of older people in order to see them as eminently knowable and predictable? allow for diversity among the old by telling stories and using discourses that explore alternatives to the prevailing ideas about old age and show it to be a contextual, contingent, and constructed category? destabilize the entire notion of categories by highlighting the ways in which older people continually challenge and subvert the meanings attached to the physical realities of aging in order to make new places and meanings for themselves? question Western ideas of independence, autonomy, and rationality as ideals of personhood by depicting our dependence on each other and our entanglement with each other at any age?

By seeing the making and viewing of film as part of a cultural struggle over meanings that are never fixed nor natural, and as part of contested practices of representation and creation intimately connected to the way we understand the various texts we encounter and to the way we make ourselves and our relationships, a critical approach to viewing popular film can allow us to recognize and create alternate ways to age. And by exploring the ways that film can make the shared meanings and philosophical foundations of aging and old age literally visible, we can work to replace derogatory narratives such as the narrative of decline with stories, discourses, narratives, myths, and philosophies that will allow the full diversity, potential, entanglement, and beauty of all who live long enough to be called old to become both visible and livable.

2

Masculinities and the Narrative of Decline

How do the negative stereotypes inhabiting the narrative of decline influence the way older men are characterized in film? In what ways does film make use of these stereotypical notions of age and gender to allow an audience to fill in the blanks, causing a word, a glance, a gesture, or a movement by an old man to mean something more, less, or different than the same sign would mean if given by a man of a different age? By viewing the movies *Gran Torino* and *Up* with a critical eye as to what is left out as much as to what is explicitly included, we can begin to see how each movie essentializes and/or denaturalizes the category old age by using tropes of masculinity to limit or expand how far any given character may believably stray beyond its bounds. And by examining how successful are a character's attempts to challenge, escape from, or subvert the ability of the narrative of decline to define his life, we can become aware of its power to corral even recalcitrant old men into its fold.

Gran Torino (2009) opens with a shot of the façade of a handsome old brick church quickly followed by a view of a cloth-draped casket in a sanctuary. The camera shows us the predominantly older congregation, leads our eyes across a white-haired man playing traditional organ music, and comes to rest on Walt Kowalski who is standing in front near the casket at his wife Dorothy's funeral. The camera closes in on Walt who, between accepting condolences from friends, snarls at the behavior of his inappropriately dressed and irreverent grandchildren. In the pews, we listen as his two sons discuss their uneasiness about "the old man's" future in an ethnically changing and increasingly dangerous neighborhood. "What are we going to do with him?" they ask each other. "Don't you think he's going to get in trouble over there ... by himself?" As Walt lowers his head to cough, they smile ruefully at the thought of someone who's "still living in the fifties" ever moving in with one of them.

The animated film *Up* (2009) quickly establishes Carl Fredricksen as a lonely, old widower as well. As a disembodied hand shuts off an alarm at 6:00 AM, we are shown a blocky old man who growls, has difficulty loosening up his creaky back on rising, and descends the stairs in a motorized chair to a breakfast of bran. Dusting the mantel after breakfast, he lifts and replaces a bird that he and his wife Ellie bought just so, reluctant to make any change even though she's gone. And when he fumbles to undo the many locks on his front door to sit on his porch, part of the reason for his perpetual frown becomes clear as the camera backs away to show the once rural house that he and Ellie restored together now standing alone in a construction zone full of high-rises.

Ageism

From the start, both Walt and Carl are depicted as widowed, retired, curmudgeonly holdouts whose futures look precarious. Their age, their inability to keep up with the times, their status as widowers in a changing neighborhood, and their potentially deteriorating health all work together to place them in a category called old, "a category that is distinct from [that of] ordinary human beings" (Bytheway 2005, 362), and one that is "socially constructed as a problem" (Cruikshank 2003, 7). Although categorization by chronological age can be seen as simply a convenient tool for quantitatively-based research and regulation — since your date of birth in contrast to your age remains the same throughout your life — it nevertheless also works to confer an external social identity. Furthermore, since categorization by numerical age is a construct that is deliberately homogenizing, it inevitably fosters ideas about sameness and difference that allow a number, or inclusion within a specific range of numbers, to become part of who we see ourselves to be, a part that is often riddled with stereotypical ideas and assumptions concerning our tastes, behavior, and abilities.

Whenever these ideas and assumptions become tied to descriptive words and phrases, categorization by age can quickly turn into a kind of prejudice that encourages tensions and conflict among age groups. Given that the prejudiced person exaggerates the extent to which members of the same group are similar to one another, and also chooses to view people belonging to different groups as being very different, such age-based prejudice can easily lead to the practice of ageism. Ageism, therefore, "gener-

2. Masculinities and the Narrative of Decline

ates and reinforces a fear and denigration of the ageing process ... and legitimates the use of chronological age to mark out classes of people who are systematically denied resources and opportunities that others enjoy" (Bytheway 1995, 14).

In "Ageism and Age Categorization," Bill Bytheway, social gerontologist and founding member of the British Society of Gerontology, discusses the two classic definitions of ageism that helped establish the notion of age-related prejudice in the popular consciousness. The first is from Robert Butler, one of the first gerontologists to recognize categorical discrimination against the elderly and the man who, in 1968, coined the term "ageism" to describe the phenomenon. The second is from Alex Comfort whose book, *A Good Age* (1976), contributed to a growing anti-ageist consciousness in popular culture.

> Ageism can be seen as a process of systematic stereotyping of and discrimination against people because they are old, just as racism and sexism accomplish this for skin colour and gender.... Ageism allows the younger generations to see older people as different from themselves, thus they subtly cease to identify with their elders as human beings [Butler, R. 1975, 35].
>
> Ageism is the notion that people cease to be people, cease to be the same people or become people of a distinct and inferior kind, by virtue of having lived a specified number of years.... Like racism, it needs to be met by information, contradiction and, when necessary, confrontation. And the people who are being victimized have to stand up for themselves in order to put it down [Comfort 1977, 35].

According to Bytheway, although both definitions relate ageism to chronologically older age and social conflict, Butler's definition asserts that it is the way individual older people look and act that leads to prejudice, whereas Comfort's definition stresses the effects of the imposition of chronological age bars and institutionally managed identity on the individual (Bytheway 2005). Butler's definition encourages us to "view aging through the prism of illness" and health (Cruikshank 2003, 35), making the state of the body all-important in the decision to categorize someone as old. *Up* director, Pete Docter, overtly engaged in this type of ageism when, in order to create a convincing old man, he and his coworkers went to an old-folk's home disguised as a Tin Pan Alley band to take notes on how the residents looked and moved. As he later told NPR's "Fresh Air" host Terry Gross in an interview, he used stereotypically "old" movements that they had observed there, such as the way the men living in the home would hike up their pants then slowly lower themselves to within plopping distance of a chair (Docter 2009), to fashion a believable animated older character.

Comfort's definition, on the other hand, leads us to view aging through the institutional prism of personhood, making issues pertaining to rights, privileges, and citizenship of paramount importance. Both Docter and Eastwood highlight this kind of ageism through the assumptions of decline and incompetence that family and authority figures make regarding their protagonists. Yet, by filming stories that allow their characters to grow, stand up for themselves, and confront efforts to control and subordinate them, as Comfort's definition suggests the old do, both directors also challenge certain stereotypical assumptions about what actions older men may be able to carry out. In an interview with AARP The Magazine, Eastwood readily admitted that Walt's character represents his "'never-too-old-to-learn philosophy' ... a rich topic at this stage of life" (Hochman 2010, 62) and said that he enjoys pushing both himself and his "audiences to think about difficult, sometimes uncomfortable issues" (62).

Despite their differences, when these definitions are taken together, we can see that ageism, like other categorical types of prejudice, is consummately essentializing, rooted in both physical appearance and in the social and political practices of age categorization, and manifested in the age-related justification of inequality, control, and subordination. Age prejudice, according to psychologist Todd D. Nelson, "is one of the most socially-condoned and institutionalized forms of prejudice" (Nelson, T. 2005, 207). Therefore, to reach a certain age is not only to be subordinated to a number and to be put into a subjective category masquerading as objective, but it is to find oneself inhabiting a political location as well. This political location is bounded and enforced by age relations—"the system of inequality, based on age, that privileges the not-old at the expense of the old" (Calasanti and Slevin 2006, 1)—which serve as a principle of social organization, a gateway to identity and power, and a point of intersection with other systems of inequality such as class, race, ethnicity, sexuality, and gender. Taken together, the system of age relations by which societies are organized and through which societies "reproduce social hierarchies by producing and giving meaning to aging bodies" (11) can seriously affect an older person's ability to obtain or retain authority, status, and the rights of citizenship, to maintain economic independence and personal autonomy, and to have social and cultural contributions recognized. Thus, it is not old age but the practice of ageism that works to rein-

2. Masculinities and the Narrative of Decline

force the narrative of decline, and the narrative of decline that justifies ageist behavior.

When Walt's sons characterize him as a problem and ask themselves what they are going to do with him they are, therefore, engaging in the oppressive, though naturalized, practice of ageism and believing in the narrative of decline. When they assume that something must be done with him, rather than fully engage him in their discussions, they are setting up an adversarial relationship with their father based on age, one that only adds to the alienation they feel from their father and that Walt feels from them. Perhaps his assumed loss of autonomy and perceived inevitable decline is best depicted in the scene in which his son and daughter-in-law arrive at his house bearing gifts on his birthday. They give him a gopher tool, "so you can reach things. It makes things a lot easier." And they hand him a phone with extra-large numbers. "This is from me. It's a phone ... I just thought, we thought, that it would make things easier.... Maybe it's time you started thinking about taking it easier." They then urge him to move into a retirement community by stressing that, without Dorothy, the house is too much to maintain and by arguing that he would be happier living around people his own age in a "home" that is "great, beautiful, really nice," just like a resort or a hotel.

When Walt snarls and ejects his son and daughter-in-law from his house along with their gifts, his angry behavior is interpreted as pathological, as a sign of senescence rather than as a justifiable reaction to patronizing and ageist attitudes and actions founded in blind acceptance of the narrative of decline. Walt then finds himself in a classic bind that Cruikshank describes as "a Catch-22, caught between a social ethic of independence on the one hand, and [an] ... ethic which constructs [him] as dependent on the other" (Cruikshank 2003, 17). From Walt's perspective, his family's unquestioning adherence to the idea that old means incompetent and to the notion that a perception of failing self-reliance gives them the right to interfere unasked *should* be met by anger. Yet, when he becomes angry and asserts his right to make decisions on his own behalf, his anger only plays right into his family's predetermined belief in the "truth" of ageist characterizations of the old as uncooperative and out of control, thus strengthening their resolve to see him as a problem.

Carl is treated in a similar fashion when a construction machine damages the mailbox that he and Ellie painted and put up years ago. When, without thinking, he hits one of the crew over the head with his cane, the understandable anger behind his quite sanctionable action is dismissed as the abnormal, even dangerous, ranting of an out-of-control-old man. His action also provides the perfect excuse to move him out of his house so that others can take control of his property. In quick succession, we see a mortified Carl hiding in his house, appearing in a courtroom with a summons, and being returned to his home by a police woman who, although she tells him "you don't seem like a public menace to me," nevertheless hands him a pamphlet on the retirement home where he will be taken in the morning. Carl, too, finds himself in a Catch-22 situation, one that Stephen Katz describes as the equation of "physical decline in old age [with] ... moral and intellectual deterioration" (Katz 1996, 89).

The connection between the physiology of old age and the waning of cognitive capacities in the old was made most clearly in the writings of physician George M. Beard in the late nineteenth and early twentieth centuries. To a narrative of physical decline, Beard added "a dimension of moral and intellectual deterioration" in which "brain disease ... and moral decay become signs of each other" (Katz 1996, 89). According to Beard, such signs as failing intelligence and decline in memory led to irresponsible behavior and "put a person's legal responsibility into question" (89). Beard's work along with that of William Osler, who popularized Anthony Trollope's satire *The Fixed Period* (1882) in which, upon reaching the age of 67, all persons living on the island of Britannula were given one peaceful, contemplative year, then chloroformed (Cole 1993), foreshadowed the growing authority of medical and industrial discourses of productivity and efficiency in defining the meaning of old age. Thus, age bars, industrial generational replacement policies, and the assumed connection between physical and mental decline and incompetence worked together to legitimate age discrimination by proffering the idea that old age itself was "a menace to the future security of America" (Katz 1996, 91).

Therefore, when Walt is encouraged and Carl is ordered to move into a retirement home, when the anger of both old men is misinterpreted as a lack of competence or control, and when Carl is thought to be a menace to society, these words, ideas, and actions are not simply descriptive of the present state of affairs, but rely on a "condensed historicity" (Butler, J. 1997, 3) which positions them as simultaneously the deliberate and unintentional effects of the present situation. It is not Walt and Carl's personal behavior alone that elicits such a response, but the underlying sedimentation and repetition of words, ideas, and actions that have become internal to the idea of an old person through time that give the response such force (Butler, J. 1997).

2. Masculinities and the Narrative of Decline

Knowledges of Old Age

Michel Foucault describes this force as the power resulting from the proliferation of disciplinary knowledges about the body and the life course. These knowledges are produced in a constantly expanding arena of disciplines, such as geriatrics and gerontology, through various methods of surveillance, classification, and documentation, and work to constitute specific subjects of power and knowledge bounded by normalizing judgment. Since judgment according to norms imposes homogeneity on a group and, at the same time, introduces individual difference by searching out abnormalities within each person, it also seeks to control or erase these abnormalities through bodily and ideological discipline. Both bodily nonconformity and ideological resistance, or reluctance to accept certain ideas and truths, are met by very real material effects, such as separation from the rest of society or loss of certain liberties. Thus, any indiscipline which challenges the fixity of a body in definite relations of domination is considered an offense and must be countered by efforts to reform or sequester the offender.

Stephen Katz draws on Foucault's understanding of the way that disciplinary knowledges have fashioned "the aged body as a coherent signification system taken to represent the inevitable difference of a subject of old age" (Katz 1996, 27) to show how the disciplining of gerontological knowledge depended on the historical differentiation of the elderly as both a separate and knowable subject and a differentiated population. With the rise of geriatrics, which referred to medicine specializing in the old, and gerontology, which concerned itself with the psychology, sociology, and demography of the old, the aged body and the elderly population became the focus of both medical and custodial institutions. Thus, the growth of disciplinary knowledge about the aged body led to the proliferation of disciplinary practices concerning old age itself, a time of life increasingly constituted as a social problem. In addition, once the medical and custodial institutions defined old age as a separate time of life, identifiable "on the basis of supposedly behavioral, physical, and moral ills specific to the age of its members" (59), life itself was divided into stages, each marked by a particular age range and by the behaviors, attitudes, and opportunities that corresponded to it.

As Katz notes, acceptance of the idea of sequence and association inevitably structured both the anticipated and the acceptable attributes of arbitrary stages of life — infancy, childhood, adolescence, adult, young old, and old old. Thus, old age, seen as the conclusion to the sequential narrative of life, came to be identified with certain behaviors thought to be appropriate to its place in the sequence rather than with those behaviors actually exhibited by older people (Katz 1996). Sequence and association thus gave rise to models, such as Erik Erikson's eight stages of life,[1] that produced both a standardization of age-graded behavior and identity, and a closed system in which the old person is unvarying and without individual intention. These models also corresponded to the bureaucratic, cultural, and economic needs of society, defining the normative age of activities such as school, work, marriage, and retirement to serve the needs of social control. By reducing human value to institutionalized stages, each with measurable productivity or burdensomeness, and by making the temporalization of life into a technology of control, Western culture "lost the power to envision aging both as decline and the fulfillment of life" (Cole 1993, 170).

Yet this closed system of stages consistently ignores many of the realities and individual differences and desires of the old person. For example, Erikson's eighth age of man, "Old Age: Integrity vs. Despair," describes being old as a time to look back and evaluate past accomplishments, and his ninth stage for the very old, added to his book, *The Life Cycle Completed*, by his wife Joan when they were in their eighties, does little but magnify the despair, low self-esteem, and loss of confidence with which his theory already characterizes the last stages of life. Even though Erikson stresses that the poles of each stage (eg. integrity and despair) create a tension or struggle that can be a source of strength and new growth, his last stages allow little space for new beginnings, continuing desires, or unexpected possibilities (Erikson, 1997).

Such a model also ignores the looping effect that the internalization of life-stage-thinking may have on social policy and the distribution of medical resources. "A society that spends virtually nothing for preventative care in effect creates illness for its older citizens, and the frailty and dependency that often accompany late-life illness appear to be natural rather than partly the result of health care policy" (Cruikshank 2003, 111). Age studies scholars such as Cruikshank stress that, rather than address the fact that old age magnifies existing inequalities in money, power, and status, as well as the cumulative effects of a lifetime of prejudice or discrimination due to gender, class, ethnicity, or environment, a life-stage model that emphasizes the inevitability of age-related deterioration and despair also contributes to the lack of emphasis on restoration of function

2. Masculinities and the Narrative of Decline

or on the fact that many kinds of physical and cognitive decline can coexist with good health. Therefore, a society conditioned to expect decline may, without thinking, attribute to aging disease and deterioration that is due to social or environmental causes or that could be treated, and will tend to concentrate on the deficits associated with old age rather than the opportunities.

Self-Reinvention

Yet, in the preface to the extended version of *The Life Cycle Completed* composed by Joan Erikson after her husband's death, she states that elders must "join in the process of adaptation [and] ... live, love, and learn openly ... for wisdom and integrity are active, lifelong, developing processes ... should we dare to hope ... unending?" (Erikson 1997, 9). It is precisely through the process of adaptation that both Walt and Carl are able to move past despair and into hope and life again. Despite Walt's initial racial prejudice, Walt and Carl's reluctance to let anyone new in their lives, and their focus on the past in rapidly changing neighborhoods, both Walt and Carl develop new relationships, care about new people, and in the process reinvent themselves in ways that defy the characterization of the last stages of life as time for reflection rather than action.

We can clearly see Walt's altered demeanor when, after several unpleasant encounters with his Hmong neighbors, the teenager Sue, of whose spunk and direct manner Walt has become fond, convinces him to attend the party they're holding for a new Hmong baby. To his surprise, he finds himself thoroughly enjoying the food, the company, and the attentions of the Hmong women. His obvious pleasure while they ply him with savory dishes in the crowded kitchen forms a picture in stark contrast to both the discomfort he felt at the wake for his wife and the birthday "celebration" he has just endured with his own family. Even after Sue introduces him to the local Hmong "witch doctor," who takes a look at Walt and immediately characterizes him as a man without the respect of his family and as someone who's worried, who has made mistakes, and who enjoys no happiness or peace, Walt barely flinches. And although he tries to hide the fact that he's ill to the point of coughing up blood, he clearly appreciates the fact that both Sue and her brother Thao show more concern for his health than does his own family. By the end of the day, Walt concludes that he has more in common with "these gooks than with [his] own spoiled-rotten family."

The Becoming of Age

By allowing himself to be drawn into this Hmong family's life, Walt begins to look forward again, not by denying his age or his infirmities, as he is often called "old man" and even ordered by Thao to lift the light end of a freezer he and Thao are moving up the stairs, but by making new connections and forging new relationships. Perhaps in part to atone for the distant relationship he has with his own sons, he becomes a role model and father figure to Thao and Sue, helping Thao to navigate American working class culture and to believe in himself, and protecting both Thao and Sue from the depredations of their cousin's gang. In spite of his unwillingness to modify the racist language he uses to describe those he considers foreign, he learns to see his neighbors as a family struggling with a new culture in a difficult situation and comes to admire their cohesion, integrity, and determination to succeed.

We first know that Carl is undergoing a similar process of transformation when, the morning after his court appearance for out-of-control behavior, two men come to transport him to Shady Oaks, the retirement home. Although he seems polite and docile enough while excusing himself to go back in the house one more time, a move that is interpreted by the men in white as an old man's eightieth trip to the bathroom, instead of returning, he inflates hundreds of balloons he has tied to his hearth, wrenches his house off its foundation, and floats away over the city. Determined to fly all the way to Paradise Falls, the place in South America that he and Ellie had dreamed about since they were children, at first he's annoyed to find Russell, a young Wilderness Explorer seeking a badge for assisting the elderly, clinging to his front porch as the house soars through the air. But after Russell successfully steers them through a turbulent thunderstorm, Carl begins to accept help and, perhaps thinking about the children he and Ellie never could have, lets the young boy into his life.

A Pixar short entitled "George and AJ" takes a satirical look at Carl's escape from the point of view of the two men, George and AJ, who came to take Carl to the nursing home. As Carl's house whooshes over them with Russell clinging precariously to the underside, we hear an alarm, see a Channel 4 breaking news segment about how Carl, a "recently convicted public menace," has probably successfully evaded capture after a fierce storm made chase impossible, and are shown a crowd of old people waving their canes and cheering. As word gets out that escape and freedom are possible, a nod to Foucault's insistence that the possibility of resistance and revolt are embedded within disciplinary discourses of power, George and AJ's pickups are constantly thwarted — by a herd of cats pulling an

2. Masculinities and the Narrative of Decline

old lady's house down the road, by a house-sized catapult and a parachute, and finally by the ignition of oxygen canisters that rocket the entire Shady Oaks building up and away. As the alarm continues to sound, we secretly cheer for the elderly, for the success of those made less than human by an overarching narrative of decline that relies on the discipline and regulation of biopower[2] to justify the perpetration of violent acts of exclusion in the name of care and compassion (Foucault 1997b). By clearly revealing confinement to a retirement home to be a means of social control, this short manages to unite us with the elderly in opposing such clearly coercive actions and, in the process, makes us realize that "they" are really not so far away from "us."

By the time his house lands in South America, Carl, still intent on fulfilling his and Ellie's dream, nevertheless finds himself concerned about and protective of not only Russell, but Kevin the snipe and her baby birds, and Dug the talking dog. When Russell asks Carl to promise to help Kevin evade capture by those who want to harm her and to cross his heart to seal the promise, something Ellie always asked him to do, Carl begins to accept the role of father or grandfather figure and to adapt to his new circumstances—to have a new adventure.

From this point on, protagonists Walt and Carl lose interest in lamenting their losses and increasingly dedicate themselves to keeping Thao and Sue, and Russell and Kevin and Dug safe. When Thao is beaten and burned by members of the Hmong gang, Walt goes to their house, manhandles one of the gang, and threatens them all with even more violence if they continue to interfere in Thao's family's life. After Carl's childhood hero, Muntz, turns out to be a villain who is out to capture and kill the snipe Kevin in order to clear his name, Carl doesn't hesitate to help his new friends escape from the wrath and the thinly veiled threats of a truly out-of-control old man. When the Hmong gang showers the house next door with bullets and sends Sue home badly beaten and traumatized, Walt struggles to control his anger while he makes a plan to ensure that the gang will permanently "go away." After Muntz tries to burn down Carl's house, Carl, in an attempt to control his anger and inspired by what Ellie wrote in her adventure book—"Thanks for the adventure! Go have a new one."—, finally decides to toss out the treasured belongings that are weighing him down and flies off in his house, making plans to save his friends from the ferocious "gang" of dogs and defeat the evil Muntz.

Rather than succumb to the seemingly inevitable decline, despair, and inertia of old age that characterizes many life course models, traits that are personified in the one-sided character Muntz who is consumed with a bitterness and a despair that make him unable to let go of the past, Walt and Carl behave in a way that conforms more closely to Gene Cohen's interpretation of the dynamics of later life. Although taught by Erikson at Harvard, Cohen later modified his teacher's ideas to construct a four-phase model to describe late life, which he called (1) midlife reevaluation, (2) liberation, (3) summing up, and (4) encore (Cohen, G. 2005), and insisted that later life was "more fluid, dynamic, and variegated" (Achenbaum 2010, 240) than Erikson's model allowed. As a physician-scientist, Cohen helped many elders solve relational problems and overcome professional obstacles in order to grow, and saw firsthand that "as long as curiosity is not shut down permanently by dogma, orthodoxy, or ... belief systems, it can flourish throughout life and be a fount of energy, vitality, and satisfaction" (Cohen, G. 2005, 31). He strongly believed that curiosity led to the kind of creativity that enabled older people to become aware of and exercise their potential in later life, leaving them in better health, and enjoying higher morale, less depression, and greater social engagement than those who felt their creative life was over. Ultimately, he argued, the actions of older people themselves "would alter prevailing notions about attributes and expectations associated with the human life course" that would lead to a "fundamental restructuring of societal institutions and generational relations" (Achenbaum 2010, 246).

By acting, that is by letting go of imprisoning pasts in order to experience what Cohen calls liberation, and by becoming aware of their potential for new endeavors or what Cohen calls encore, both Walt and Carl creatively reinvent themselves and regain their self-respect, confidence, and strength in the process. Through their own actions, they reveal, as Margaret Gullette says in her essay, "Our Best and Longest Running Story," that both progress and aging are stories, the kind that although they never happen "in the vacuum of a solitary mind" (Gullette 2009, 29), can be individually rewritten based on judgments about the underlying directions of a changing self in spite of the existence of constraining cultural narratives.

Gullette uses the conversations between Simone de Beauvoir and Jean-Paul Sartre, when he was 69 and in poor health, to illustrate that progress story-telling that defies the narrative of decline is still possible even in the worst circumstances. Perhaps Beauvoir, who had published *La Vieillesse*[3] a few years before, was curious as to how well Sartre's belief in the "underlying direction of value" (Gullette 2009, 30) of a life course had

2. Masculinities and the Narrative of Decline

held up now that he was going blind and finding it difficult to write. But when she asked him how he felt about his own progress narrative, he replied, "I always thought life was progress up until death — that it must be progress.... As I see it, the moment itself is already progress. It is the present and it flows on toward the future, leaving behind it the poor, disdained, despised, denied past. For this reason, I've always readily admitted misdeeds or mistakes, since they were committed by someone else" (Beauvoir 1984, 414–415). Sartre's account evaporates his past selves and allows him to concentrate on being alive now. For him, decline and loss are not the dominant story of old age, as if there were only one story and only one self to lose, but the story and its often reinvented self continue to the end.

Sartre's attitude both decenters his body as the most important marker in the narrative of aging — although not through denial of physical loss or disguise of physical symptoms — and provides him with a sense of personal continuity, paradoxically achieved by leaving his past selves behind. Such an attitude challenges society's right to deny a feeling of progress (hope, growth) to an entire category of people, and argues for each of us to wrench our personal progress narrative from the overarching cultural narrative of decline. It allows us to separate ourselves from the "idea" of the old person that Hacking talked about, and to be for ourselves. Despite the fact that consistency and stability, "the necessary requisites [for maintaining a progress narrative] have been becoming more elusive ... over the last thirty years" (Gullette 2009, 25), and that progress narratives for older people are constantly assaulted by the specter of loneliness, insecurity, downward mobility, and poverty, Sartre's attitude can give us enough hope to believe that change is possible.

Both Walt and Carl embody the effects of Sartre's attitude when their anger at being stereotyped and treated as children combines with the hope that things could be different and results in actions that return to them an "individual sense of control and social engagement" (Perlstein 2010, 254), changing the way they view themselves and their capabilities. In *Gran Torino*, through the act of strategizing to solve the gang problem permanently, Walt regains a sense of mastery of the situation. In *Up*, Carl's newfound resolve allows him to fling himself back into life and interact creatively with a new and dangerous environment. They both demonstrate what Erikson called vital involvement, or "the process through which we, at any age, participate in life's activities, responsibilities, joys, and hardships, and through which we incorporate the influences of all these into the ... self we are constantly becoming" (Kivnick 2010, 424). Since vital involvement underlies both individual creativity and social relations, it allows us to use obstacles and challenges that previously might have forced us to withdraw to "engage meaningfully with ideas ... and one another ... by expressing new or different strengths ... and by continuing to develop new ... abilities" (425).

Mapping the Life Course

The self-reinvention that vital involvement can occasion in older men can also be interpreted as a self-sustaining reaction to the realities of marginalization and loss of power that occurs in contemporary post-retirement life. Walt's pride in the fact that he actually built part of his classic Gran Torino and his willingness to use the "proper" tool to "fix things," and Carl's novel use of balloons, the tools of his trade, to make his escape and chase his dream, can be seen as a way of resisting the marginalization of retirement by demonstrating that the knowledge acquired during their working years is still relevant.

The intertwining of the ideas of marginalization and retirement that both characters experience is documented as far back as medieval times. Although old age as a stage of life was not yet set apart by specific rituals or customs, since most people had little idea of their chronological age, the use of retirement contracts allowed for the transmission of resources to the younger generation while making provisions for lifelong maintenance in a separate residence for parents (Cole 1993). Therefore, although no longer involved directly in the day-to-day operation of a farm or a business and, in that sense, marginalized, the expertise of the elderly was neither discarded nor out of reach. The principle of familial provision for the aged was also reflected in England's Poor Law of 1601 which "stipulated that children provide for their elderly parents" (Katz 1996, 53), a practice which required contact between generations rather than leaving the old isolated and dependent on charity or the state.

If the aged had no family to care for them, as was the case of many in America, they could enter the almshouse, a last resort place where the able-bodied poor of any age could work in order to receive relief. But, as Katz points out, when the number of persons needing relief rose sharply during the nineteenth century, in part due to the redefining of unemployment and poverty as individual rather than social problems, gradually the almshouse came to function as an institution of reform as well as a humanitarian refuge. Given that the majority of the inmates were elderly, it soon

2. Masculinities and the Narrative of Decline

became clear that the old, unlike the unemployed, the mentally ill or the criminal, could not be reformed through self-discipline and hard work. Thus, it was the condition of the elderly in the almshouse, not of the elderly who remained with family, that unwittingly provided the basis on which authorities began to associate old age itself with poverty and dependency and to mark the elderly with the subjective homogeneity of a distinct population (Katz 1996).

According to Stephen Katz in his book, *Disciplining Old Age*, if the almshouse was a technology of differentiation that "created a marginalized social space" (Katz 1996, 61), a space both visually and viscerally depicted by Walt and Carl's sense of isolation at the beginning of the movies, then the development of pension and retirement programs was a technology that "created a marginalized social time" (61), evinced, although in contradictory ways, in the scene in which Walt sits on his porch with his dog Daisy, drinking beer after beer until the cooler is empty while losing track of time, and in Carl's near obsession with time in the opening scene when he wakes up at 6:00 AM, dresses, eats, dusts, and checks the mail even though he has no obvious reason to be so punctual. Although the idea that only the old should inhabit this marginalized time dates back to a public pension plan for Civil War veterans in which age alone qualified one for benefits, its true roots lie in the twentieth century desire to rationalize and control labor by legitimizing unemployment as retirement. If the elderly could be characterized as slow, inefficient, and unable to keep up, as both Walt and Carl have been, then a normative age for old age could be constructed after which workers could be excluded from the workforce, Katz argues. By 1935, the year the Social Security Act was passed, sixty-five was widely accepted as the minimum retirement age, an age that better suited political and economic imperatives than the actual needs of the elderly.

Another way to understand the correspondence between old age as a stage and the characteristics ascribed to it is by seeing the ordering of life as a series of stages as the effect, and not the cause, of the mapping of or laying out of a grid over the life course. As with the mapping of any geographical area in which a grid arbitrarily marks off areas previously delineated by their physical properties and embedded histories, mapping appears to record and make intelligible "natural" categories. Yet "many quite real things had to be reorganized to make the world appear to separate cleanly along its new divide" (Mitchell 2002, 93), and to the extent that the map or the representation takes precedence over the lived reality, the violence done to an individual life course involved in this reorganization is effectively erased. By abstracting old age from its context within a whole life and from its connection to lives of other ages, an abstraction that often manifests itself in ageist behavior similar to the kind that both Walt and Carl experience, mapping life allows the problems associated with aging to be seen as natural rather than political and encourages solutions that other and exclude the old. This depoliticization also allows the social and structural issues of retirement to cease being a question of power and control over people's resources and lives and to become a problem of management (Mitchell 2002), a problem often "solved" by coercive efforts to place the old, like Walt and Carl, in retirement homes. Ironically, retirement, according to the map of life, signifies "an unmapped space at the end of the life course — a space not literally but by social definition 'empty'" (Walker, M. 1999, 105) "even if there's a lot of life left" (104).

Although economic and social technologies that control working lives and overarching grids that squeeze lived experience into a premapped life course are attempts to corral the old and retired into a marginalized and empty space and time, ironically they simultaneously create a homogenous subjectivity that allows older people to constitute a strategically essential position[4] from which to demand their collective rights and privileges. This position increases their ability to challenge the boundaries and constraints constructed around them by rigid life course perspectives, as evidenced by Eastwood himself when he says, "[retirement] is not for me" (Hochman 2010, 62). Thus, retirees now deal with not only the derogatory and historically sedimented "social perception of retirement as a marker of irreversible entry into old age" (Calasanti and Slevin 2006, 236) in "a culture and society which systematically devalues, marginalizes and discriminates against older people" (234), but with unprecedented opportunities for individual choice and for living outside the lines or in the empty space that release from the time and relational constraints of paid work may confer.

In "The Aged Traveler: Cinematic Representations of Post-Retirement Masculinity," Gabrielle Mueller characterizes one opportunity opened up by the dialectical struggle between cultural identity and self, structural constraints and personal freedom, as a reaction to the way retirement can be seen and felt "as a process of emasculation" (Mueller 2009, 151). She sees both Walt's internal journey out of racism and isolation into multicultural caring and connection, and Carl's literal journey to South America that results in new "family" connections as a type of road movie,

2. Masculinities and the Narrative of Decline

a quest narrative that transforms their experiences of self. As in road movies with younger protagonists, Walt and Carl's marginalization does not result in unquestioning conformity to the social role they are expected to play, but rather in what Mueller calls "a male escapist fantasy of freedom" (154) and transcendence, and an exploration of subversive possibilities. Yet, in contrast to road movies with younger characters, these films also offer "an affirmation of conservative social norms" (154). "If the journey in a road movie is usually coded as a process of defamiliarization, here the characters' motivation to undertake the journey is their desire to reclaim the familiar and to re-establish the intergenerational relationships on which their masculine identities were constructed" (155). Thus, Walt and Carl's journeys take them away from a despised social location not to remain outsiders, but to discover a way to return, changed in some way, to a place from which they feel they have been ejected. These films, therefore, both indict the way in which men are socialized in an industrial society where their value is determined almost exclusively through their past involvement in paid employment and offer a cultural critique of the identity crisis caused by pressure to conform to the new social role of elderly characterized by inactivity, failure to communicate, loss of dignity, isolation, and the threat of institutionalization.

Their journeys can also be seen as attempts to reclaim their age-threatened masculine identities by offering a conservative discourse of masculinity as triumphant. In "Eastwood Bound," Paul Smith discusses what he sees as the three stages that form an orthodox structuring code for action movies, including the majority of Eastwood's movies. In the first stage, we see the male body as still strong, though older, and the masculine things it does, in Walt's case "manning up" Thao and actions involving cars, tools, guns, and saving Sue, although not your typical helpless female, nevertheless a female in distress. In the second stage, we see the male body endure some type of destruction that makes it seem out of control, such as Walt's undisclosed yet potentially life-threatening illness. And in the last stage, we see the hero emerge triumphant by transcending, through regrowth, rebirth, or sacrifice, the "text" of his body, in this case Walt's choosing death in a way that is cinematically reminiscent of the figure of Christ, seen by the position in which his body is found, and symbolically reminiscent of the triumph of life over death.

When we view *Up* as an action movie that "tests" the masculinity of an aging protagonist, Carl's persona also conforms quite closely to this three-stage structuring code. His characterization as a stubborn old man trying to protect his property, followed by his brief encounter with the law due to his out-of-control behavior, resulting in his decision to embark on an adventure where he, through masculine strength and determination, triumphs over evil and is, in a sense, reborn does follow the general pattern of masculinity threatened, changed, and triumphant. Smith further argues that all three stages "must serve the end of the hero's triumph" (Smith 1995, 88) and must show masculine control over an out-of-control body at the moment it is falling apart. That the moment of regaining control serves the further purpose of "saving" Thao and Sue or Russell, Dug, and Kevin through sacrificing the past and, in Walt's case his future, simply strengthens a reading of these films as both escapist fantasies of freedom and as attempts to reclaim a threatened masculinity through the creation of new stories to replace the despised narrative deemed appropriate for retired life.

Counterstories

Yet, to what extent do Walt's choices, his vital involvement, self-reinvention, reconstructed identity, and attempts to escape the emasculating and destructive ideology of the narrative of decline succeed in breaking its hold on his life? Is he able, like Sartre, to leave behind his past with its expectation of decline and concentrate on being alive now? By the end of *Gran Torino*, Walt has forged a bold and secret plan to save his friends from the Hmong gang that has been terrorizing them. He has confessed and made peace with himself and the church, has made final arrangements for his passing, and has put his affairs in order even to the point of leaving his dog, Daisy, with the gruff Hmong grandmother next door. As he approaches the Hmong gang's house, without police support, with the priest gone from the scene, and with the angry and impulsive Thao safely locked in his cellar, what kind of story do his actions and the reasoning behind them tell?

In "Stories of My Old Age," Hilde Lindemann Nelson calls the self-transformative process that Walt is undergoing the creation of a counter-story, a story that will allow us to resist an oppressive identity by rejecting the cultural fragments out of which it is constructed and replacing them with a more respectful understanding of who we are. She argues that identities are never natural or essential but are narratively constructed in two profoundly social ways: by drawing fragments of stories from the background noise of culture to apply to ourselves and, at the same time, by

2. Masculinities and the Narrative of Decline

being subjected to the identities that others impose upon us through their own narrative activity, whether we will them or not (Nelson, H. 1999). Thus, any personal identity is put together out of the actions, experiences and characteristics that are important to our self-narrative as well as the roles and relationships that are culturally available and by which others identify us.

Nelson further argues that "the narrative figurations by which other people identify [us] can do [us] serious harm" (Nelson, H. 1999, 85) when the stock character imposed on us by others identifies us in a way that keeps us from exercising a social role that is an important part of the way we identify ourselves.

> A great deal of discrimination against the elderly tends to work in this way. The elderly person, identified as a stock figure, becomes a character in ... a narrative of decline, and the person is then required to behave according to the specifications of that particular plot (Gullette 1997). The decline narrative generally harkens back to a golden age in which the person possessed desirable qualities— ... physical strength, a sense of the Zeitgeist — and then moves to the present, in which the person has sadly, or in the nature of things, lost these qualities.... In particular, narratives of decline are oppressive when they are used to block or restrict a person's access to a valuable role or relationship that might otherwise still be acquired or retained ... [Nelson, H. 1999, 85].

When trapped in some version of the narrative of decline, the construction of a counterstory may allow us to reclaim a part of our identity that is threatened. But if we wish to invent a counterstory, it must not only break through our own internalized ageism, but be recognized and not dismissed as offensive or ridiculous by others in order to work. A good counterstory must break through the "firewall" that makes practices and structures of discrimination seem so natural and normal that any objection to these practices as injurious simply cannot be recognized as legitimate. Since firewalls are constructed by privatizing or confining people "to private spaces in a way that ... makes unkind or violent treatment of them disappear behind closed doors" (Nelson, H. 1999, 89), by naturalizing or producing the appearance of inevitability of a certain course of action, and by normalizing or making a presumption that certain behaviors "are standard and normal ... rather than wondering why that particular set of behaviors is necessary" (89), to have a counterstory seen as legitimate knowledge, we must be socially authorized to speak or, as Foucault would say, we must be part of the discourse. But given that the master narrative of aging as decline, decrepitude, and incompetence is part of the firewall, thus preemptively disqualifying an older person from speaking authoritatively, the real meaning of an elder's counterstory is often ignored, deflected, or coopted by the already existing dominant narrative.

When Walt confronts the Hmong gang alone and unarmed, knowing that as he reaches for his lighter they will assume he's going for a gun, fire on a defenseless old man, and end up in prison, he certainly is exercising his agency to create a counterstory. But what does it say? From fragments of other narratives, he constructs a new story for himself in which he can finally relieve himself of the burden of having killed someone in Korea he believes didn't deserve to die, sacrifice himself for the good of the young Hmong he has come to care for, and die honorably before the disease he has can rob him of his strength and independence. But to what extent do any of these justifications for his action really go against either his internalized ageist assumptions or the external narrative of aging as decline?

Maybe *Gran Torino's* story is so appealing precisely because it conforms to the expectations the dominant narrative has given us, rather than breaking with them. Walt is old and his family regards him as increasingly dependent and a burden, yet his conflicts with and alienation from his family have been privatized. He values his "manly" strength and feels he must protect, by the use of guns and violence, the friends for whom he has taken on a grandfatherly role, yet, at the same time, he naturalizes the diminution of his physical strength and exaggerates the importance of its loss. He is sick and probably dying (although we never really know what illness he has) and, rather than face the possibility of debilitating treatments or a future of rapid physical deterioration leading to a further loss of autonomy, he normalizes the course of his disease as unrelieved decline and loss and chooses to bypass the abhorred physical states associated with age and illness by arranging his own death before he becomes infirm.

The Choice of Death

According to Jacques Derrida in *The Gift of Death*, to choose death in this way is to recognize our absolute singularity. Derrida argues that death gives us a sense of irreplaceability and is, therefore, a call to responsibility. Since responsibility can only be felt due to our relationship with the other, death can thus be seen as the ultimate freedom, our only real choice. "I cannot die *for* another (in his place) although I can die *for* him (by sacrificing myself for him)" (Derrida 1995, 43). Only by choosing

2. Masculinities and the Narrative of Decline

death, says Derrida, do I have access to what is absolutely mine, to what no one else can decide or do for me. It seems reasonable to assume that Walt may feel, due to his special relationship with Thao and Sue, that only he can save them, that by sacrificing his life for them he is exerting control over the situation in a way that only he can.

Yet, although reclaiming our singularity and our freedom to be in control and write our own story from the homogenous muck of the depersonalizing narrative of decline is in large part what the construction of a counterstory is designed to do, Derrida's description of the choice of death as absolute freedom ignores the fact that Walt's choice is not made in a vacuum. Margaret Gullette posits that losses due to ageism as a cultural and collective phenomenon, not to aging itself which is a more personal and singular experience, are what push older people into despair and often make them conclude that "despair is a rational response to normal aging" and that "perhaps they should make an exit before they become a 'burden'" (Gullette 2011, 43). Yet despair and depression in later life are not at all inevitable. Though the term "geriatric depression" implies that there is a distinct kind of depression experienced in old age and leads many doctors to consider it normal and acceptable in older patients, "in fact older people do not suffer higher rates of major depression" (53) than others.

Rather than depression, it is more often internalization of decline ideology over a lifetime that leads to approval of suicide as an option, recasts it as the freedom to die, and even colors it as a strategy for cherishing earlier and possibly healthier parts of later life. Retirement and the loss of social capital it brings can exacerbate vulnerability to seeing self-murder as a rational option. The sense of personal failure, reduction of self-esteem, and the relentless bombardment by the hostile rhetoric of unproductivity and burdensomeness that retirees often experience can feed into a suicidal belief system that interprets the right to choose death as an issue of control. The cultural outcome of such a belief system can reduce the will to live enough to make "suicide ... seem the responsible thing [to do]" (Gullette 2011, 55) and can even convince many that it may be "for the good of the victims themselves" (Bytheway 1995, 27).

Gullette calls this trend the fantasy of the desirable self-inflicted death and argues that it is proliferating so much in novels, film, and everyday life that "suicidal ideation is becoming familiar to millions of Americans in a casual, conversational way" (Gullette 2011, 55). Yet, this fantasy takes no note of the cultural context of sexism, ableism, classism, racism, and ageism in which it exists. Neither does it recognize that the emphasis on personal choice in decisions regarding elective death also reflects the realities of a callous lack of collective social support for the elderly, increasing difficulty in accessing adequate and age-conscious health care, and the ever-present and oft-repeated incantation that the old are a drain on scarce economic resources.

This fantasy also leaves unexamined the fact that personal ideas of an afterlife both give meaning to and affect our behavior and choices in this life. In *Speaking of Death*, Michael Bartalos compiled information on modern Americans' attitudes toward and beliefs about the afterlife and found that more Americans believe in the afterlife than believe in God. He discovered that, due to the proliferation of religious options and the erosion of surety as to the "rightness" of a particular religion, heaven is now considered more of a democratic entitlement than a reward, and is structured as a place in which work, personal identity and growth, and competitive notions of progress survive (Bartalos 2009). Whether an afterlife is conceived of as a place of literal bodily resurrection or of an immortal and transcendent soul, when the fantasy of the desirable self-inflicted death takes hold, we fail to see the contradictions inherent in believing simultaneously in the continuing existence of an identity built up in this life through personal, bodily experience and the erasure or renewal of the very body in and through which that personal experience occurs. Therefore, how we conceive of an afterlife may make suicide, thought of as an escape from the pain of the identity-destroying losses of old age, become a reasonable option.

Walt's choice to die, contrary to allowing his actions to tell a new story, conforms closely to the demands of the narrative of aging as decline. Rather than being made in a context marked by individual freedom, singularity, and control, his choice is conceived within a web of cultural ideas about the questionable worthiness of the old, perceptions of the old as burdensome and useless, and notions of self-inflicted death as both a religiously defensible and a rational choice. Furthermore, it precludes an exploration of other roles for the elderly and of ways to live with disease and disability that refuse the equation of the value of a life with youth and perfect health, thus foreclosing the possibility that frailty and physical dependence can coexist with strength and independence of spirit. Even though Walt initially breaks with the decline narrative's stereotype of the old as inflexible and unchanging, he ends the story before an effective counterstory can be told.

2. *Masculinities and the Narrative of Decline*

Alternative Masculinities

The ending of *Up*, at least, allows more room to maneuver. When Carl decides to break the ties to his past that are literally holding him down, he also breaks with the picture that we as viewers, and he as a character, hold of his physical capabilities. Even though leaping on top of a moving airship and running across it to catch a dangling rope at the very last moment are feats of strength that only an animated character could manage, they nevertheless have something to say about how we think about stereotypes of aging, strength, and masculinity. In "Maintaining Manliness in Later Life," Robert Meadows and Kate Davidson argue that manhood is constructed by reference to age in ways that subordinate old men in relation to young men. They maintain that, although there are always multiple masculinities, hegemonic masculinity is "the dominant, most 'honoured or desired' form" (Meadows and Davidson 2006, 296), encompassing behaviors that legitimize patriarchal authority and lionize traits such as physical strength, self-control, and aggression. But since hegemonic masculinity also favors youth, retirement, diminishing physical strength, or illness can weaken a man's position within this dominant ideology, resulting in exclusion from masculinized spaces and designation as "other."

Older men, therefore, often feel forced to choose between attempting to continue approximating hegemonic forms and possibly facing failure, and formulating an "alternative masculinity" that can incorporate behaviors that do not derive from physical strength or patriarchal control (Meadows and Davidson 2006). One way older men may choose to continue to perform masculinity is by associating "aging with physical decline, not chronology per se, and ... demonstrat[ing] ... their youthful manliness by illustrating what they can 'still do'" (302). Carl's behavior in the daring rescue conforms to this strategy, as does his lack of need for the three-pronged cane he relied on until that point in the movie. Although disassociating chronological age from physical decline may seem a route ultimately leading to a dead end, given that perceptions of age, as Becca Levy discovered in her studies, can contribute heavily to how long and how energetically one may live in old age, it may well be worth the tenacity and energy required to maintain a distance, no matter how illusory, "between stereotypes and experiences of the aging self" (303).

Whether Carl's newfound strength and zest for life is the result of distancing himself from the image of the stereotypical old person or corroborating evidence of new research that finds that "many of the supposedly unavoidable and debilitating physiological effects of aging are [themselves] illusory" (Reynolds 2011, 81), by the time Carl arrives home, he not only is enjoying his renewed masculine physicality, but has also embraced the alternative masculinity of a caring relationship with Russell. From one point of view, his choice to fulfill the caring role as a grandfather figure appears to conform to the dominant narrative about aging, given that it can be seen as a service role, one conferring substantially less status and fewer rewards than roles considered suitable to hegemonic masculinity. Such a role can be appealing since it often fulfills the expectations of others and "since those who serve ... are unquestionably useful" (Cruikshank 2003, 41). But the service role can also mask "doubt that the old are worthy in and of themselves" (41), given that it "locates their value in action, not in being" (41), and can lead to a need to justify their continuing existence in terms of utility. The idea of having to justify the existence of the old is well expressed in "The Geezer's Crusade," an article by David Brooks ostensibly celebrating the ability of elders to demand change by leading a nonselfish revolution in generativity[5] that will better the lives of their grandchildren. Yet underneath the praise, Brooks sharply criticizes the older generation for neglecting to sufficiently serve the young, a role that he unilaterally deems infinitely more satisfying than attending to one's own wants and needs (Brooks 2010). Justifying the existence of the old by requiring of them actions not necessarily asked of other age groups and "on the grounds that they serve others is narrowly utilitarian and devalues those too infirm to give assistance to others" (Cruikshank 2003, 42) as well as those who receive assistance. It assumes that old men and women are a monolithic group and denies them the individual choice of whether and how much to serve.

From another point of view, many older men successfully incorporate caring activities into their lives when they "do not perceive caring as a burden, manage to maintain their autonomy, and gain increased self-esteem, admiration, and gratitude" from activities associated with caring (Meadows and Davidson 2006, 306). This attitude towards caring defies the narrative of decline in that it leaves men like Carl open to continued growth and development (shown by the fact that his airship, a symbol of freedom and autonomy, is moored in the sky above him), and a future of reciprocity and mutuality. It opens up Carl's world to

2. Masculinities and the Narrative of Decline

the possibility of care being an apprehension of "the world from the other's reality ... on the basis of the other's understanding of [him]self and [his] needs" (Fiore 1999, 248), rather than an apprehension based on values and needs defined by negative cultural attitudes toward the aging.

Care as reciprocity goes beyond performing the grandfather role and becomes friendship care, a kind of care whose "ethical possibilities ... exceed those of other forms of care because of its unregulated character. Relative to the conventionally designated obligations of kin ... friendship provides the condition for the possibility of freedom in an age of comprehensive social regulation" (Fiore 1999, 250). As feminist Carol Gilligan argues concerning the devaluation of an ethic of care, substituting a morality of responsibility with its consideration of relationship and reciprocity for a morality of abstract rights and rules with its emphasis on separation and difference can lead to an alternative view of the world. In this view, notions of interdependence, reciprocity, and respect alter both the way we judge ourselves and others (Gilligan 1997). Care as friendship and reciprocity, structured on values of mutual give and take and ageless respect, therefore, can often sidestep the questions of utility and social control, and better allow both parties to relish just being and becoming in each other's company.

The changes we see in Carl when he returns home, although resulting from a conscious decision to live outside the lines, nevertheless remain more ambiguous as to their status as a refutation of the dictates of the narrative of decline. It is left to the viewer to decide if the level of physical performance displayed in his adventures reaffirms the importance of strength as a marker of hegemonic masculinity, thus leaving the old who are physically frail firmly in the grip of devaluation and decline, or if his actions rather confirm mounting evidence that declining physical performance is tied more strongly to a sedentary lifestyle than to increasing age (Reynolds 2011). It is also up to the viewer to determine if Carl's newfound role as carer ties him more tightly to the dominant picture of the old as generative servants or frees him to express alternative forms of masculinity that acknowledge mutual dependence and reciprocity. Given that most moviegoers are themselves thoroughly indoctrinated into the narrative of aging as decline, the possibility that any will break through the firewall and recognize a counterstory in Carl's self-transformation is slim, but at least it exists.

Conclusion

At the end, as the credits roll, as Thao drives off with Walt's dog, Daisy, in the Gran Torino (significantly, an old car in mint condition) and Carl and Russell and Dug eat ice cream on the curb while counting cars, we need to ask ourselves if we're left feeling satisfied and comfortable, as if things turned out as they should, or if we're left with a slight sense of discomfort, wanting something more. For although it's good to have movies with aging protagonists, and great to make an audience regard them with affection and to root for their success, as critical consumers of popular culture, we need to ask ourselves if the meanings and myths, and the philosophic positions about age underlying the storyline really work to undiscipline aging and old age. Do they allow an aging character the freedom to create a believable counterstory that affirms the worthiness and the present and enduring value of the old even in the face of physical or cognitive decline? Or do they function as a tool of oppression — exaggerating the significance of loss, papering over strengths, abilities, and talents that someone might still be developing, blocking access to dreams that could still be realized, roles that still could be filled, and relationships that still might blossom?

Although the stories in *Gran Torino* and *Up* are individual, the shared meanings through which we make sense of these stories are similar. Both movies initially rely on easily recognizable stereotypes, discourses, and myths about old age and specifically masculine aging processes to set the stage for the action to come. Both movies then work to bring these stereotypes, discourses, and myths, which exist at a level of practical consciousness and therefore are not easily accessible to critical thought, to the level of discursive consciousness[6] by allowing their protagonists to breach the firewall constructed by ageism in a way that forces us to question the essential nature of certain characteristics ascribed to the old. At that point, we may begin to entertain the possibility that the category old age is, at least to some extent, socially constructed and vulnerable to the looping effect. But, rather than leave us with characters who might be permanently transformed in a way that would make them ambiguous or unrecognizable in the context of the narrative of decline, and thus socially threatening, both movies ultimately rein them in by reinserting them into culturally acceptable positions through re-equating old age with illness and death, with sacrifice for the younger generation, and with usefulness and service through the grandfather role.

2. Masculinities and the Narrative of Decline

The way that *Gran Torino* and *Up* make use of the narrative of decline is reflected in the storylines of many other movies about older men, as well. For example, in *About Schmidt* (2002), the combination of Schmidt's reluctant retirement and the death of his wife lead him to decide to take to the road to discover aspects of himself he hadn't understood and to change the way he relates to his family and to a young boy he sponsors. Yet, after several mild adventures, the film ends with Schmidt right back where he started, ultimately unable to change how he gives meaning to growing older. The two older men in *Secondhand Lions* (2003), though reclusive as are many older men in film, present more interesting characters due to their refusal to let age seriously limit their dreams and pursuits. Yet, even though an unexpected relationship with a young boy inspires them to partially rejoin society and to undertake even more adventures, they die before their fears of losing their masculine strength and their autonomy can be realized. In *Get Low* (2009), a curmudgeonly old hermit, who takes pains to show that he is still strong, publicly admits to past mistakes and successfully reintegrates himself into society only to succumb to a mysterious illness and die before he truly becomes old. In *Red* (2010), although the use of truly older actors to comically highlight negative ageist stereotypes in order to bring them to our attention is commendable, the effortless way the characters relive their youthful exploits promotes individualist ideas of "successful aging" based on continuing athletic prowess and unremarked class privilege that leave untouched the larger social contexts in which we age.

Each of these films relies excessively on the narrative of aging as decline and deterioration to cut short the life of, present as an aberration, or portray as dangerous to society and self, as comic, or as an exception any character who successfully subverts this narrative's dictates. This tactic keeps invisible and, therefore, unknowable, alternate conceptions of old age that might deal with the realities of growth and becoming despite disabilities and losses. It also diverts our attention from the difficult social and personal questions raised by deep old age, a time when a majority of those who survive will do so with significant mental and physical impairment. But most of all, it keeps us from recognizing that old age, just like any age, is filled with contradictions, ambiguities, and individual differences that should be nurtured and allowed full expression.

Learning to critically view films that deal with men's aging and old age doesn't mean we can't and shouldn't enjoy them, since many of them are excellent films, but it does mean that we will begin to notice how deeply the cinematic treatment of old age influences how we ourselves perceive, interact with, and value those who are old. Do we concur when a film denies the old the same hopes and dreams we would give ourselves, or do we, like Sartre, argue that life itself, young or old, strong or weak, valued or seemingly useless, is a continuing story of progress and hope? Do we let the old tell their own counterstory or do we insist that their story ultimately conform to a preconceived ageist narrative? Recognizing how we deal with representations of aging and old age in film can be an all-important first step in learning to recognize, resist, and replace the real-life narrative of decline.

3

The Silence and Invisibility of Older Women

How do negative stereotypes about aging and old age intersect with those about gender to influence the way older women are portrayed in film? To what extent do sexism and ageism devalue older women "not only in relation to men but also in relation to their younger counterparts" (Calasanti and Slevin 2006, 13)? How is this "double-double standard" of women's aging represented in films? In what ways do older female characters deal with the almost universal judgment that their bodies and faces naturally become unattractive with age, rendering them "justifiably" subject to the silence of social exclusion and the invisibility of cultural irrelevance? To what extent are movies complicit in concealing the structural causes of this seemingly natural social exclusion and cultural irrelevance?

Death, the Ultimate Silence and Invisibility

Before considering movies in which "older women" play a leading role[1], let's take a moment to look back at *Gran Torino* and *Up* in order to examine the roles that Dorothy, Walt's wife, and Ellie, Carl's wife, play in these movies. Although already dead when the movies begin, and therefore truly silent and invisible, Dorothy and Ellie's ever-present influence on Walt and Carl, evidenced by the way their husbands miss them, "talk" to them, and make decisions that they believe would please them, in a sense makes them main characters as well. In death, both Dorothy and Ellie are cast as carriers of pathos who cannot speak for themselves but are spoken for by others (Cruikshank 2003), as older women whose lives held no meaning or interests aside from caring for husband, church, or family, or in the case of Ellie, wished-for-family. In *Gran Torino*, for example, the priest conveys his conception of Dorothy's wishes to Walt in conversations about Walt's relationship to religion and Walt himself takes his understanding of her desires into account when he decides to leave his house to the church. In *Up*, Ellie is spoken for by the pictures and note she leaves for Carl in her adventure book, his interpretation of which greatly influences the course of his life, and by a series of sentimentalized images depicting Carl and Ellie's childhood, romance, and married life together. Although these pictures are beautiful, according to *Up* director Pete Docter, they are a blatant attempt to establish Carl's past relationship with his wife through the use of lyrical drawings, absent dialogue and sound effects, in order to construct a "shadow of a past that ... [is] abstract and emotional" (Docter 2009, 9) rather than to give substance to the woman Ellie was.

The manner in which these movies represent Dorothy and Ellie clearly reflects the influence of ageism and sexism on decisions about who will be allowed to speak and whose voice will be heard. If, as Linda Dittmar suggests in "The Articulating Self," we think of voice as not only a vehicle through which we express opinions, judgments, and will, but as an activity that symbolizes and interprets our personal experience and negotiates our access to well-being, then what is important about voice is not ownership but our ability to use voice as a tool to position ourselves and others in society (Dittmar 1994). By understanding the use of voice in film as an "arena for the clash of differences" (Dittmar 1994, 392) across social relations rather than simply as an instrument of personal expression, we can see how film uses access to voice to diminish or enhance a particular speaker in relation to an implicit hegemonic norm and to establish unspoken connotations of inferior or superior status. Thus, the filmic treatment of older women often encodes a problematic relation to speech as integral to a woman's gender and age, awakening unbidden in the listener stereotypical notions of older women as not worth listening to, as culturally irrelevant — dead or alive.

Ironically, stereotypical notions of older women's bodies as not worth looking at are also evoked by the absence, and therefore the invisibility, of their literal bodies. In *Gran Torino*, the fact that the only picture we see of Dorothy shows her as Walt's young bride allows the predominant discourses and narratives surrounding aging to paint a picture of her for us. If we think of her appearance at all, most likely that picture will be painted with "the matronly spread and shrivel" (Frueh 1999, 213) often attributed to older women's bodies, a picture whose reception works "to teach an

3. The Silence and Invisibility of Older Women

older woman to recede into invisibility" (Woodward 1999, xii). In the case of *Up*, although we do see images of Ellie when gray and ill, their deliberate sentimental and nostalgic nature precludes any serious examination of the effects of age and illness on older women's bodies. Thus, the strategy of invisibility, or visibility only through the eyes of another, keeps us from having to confront the dominant conclusion that "old age is bad, repulsive, and ugly" and "facilitates the construction of 'a culture that discards old [women]'" (Clarke 2011, 29) by silencing and making them invisible.

Kathleen Woodward argues that the invisibility of old women reflects a decidedly ageist cultural phenomenon. In the introduction to *Figuring Age*, she illustrates this phenomenon by retelling the story of 86-year-old Anna Gerbner who, while leaving a senior center, was run over by a young man on his bicycle and died of her injuries. When asked what he had to say in his defense, the young man replied, "I didn't see her" (Woodward 1999, ix). Woodward classifies Anna's demise as "death by invisibility" (ix). It is also death by silence; he never heard her voice either. Although women's increasing longevity (they now outlive men by an average of eight years as opposed to three a century ago) may indicate that natural "selection favors robustness after menopause" (Cruikshank 2003, 193), due to social policies that often deprive women of adequate income and health care, many of these hardy women "are poor ... and powerless, invisible and without voice" (Woodward 1999, xxvi). And although older women are on the front lines of what is often described as a battle for the ages— for their own economic security, for that of those for whom they care, and for some measure of justice in the skewed distribution of economic advantage in later life—they are rarely listened to or credited with the knowledge their experience has provided.

When we consider the fact that most of the old are women, their invisibility and lack of voice in film is truly remarkable. Statistically, Dorothy and Ellie should have been the stars, with Walt and Carl leaving them to fend for themselves while "talking" to them from the grave. It is an interesting exercise to imagine how differently their counterstories might have played out given the same possibilities and constraints their husbands faced. What steps would Dorothy and Ellie have taken to overcome a growing sense of isolation, make new relationships, transform themselves, or uncover their hidden "feminine" strengths? In "Misrepresentation Again," a comment posted on the rinaross film blog on March 21, 2011, Rina Rosselon, researcher on the representations of old women in feature films, argues that the gender reversal that causes older women's invisibility relative to older men, including their two-dimensional or stereotypical presence and lack of central roles in films that are widely distributed, is due to the lack of awareness by the entire chain of film industry workers of the value of older women both as subject of films and as audience.

We can see the effects of this lack of awareness in both the production and the reception of many major films. In *About Schmidt* (2002), Helen, Schmidt's wife, about whose physical appearance Schmidt is already feeling queasy, dies early in the story while cleaning the floor. As with Dorothy and Ellie, she is subsequently spoken for by her family and we never get a chance to know her except through their memories, some of which cast her in a distinctly unflattering light. In *Get Low* (2009), Felix, who has lived his life as a hermit in order to atone for the death of a young married woman with whom he had had an affair years ago, rejects the "advances" of Mattie, the young woman's sister, who was, and still is, in love with him. His fixation on the memory of his young love blinds him to the older woman's presence, making her, in a sense, invisible, thus depriving himself of companionship and love in his old age and her both of his company and of a larger role in the film. Even those movies that feature older women as protagonists often make them visible in a comic, fairy-tale-like way that forecloses the possibility of anything but a grandmotherly role for an older woman, as does *Nancy McPhee* (2010). In this film, as one reviewer wrote, the elderly female lead is a "warty, cronish, snaggle-toothed eccentric" who, aided by her even older friend, a "sweet-souled dodderer with moonstruck moments," can disclose her inner appeal only through the exercise of her tough-minded generativity. And if a movie does manage to escape the two-dimensional stereotype of older women and reveal the beauty and desire that an aging woman can still feel, as does *Innocence* (1991), the passionate love story of a couple who reignites their romance after fifty years apart, it will generally lack both sufficient press and distribution to make it widely known.

Given the cultural devaluation that older women face, ignorance about their value and reluctance to publicize the movies that do feature them could certainly explain their lack of prominence in film. But just possibly Barbara Walker has uncovered a deeper reason for their silence and invisibility: the timeless fear of women who live outside of male control. Walker argues that "the real threat posed by older women in a patriarchal society may be the 'evil eye' of sharp judgment honed by disillusioning experience, which pierces male myths and scrutinizes male motives in the hard, unflattering light of critical appraisal" (Walker, B. 1985, 122). When we watch movies that include or feature older women, let's imagine that we have an evil eye of critical appraisal that enables us to move past the predominant ageist and sexist stereotypes in order to see bodies that are invisible and hear voices that are silenced. Furthermore, let's imagine that by really looking at these bodies and listening to these voices in the unflattering light of critical appraisal, we can learn to see and hear old women differently, understand the institutional and structural causes of their apparently "natural" slide into silence and invisibility, and transform the way we value and experience women growing old both on film and in "real" life. Such an imagination could be the beginning of true change.

The Gendered Imagination

Saving Grace (2000), starring 54-year-old Brenda Blethyn as Grace, and *Calendar Girls* (2003) featuring 55-year-old Helen Mirren as Chris, are films with protagonists who find creative and empowering ways to deal with the problems that turn on the silence and invisibility imposed on women growing older. Although comedies made in the tradition of modeling women's subversive, rebellious behavior only to later contain it, these films tell stories that both bring out the practical and existential necessity for opposition to the gendered hegemonic narratives that work to narrow the female protagonists' lives and celebrate the real threat their oppositional stance poses to the continuation of a narrative (Carson 1994) that works to reduce older women's options for either financial or personal growth. Therefore, when we watch these movies, we need to be aware of the way notions of femininity and age combine to simultaneously restrict and expand the protagonists' options, and how these options work to both release them from and reinstate them within hegemonic patriarchal norms.

Like so many movies about aging, *Saving Grace* opens with scenes of a grave being dug, followed by a funeral and a wake at the widow Grace's home. She, like Walt, though graciously serving food and drink to her friends, seems uncomfortable and in need of time to consider her situation by herself. Although at first we aren't aware of the extent of Grace's problems now that her husband is gone, we do know that he died jumping from an airplane without a parachute, a fact that the other older ladies at the funeral find curious, and that an unknown woman attired in black attended the funeral, a fact that Grace finds particularly upsetting.

Stunned, Grace seems unable to understand why her husband would kill himself until she gradually comes to the realization that, in addition to leaving her with no money, he left her with a mortgage of 2000 lbs. a month on the house, which he used as collateral to raise money for secret business ventures, and a debt of 300,000 lbs. to the bank. Knowing that her husband lied to her about everything including the nature of his business dealings, for a time she is unable to process her predicament and hides her head in the sand, leaving her mail unopened, her phone unanswered, and her person uncared for, silent, and invisible. Sleepless and smoking again, she calls her late husband a "liar" and a "bastard," and even walks by night on a cliff overhanging the sea, possibly contemplating an easier way out.

Although her friends and neighbors in the small town where she lives try to protect her by "losing" her account at the local store and refusing to let her donate money to a good cause, they can't keep her mower from being repossessed, her furniture and jewelry from being sold, or the bankers from attempting to contact her in order to auction off the house. Feeling totally unsuited for any job other than gardening and aware that the bankers see her as nothing but a "middle-aged woman with huge debts and no income," she asks herself, "What in God's name am I going to do?" And what does a single older woman do when facing the often sudden, always frightening prospect of homelessness and poverty? How did she end up in such a vulnerable position? To what extent was it due to personal choices or to structural causes based on historical assumptions over which she has no control?

Before examining the creative and rather radical way that Grace manages to extricate herself from her predicament, it is important to identify the problem itself, one that most movies with older women characters manage to avoid confronting by killing them off, making them independently wealthy, or sticking to a storyline that ignores economic questions. Exactly what challenges might an older woman left on her own due to the death of a spouse, divorce, or lack of children or family members who might offer to help care for her face? How vulnerable are older women to finding themselves in a situation similar to Grace's? And how aware are women of the reasons for this vulnerability? In *Make Way for Tomorrow* (1937), filmed during the Depression at about the time social security became law, the predicament of an older woman without resources was

3. The Silence and Invisibility of Older Women

shown to be dire indeed. Portraying the story of a couple who has lived together happily for fifty years, this movie provides an unsentimental look at what can happen when an older couple loses their home to the bank, is left without any money, and has to move in with grown children. Separated from each other in the homes of different children, and gradually wearing out their welcome with the very real problems their presence causes, Lucy and Bark's sadness at the knowledge that they will never live together again is only offset by the dignity with which they face the prospect of being apart. Bark is to be sent from New York to California to live near an unseen daughter, and Lucy, sympathetic to the strain she is placing on her son's marriage, feels that she has no choice but to agree to move into a home, even though she recognizes that life there will be lonely and dismal. The poverty she faces, both financial and emotional, after a lifetime of care work is truly heartbreaking.

Though much has changed, recent studies find that poverty in the United States, due to outliving one's income as well as one's spouse, is overwhelmingly an older women's issue. Nearly 20 percent of unmarried elderly women are poor and four times as many widows live in poverty as do married women of the same age. Even though the incomes of married women are increasing, the incomes of widowed, separated, or divorced women are in decline (Cruikshank 2003), due in part to the inequitable nature of the redistributive features of a Social Security system that persists in conforming to norms based on male work histories. As long as these norms devalue "women's work" and attach less economic value to the work of care giving—whether of the home, children, elderly, or disabled relatives—taking time off to care will constitute "a net economic loss for women" in old age (Holstein 2005, 31).

Susan Jacoby, author of *Never Say Die: The Myth and Marketing of the New Old Age*, documents that women who interrupt their careers to care for children or elders for little more than two years can lose 18 percent of their earning power, and up to 28 percent if they work in business and finance. In addition, only 40 percent of women who leave a job for care giving responsibilities ever find full-time jobs to which they can return (Jacoby 2011), a statistic corroborated by the fact that unemployment among those over 55 is the highest it's been since the 1940's (Rand 2010). Given the penalty that women pay for taking time to "care" and the difficulty they may experience in finding financially rewarding work with benefits when they return to the labor market, the price tag for taking time off from "work" can become dramatically and suddenly apparent if they undergo a change in marital status or with the approach of deep old age. The long-term consequences of what appear to be individual choices but in reality are choices made in the context of a normative life course that does "not reflect women's experiences" (Holstein 2005, 31) can be severe. For whenever circumstances that are understood as individual and private, such as divorce and widowhood, are experienced in the context of public policies based on the presumption of lasting marriage and fashioned on male norms, the consequences will reveal themselves in the concrete existence of a "world in which nearly all women become poorer" (Jacoby 2011, 132) as they age.

With these statistics in mind, at what point do individual and social/cultural responsibility for Grace's dire situation meet? We can better answer that question by looking at Alice Kessler-Harris' book, *In Pursuit of Equity*, that tells the story of how the "gendered imagination," a set of unquestioned beliefs about the natural order of gendered life, shaped apparently neutral social legislation in a way that limited the full participation of women in social, political, and economic life. In American thought, this social imaginary is directly traceable to the Enlightenment with its dualistic notions of the superiority of mind over body, reason over emotion, culture over nature, and its attribution of mind, reason, and culture to the male, and body, emotion, and nature to the female. In *Imaginary Bodies*, philosopher Moira Gatens discusses one way this gendered imagination functions by comparing the seventeenth-century birth of the human subject to the birth of the body politic or the state. Arguing that the state was created as a way to protect the abstract human, yet markedly masculine, subject and its needs from nature, Gatens maintains that woman was relegated to a position outside of the contractual relations of the body politic from the start. Therefore, even when accorded various types of equality, unless the significance of the sexed body as it is imagined and lived in culture was ignored, woman's supposedly essential nature and position as the subordinate term in the Enlightenment binaries on which the state was founded often rendered such equality purely theoretical rather than practical (Gatens 1996).

The propensity of enlightened thought to make binary oppositional categories based on the essential nature of things is not new, as it reflects ideas that go as far back as Aristotle and his essentialist ordering of the world. In Book I of *The Politics of Aristotle*, "The Theory of the Household," Aristotle set out his belief in a principle of rule and subordination in nature at large that made one person a master, or someone

3. The Silence and Invisibility of Older Women

in possession of a rational faculty of the soul, and another a slave, or someone who possessed bodily power along with the ability to understand the master's directions (Barker 1958). When Aristotle extended that principle to gendered relationships he argued that, since "the relation of male to female is naturally that of the superior to the inferior" (Barker 1958, 13), "the male is naturally fitter to command than the female" (32) and should be head of a household in which the female is subordinated.

The idea that the normal order of family life naturally subsumed women's desires and needs as secondary to those of other family members was remarkably persistent through time, serving to legitimize, justify, and rationalize policies that generally benefited men by virtue of their work and their position as head of a household, and women by virtue of their status as members of a family. Though debated by first-wave feminists, such as Charlotte Perkins Gilman who argued that women would remain second class citizens without the same economic rights as men, and by men sympathetic to their cause, such as John Stuart Mill who demanded equal education and employment opportunities for women, the majority of "rights, obligations, and benefits granted to women ... [were] based on traditional gendered images of work and family" (Kessler-Harris 2001, 15). Though contested, this gendered notion of fairness, argues Kessler-Harris, was inscribed into the social policies of the twentieth century that still frame our lives today, such as the fact that access to old age pensions and medical care are vested in each person's "work" record rather than in a person's citizenship. These policies left many women — those never-married with or without children, widowed, divorced, poor, old — without resources (Kessler-Harris 2001), often despite a lifetime of hard work.

Even though over time Social Security has expanded coverage to homemakers, widows, and the divorced if they meet certain criteria, and it and other social programs have greatly improved the overall economic security of the elderly, the gendered social imaginary under which these programs were enacted has led to exacerbated gendered disparities in well-being among the old. For example, when retirement is looked at through the prism of women's life experience, a pattern of structural socioeconomic disadvantage emerges. "Women's retirement income is lower then men's because of their lower pay, interrupted work history, ... workplace gender segregation" (Cruikshank 2003, 128), and the refusal to recognize their care work as a public good supportive of economic growth (Holstein 1999). Yet, due to their longevity, women are more likely to be retired longer than men, lose one-third of their Social Security benefit when a spouse dies or not yet be eligible for Social Security benefits, have a chronic illness that occurs before they are eligible for age-based social programs, or suffer from a condition with needs that extend beyond the protections offered by old-age policies. No matter a woman's individual choices and personal circumstances, "her late-life income is largely determined by family and workplace structures and by public policy" (Cruikshank 2003, 131) that favor the normative life course of a white, middle-class male. Therefore, emphasizing the importance of individual effort in determining the economic position of an older woman while ignoring the "clear pattern of 'structured diversity'" (Hudson 2005, 11) and cumulative advantage or disadvantage under which she lives, only disguises the myriad inequalities built into the system. Clearly, the situation in which Grace finds herself is not all of her own making.

Even though Grace's husband was a cad who, without consulting her, made financial decisions about their future for which she is now responsible, and even though she may have at times willingly turned a blind eye to his affairs and machinations, they both acted in the context of discourses and narratives about gendered behavior that they internalized from the social institutions, laws, policies, and customs that framed their lives. Living within that frame, it is likely that Grace's "job" of caring for her husband, her "lovely, lovely" home as her tea-time friends described it, and members of her community like Matthew, her friend and gardener, was precisely the job that both she and her husband expected her to do.

Yet, public commitment to a male-breadwinner family structure such as Grace's is exactly what ended up producing different social rights and divergent types of citizenship for men and women. By divorcing social citizenship, or the tasks of care and concern for which there are no publicly conferred benefits and thus little chance to escape dependency, from economic citizenship, or the tasks of remunerative work for which one gains not only independence but various publicly financed benefits (Kessler-Harris 2001), gendered assumptions and expectations were built into the system. "Ideally, espousing economic citizenship should not diminish caregiving as an equally enabling access route to democratic participation" (Kessler-Harris 2001, 13). But, even though the collective efforts of women such as the social feminists of the early twentieth century had enormously beneficial effects on community and working life,[2] contemporary beliefs about the sanctity of the market,[3] what constitutes "work," rugged individualism, and independence rely on certain essential ideas about gender and age for their meaning and continue to make access to the market the only real path to voice and visibility as an individual citizen (Kessler-Harris 2001).

A Utopian Turn

It's quite possible to conclude that part of Grace's anger at her husband and the financially precarious situation in which he has left her is really anger at the way invisible "background conditions mediate[d] life's possibilities and reinforce[d] conditions of inequality" (Holstein 1999, 242) across her life course. Philosopher Martha Holstein and economist Amartya Sen argue that, in order to remedy entrenched gender injustice, societies ought to support the development of basic capacities that give individuals maximum agency and choice whether they "work" or do non-work-related activities in order to benefit others that may, under the present system, negatively affect their future well-being (Nussbaum and Sen 1993). Nussbaum calls this type of support the capabilities approach and asserts that governments should focus on "human capabilities, ... what people are actually able to do and to be" (Nussbaum 2002, 49), rather than on what they do and are, in order to make visible the way that the hierarchies of power and opportunity internal to a society consistently discriminate against certain groups. By treating each person as an end in her own right rather than as a supporter of the ends of others, each becomes a bearer of value and a contributor to the collective well-being. This approach reconceptualizes human lives as characterized by profound neediness as well as by independence and recognizes, as Sen has written, that, since political rights both formulate and fulfill states of need and dependency, potential inequalities in the experience of these states must be part of political thinking from the start. Only then can gender disparities in access to resources and opportunities, in participation in defining what counts as work, and in social and economic security in childhood, old age, and other times of need be fully noticed and addressed. As long as atomistic individualism based on gendered concepts of rights and citizenship that ignore values of community, intergenerational solidarity, and obligation is the prevailing narrative, the chances for an older woman like Grace to live a creative life that lets her develop to her full potential on or off the screen will be severely reduced.

"What could I do? Can I get a job?" Grace asks while consoling Matthew about the loss of his position as her gardener. Instead of commiserating with her or despairing over his own loss, Matthew tells Grace that she's the best gardener in the world and asks her to come with him that evening to look at some sick plants. Sneaking behind the vicarage in the dark to find the plants, Grace diagnoses the problem and they take the ailing "hemp" to her greenhouse to see what can be done. At this point the movie takes a utopian turn. Instead of projecting a future based on what we "know" about the silence and invisibility imposed on older women, the story breaks with the status quo and begins to imagine a world where an older woman like Grace can live differently. Rather than see life as a rational plan that can only be fulfilled by having a career that defines who we are, Grace is now free to visualize life as "seriatim selves," each with its own job in its own time, none of which is life-defining (Nelson, J. 1999).

In *Feminism, Economics, and Utopia* (2008), Karin Schonpflug traces the importance of utopian moments throughout history, describing them as thought experiments that present positive alternatives that can be used for inducing social and political change that could lead to a more desirable future. According to Schonpflug, "utopias function as metaphors for carrying complex beliefs and models ... that ... critique ... the current state of affairs" (Schonpflug 2008, 11), allow us to understand that the current situation is not ahistorical, and give us a venue to present ideas about what is just or ethical in the form of an example. Utopian thinking destabilizes what Foucault describes as unconscious control mechanisms embedded in dominant discourses and enables us to imagine a world in which hegemonic norms no longer constrain either thought or action. Recent studies also find that utopian thinking may "be hardwired by evolution into the human brain" because, "to make progress, we need to be able to imagine alternative realities" (Sharot 2011, 42). Utopian thinking, therefore, permits us to be shaped by ideas about the future as well as stamped by the past.

The utopian moment in *Saving Grace* also resonates with the aims of feminist science fiction, such as those of Joanna Russ's imagined society Whilaway in *The Female Man* (1975). As an alternative to the way our present economic system treats older women, Russ creates Whilaway, a world in which older women do all the creative and skilled work. Only

3. The Silence and Invisibility of Older Women

older women can reach "the highest status. [They] never cease to work, until they die — because it is such good fun" (Schonpflug 2008, 110). Instead of being perceived as a burden and a drain on the economy, older women's life experience qualifies them to be the creators of a better future for everyone. The utopia on Whilaway denies neither the physical reality of aging nor of death, but it does offer a concrete example for implementing many of the ideas contained in Nussbaum's capabilities approach. Grace and Matthew's plan for paying off her debt with money earned by growing and selling marijuana certainly calls for creativity and planning on Grace's part. It also allows her to use all the capacities she has developed as a gardener through the years, shows intergenerational cooperation in the partnership between Grace and Matthew, and demonstrates reciprocal caring between Grace and her community in her concern for Matthew and his pregnant girlfriend, Mickey, and in the way the community at large supports her efforts to save herself— and to carry on the local tradition of "complete and utter contempt for the law" by ignoring the fact that her plan, though brilliant and "beneficial" to many members of her community, is quite clearly illegal.

With the new plan underway, Grace begins to enjoy herself again, laughing at the audacity of their project, giggling and dancing while "trying out" their finished product, and indulging herself in the out-of-the-box thinking that Gene Cohen says characterizes the liberation from social constraints that often accompanies aging (Cohen, G. 2005). Rather than wallow in the slough of despond created by statistical evidence that shouts out the overwhelming odds that women will die poor and alone (Jacoby 2011), Grace's optimism about her personal future remains incredibly resilient, embodying what biologist Ajit Varki describes as the coevolution of the knowledge of certain death with the bias towards irrational optimism that enables even older humans to always picture a bright future (Sharot 2011).

In this sense, Grace's utopian moment provides us not just with an entertaining story but, combined with the "evil eye" of critical judgment that contests the naturalness of her predicament, with "serious indicators for political action" as well (Schonpflug 2008, 2). For whether we approach change in the ways we hear and see the aging and older women among us by optimistically touting their never-ending potential for development and growth, as Cohen does, or by pessimistically uncovering the fantasy and hype that conceal the dire prospects that await them, as does Jacoby, the ultimate goal is the development of more humane ways to listen to, see, include, respect, value, and care about all of us as we age. And we need to be aware of both present realities and imagined utopias in order to accomplish that task.

The Bodies of Older Women

Before discussing how Grace's adventure turns out, it would be instructive to look at *Calendar Girls*, a movie that has a different take on how women might handle the silence and invisibility that begins to surround them as they grow older. *Calendar Girls* is based on the true story of the creative and unusual way a group of seemingly staid, mature women who belong to the Women's Institute (WI) in Knapely, Yorkshire, raises money for the cancer ward at the local hospital. Opening with a view of the women exercising on a hill overlooking the picturesque village, the scene quickly shifts to a less-than-exciting WI meeting, accompanied by an out-of-tune piano, the sounds of several women dozing, and the laughter and inappropriate comments of Chris Harper, who thinks the WI should loosen up a bit, become more about fun and friendship. Through a succession of short scenes in which we see Chris enter and win a sponge-cake-baking contest with a store-bought cake, laugh at the playboy-type magazine she finds under her son's bed, and support her best friend Annie whose husband has leukemia, we get to know Chris as a woman who loves fun, family, and friends, but who chafes a bit at the narrowness of a life full of caring for her son, husband, and their flower business in the conservative atmosphere of Knapely.

When Annie's husband John dies, Chris reads the speech he had promised to give to the WI and becomes determined to raise money for the hospital in order to help others with needs similar to Annie's. Inspired by the way John had compared the flowers of Yorkshire to its women, and by a "girly" calendar she sees in the shop where her son's bicycle is being fixed, Chris comes up with the idea that she and her friends should pose nude for the yearly WI calendar. Such an "alternative calendar" would be much more interesting than the usual pictures of the local scenery, she reasons, and would honor John's idea that the last phase of growth for both flowers and women is "the most glorious."

After convincing her friends that a nude WI calendar is a good idea, the group decides to take practice pictures in which, although the women are naked, some object associated with women's traditional tasks—fruit, knitting, music—softens the effect and covers their more intimate parts.

3. The Silence and Invisibility of Older Women

When Chris's son, who is already embarrassed by his mother's strange behavior in the bike shop, walks in with a friend and sees his mother undressed, hiding behind a basket of buns, he most likely concurs in the assessment of his friend's dad that women go through a "difficult age" when they get "all odd and irrational and difficult to predict." From this point on, an atmosphere of tension exists between mother and son that gives the story space in which to contrast stereotypical notions about the bodies and sexuality of older women formed from the gaze of youth with the women's feelings and beliefs about their own bodies and sexuality.

This contrast, argues Margaret Gullette, is not natural but is culturally and historically manufactured by the way our culture's privileging of youth categorically denies and obscures the existence of women's physical beauty and sexual expression in later life (Gullette 2011). Spurred on by the cultural imperialism of youth, this denial contributes to the construction of age cohorts, or, as Hacking explained, the construction of categories in which to contain supposedly essential yet arbitrary and fictitious collective identities. Since age cohorts can be used as a "linguistic trick for othering" (Gullette 2004, 56) and as a tool to separate out inherently diverse groups of people based on chronology alone, they can result in the perception of generation gaps that undermine commonalities between parents and children and destroy any sense of life course continuity or intergenerational connection. Together, cohorts and gaps can result in a generational culture war that encourages "'the young' to parrot negative, dismissive feelings against another age group" (58) and that keeps us all from seeing how the master signifier, age, works to render invisible other characteristics that might unite people of various ages across cohorts and generations. No matter how an older woman may feel about her body and her sexuality, and may wish to connect with another group, unwilling interpellation into a cohort or generation can make it extremely difficult to live outside the label.

Although *Calendar Girls* treats these culturally constructed differences in a comedic manner—as in the scene where Chris picks up the practice photos only to find the young girls at the counter flipping through them laughing—slicing life into mutually hostile stages is, in reality, a crime against the life course (Gullette 2004). This crime foments existential and bodily anxiety about growing older in young and old alike and, for aging women, "poses a huge threat to women's sense of identity, perceived femininity, and sexual desirability" (Clarke 2011, 2). Therefore, when Chris, visibly shaken after the encounter with the young girls in the store, shows the practice photos to the rest of the group, they agree that they are unable to combat their cultural devaluation alone and unanimously decide that they need a professional photographer, an artist, to make the photos "look OK."

Although they insist that they needn't undergo any special preparation for the photo session and that, in the spirit of John's declaration that the last phase is the most glorious, they should come as they are with "gray hair, cellulite, and the lot," the next scenes show them having their hair done, tanning themselves, exercising, and eating lots of celery. Their behavior mirrors precisely the dilemma that older women face in an androcentric and ageist culture: they are simultaneously required to engage in beauty work in order to be deemed acceptable to themselves and to others, and are held in contempt and seen as shallow and narcissistic for doing so (Clarke 2011). The ambivalence these women feel, both as characters and for Helen Mirren in "real" life where she simultaneously basks in and ardently resists and disavows her recent characterization as a sex symbol, makes clear both the embodied nature of ageism and the struggle women undergo when their internalization of ageist beauty norms clashes with their resistance to its impossible demands.

The Split Subject

One way to theoretically explain the prevalence and intractability of this ambivalence is through the idea of the split subject, a subject that distinguishes "itself ... from its own body, over which it [tries] to establish hierarchical ... control" as if its body were an object[4] (Grosz 1995b, 47). Once split, the subject becomes alienated from itself and forms a relationship with itself. This relationship is not between a natural biological body and a constructed cultural body, since natural and biological are terms whose meaning depends on a particular cultural and historical context but, as Foucault explains, between two registers of the cultural body. The first or intelligible body is created through "subjectification," or being seen as an object by others who judge a subject's adherence to cultural conceptions of the body, such as norms of beauty, health, or independence. The second or useful body comes about through "subjectivization," or the ways a subject itself engages in the practical rules and regulations that train and shape the living body to respond to these norms (Bordo 2004 and Barber 2004). Elizabeth Grosz refers to these two bodies as inscriptive and lived, the first more

3. The Silence and Invisibility of Older Women

"concerned with the processes by which the self is marked ... and constructed by ... institutional, discursive power as a particular kind of body" and the second with "the body as it is experienced and rendered meaningful" (Grosz 1995a, 33).

We can better understand the difference between the intelligible and the useful body by looking at the way many women responded to the 1960's scripting of menopause as a deficiency disease marking the onset of old age that could be "cured" by replacing "lost" estrogen. Even though the intelligible body may have been marked by this cultural script and suffered the consequences in terms of fear of aging, lowered self-esteem, or postmenopausal social exclusion, if a woman chose to "stay young" according to this script, the useful body actually had to practice what was required, take the synthetic estrogen, assume the associated risk of cancer, and thus incorporate both the cultural message and the material substance into her body in order to fully conform to the norm created by the cultural script. To the extent that Chris and her friends subject themselves to practices in order to make their bodies more acceptable and youthful, they actively incorporate the meanings, values, and norms about aging and old age with which the intelligible body has been marked into the useful body, coding their living bodies with and as a sign inhabiting a particular culturally determined social location and position.

Although it may be useful to theorize these two bodies separately, they are always part of the same discourse, one that positions the body as neither fully essential nor completely socially constructed. Within this discourse, these "separate" bodies at times agree to the same narrative, at times argue over it and oppose each other, making the body a site of often unconscious personal and political struggle. For older women raised "in the context of cultural inferiorization and predominantly other-oriented training" (O'Grady 2004, 96), this struggle can lead to an attitude of self-criticism and self-policing that internalizes as personal deficiencies and moral failures what are in reality cultural structures of gendered and age-related inequity. It also can create an overseer relationship between the two bodies that "precludes spontaneity and diminishes possibilities for self-fashioning" (96), leaving older women discontented, disempowered, and disenfranchised. Chris's struggle over how much responsibility to take when, in the wake of the publicity surrounding the calendar, her son begins to misbehave and her husband implies that she has been ignoring their son's problems, is a clear example of such culturally induced self-criticism.

The Anti-Aging Industry

This struggle also opens up endless avenues for the anti-aging industry to ply its wares. Though anti-aging is a term that "was originally defined primarily in terms of longevity and the maintenance of health" (Clarke 2011, 74), it is now associated with the fight to maintain a youthful bodily exterior in order to remain socially relevant. Margaret Gullette argues that the current commerce in anti-aging products with its promises of vigorous health, suitable youthful appearance, and greater social acceptability should "more aptly be called the 'uglification industry'" (Gullette 2011, 34). The uglification industry works, she explains, by looking at the body as an assemblage of discrete parts (Clarke 2011) and exaggerating or creating, then publicizing, flaws in those parts for which it has developed cures and nostrums. We can see the effects of the uglification industry's partition of the body in the way the WI women target certain aspects of their bodies for improvement, such as hair or skin or size, before the photo shoot. But we can also see the effects in the way the church organist wants to show her breasts, a part of her body she believes still meets the industry's standard of beauty. Thus, a woman's personal dissatisfaction with or pleasure in her body is manufactured, along with the cure, by a commerce in aging that invents imperfections, ties them to growing older, and does so in lock step with the pace of developing aesthetic medical technology.

As Jean Baudrillard explains, the uglification industry functions like this in order to produce a system of needs that is the product of, rather than the impetus to, the system of production. Consumption of these products thus not only promises to fulfill these newly created needs and desires, but to place the consumer in a category of persons marked by the sign of the object consumed (Poster 1988) rather than in a category marked solely by biology and chronology. Bodily appearance then becomes not just a marker of age, but a barometer of adherence to a certain level of consumption that, while it richly rewards physicians and participating companies, costs older women dearly in terms of both decreasing self satisfaction and social currency.

In *The Beauty Myth* (1991), Naomi Wolf elaborates on the idea of beauty as a kind of currency, arguing that, in the economy of beauty, women are assigned value "in a vertical hierarchy according to a culturally imposed physical standard" (Wolf 1991, 12) of attractiveness that largely ignores other qualities and values. Using this value as currency, a value

3. The Silence and Invisibility of Older Women

that invariably declines with age, they are forced to compete with each other within and across generations for male-controlled resources and attention. When looked at as a system determined by an androcentric culture rather than as a naturally occurring hierarchy, Wolf continues, the beauty economy is clearly an expression of power relations, part of a political and medical system that perpetuates male dominance through the naturalization of sexist and ageist strategies of exclusion and discrimination. Seen in terms of the beauty economy, the women pictured in the WI nude calendar are not only contesting the low value assigned to older women's bodies, but are making a political statement that challenges the entire basis of their exclusion.

The uglification industry's devaluation of older women's appearance and the support it receives from the medical profession is also reflected in the demonization of women's sexual aging that the related dysfunction industry promotes. "For the commerce in aging to flourish, victims must be taught that fun and intensity equals 'youthsex,' that later such pleasures cease, and then sexual difficulties ... and dysfunction begin" (Gullette 2011, 126). The industry's discursive strategies mirror Foucault's argument that sex and sexuality are not natural things to be known, but are the effects of a particular cultural discourse. As with beauty, this discourse treats female sexual aging as a series of inevitable physiological losses and promotes consumption of its products as the only way to retain sexual currency. This strategy not only limits the cultural imaginary of women who are labeled older by denying them an erotics of their own (Frueh 1999), but ignores research that finds it impossible to distinguish women by age when speaking of the quality of their sexual relationships[5] (Gullette 2011) or the intensity of their desire. Moreover, due to a lifetime of experience, older women may be "more rather than less open to change and possibility" (Connids 2006, 129) than younger people, often constructing relationships in which they see themselves as sexual subjects rather than objects. Nevertheless, one of the main effects of the dysfunction discourse can be seen in the contrast between the tacit approval Chris feels for her son's burgeoning sexuality and the shame and embarrassment her son feels when confronted by the reality of his mother's and her friends' sense of themselves as still sexually attractive beings.

Thus in our culture, as women age, they become not only financially poorer, but they have diminishing social currency, voice, and visibility as well. Yet, the connection between older women's poverty, silence, and invisibility lies at the heart of gerontological knowledge. Modern geriatrics began with Jean-Martin Charcot's studies of old age in the latter part of the nineteenth century in Salpetriere, a Parisian hospital and poorhouse for women. Although Charcot's project was to identify the pathologies of old age, he did so not by looking at a broad population of elders, but by examining elderly, destitute, yet generally healthy older women (Katz 2005). Despite their preponderance of good health, Charcot, combining acceptance of the male body as the norm and pervasive negative cultural attitudes toward post-menopausal women, identified these aging female bodies as inherently pathological, "biologically fouled misadventures" (Katz 2005, 46) that reverted to a "neutral man-woman state" (166) in later life. The irony is, as Katz notes in his study of the genesis of geriatrics, that Charcot's distorted vision of older female bodies and sexuality forms the discursive background for a gerontological knowledge formation that generally works "to silence, regulate, and negate" (50) the very bodies that made it possible.

Aging women, therefore, are placed in an untenable and paradoxical position by the very discourses that define them: they are endowed by geriatric and gerontological knowledge with a body that is naturally and increasingly deficient, yet simultaneously assumed to possess the emotional, physical, and moral ability to defy this body's natural, biological decline if they only will conform to the exhortations of the anti-aging industry and consume enough of its products. In this situation, it falls to the individual woman to manage how she ages, to choose where she will set the boundaries between "natural" and "produced." She must decide whether she will embrace what were once considered the limits of the human and age "naturally," refusing to see her youth as a lost object to be recovered and instead choosing to see the marks of age as a record of her life through time, too valuable to be erased (Woodward 1999). Or she can decide to subscribe to "the constant work of modulation, adjustment, improvement ... [and] self-scrutiny ... in the name of maximizing ... her potential, recovering ... her self, shaping ... [her] life" (Rose 2007, 223) that the anti-aging industry promotes. In this industry-driven context, the ultimately doomed battle against aging and aged appearances becomes not only a physical but an ethical encounter as well, one that can render those who "fail" to uphold a youthful standard responsible for their own decline due to their morally irresponsible choices, and therefore deserving of their subsequent silence and invisibility.

3. *The Silence and Invisibility of Older Women*

Utopian Empowerment

At this point, events in the lives of the real women on which *Calendar Girls* is based take a surprisingly utopian turn. As did the real-life characters, Chris and her friends, drinking wine in their bathrobes while their husbands wait anxiously in a bar, call in Laurence, the artist-photographer who has agreed to work with them, and the photo session begins. After a rough start, Laurence compliments them on their beauty and, as if he were channeling Louise Nevelson, a sculptor who age-studies author and scholar Kathleen Woodward argues remained well aware of her own power and potential even in old age,[6] calms them down and makes them feel as if they were women whose image reflected back to them not aging matrons but vitally creative and self-confident women (Woodward 1999).

The idea of burgeoning female creativity and confidence that may come with age continues in the scene where Chris and Annie go to the National WI Federation conference to defend the calendar against their local leader's charges that it will look like porn and thus defame the WI. Although Annie finds herself rather tongue tied in front of such a large audience, Chris, whose relationship to speech has previously been coded as less than dexterous, finds her voice, passionately defends her plan to honor John, her friend and a man she loved, by raising money through the sale of this nude calendar, and wins the argument. Returning to Knapely and a press conference, both women are greeted by wild applause and a newspaper and TV press eager to give them enough publicity to make it difficult to keep up with demand for the calendars.

Instead of causing a scandal, the project to raise money with a nude calendar featuring older women's bodies resonates with thousands of women, making them feel less alone, allowing them to openly express their troubles and desires and to give voice to previously silenced stories of their everyday worlds. The project also empowers women to face their losses and recognize their gains, to accept their aging bodies, and to live their lives with renewed courage and self-confidence. Such an outpouring of support and encouragement exposes a fundamental error in neoliberalism's attempt to privatize the experience of aging by construing life as the outcome of a series of individual market-based choices, and clearly reveals aging and the vicissitudes that accompany it to be a collective social and culturally inflected process.[7] Moreover, the enthusiastic response to the way the calendar resists and subverts ageist and sexist norms underscores and gives voice to older women's radical dissatisfaction with the way their bodies are described and evaluated. This reaction confirms another fact discovered by Clarke in her study: older women feel "bombarded and angered by ageist media messages ... and balk ... at the societal demeaning of aged bodies and appearances" (Clarke 2011, 128). Like the fictional utopian moment in *Saving Grace*, the utopian turn modeled on real-life events in *Calendar Girls* empowers older women to believe in themselves and to embrace change as opportunity and hope rather than as failure and decline.

Some of the parallels in the way *Saving Grace* and *Calendar Girls* make use of this empowerment to develop their stories are striking. Grace resists ageist stereotypes and dares to smoke a joint; Chris and her WI friends resist the devaluation of older women's bodies and dare to pose nude. Grace summons up the courage to confront Honey, the other woman, and to face the fact that her husband mistakenly thought she was uninterested in sex; Ruth, one of the calendar girls, finds the courage to confront her husband's mistress, to face the fact that her husband considered her as good as dead, and to relish the prospect of life on her own. Grace, though nervous and discouraged by her friends from making such a dangerous trip, is determined to go to London, find a dealer, sell her crop, and clear her debt; Chris, despite her son's rebellion and arrest for smoking what turns out to be oregano and her husband's worries about their business, is determined to make the most of the chance to go to Hollywood in order to promote more sales of the calendar. When Grace meets Jacques, the dealer, instead of being a perfunctory meeting, the encounter exudes a sexual tension between older people; when the calendar girls appear on the Jay Leno show and on the set to make a commercial, the sexual connotations of having posed nude despite their age are emphasized. Grace's plan for selling her crop literally go up in smoke when she decides to burn the marijuana before it can be sold; the calendar girls' plan for further promotion of the calendar in the U.S. is cut short when, due to what they consider inappropriate expectations for its marketing, they decide to leave before finishing their tour. At the end, Grace marries Jacques who fully supports her new career as an award-winning author; Chris returns to Knapely to her son, who has inexplicably resolved his problems with her actions, and her husband who, though he had trouble running the business without her, cheered for her success and thinks what she did was "brilliant."

3. *The Silence and Invisibility of Older Women*

Fairy-Tale Endings

Looking at these stories, one fictional and the other based on fact, at first it appears that Grace and Chris have shattered the aura of silence and invisibility that tends to surround aging and older women, have broken through their own internalization of sexist and ageist norms to discover truer preferences and desires, and are on the way to developing their capabilities more fully, as Nussbaum would put it. Such a breakthrough would fit well in the feminist utopian tradition of making older women both visible and vocal, of imagining and working to create an environment in which older women are free to follow their talents and abilities, to achieve financial independence and security, to freely express their sexuality, and to structure family relationships in ways that don't blindly conform to patriarchal assumptions concerning unpaid and unrecognized female care. But a closer look at the way these movies end reveals that much of that utopian promise has been betrayed. These endings, rather than using the transformative potential of utopian visions to explore what a less sexist and ageist world might look like and what the process of achieving it might entail, spend their creativity on fairy-tale strategies that curb the excess ambitions of older women and reinfold them in the status quo of androcentric culture and patriarchal institutions (Mangum 1999).

According to Bruno Bettelheim, fairy tales are a way to integrate contradictory emotions and experiences that might threaten a child's sense of security. They accomplish this integration by splitting a character into two separate people, one benevolent and promising continuity, the other frightening and threatening change, such as the kindly grandmother and the evil wolf in "Little Red Riding Hood." Fairy tales externalize the evil part by projecting it onto the threatening character and using it to warn of the dangers and possible tragic consequences of rash wishes and unthinking actions. By attributing the evil character's strange ideas and behavior to some kind of innate difference, fairy tales can ignore, marginalize, or destroy the bad character and bring the true, good one home. For a child first experiencing the internal and external contradictions and ambivalences of life, splitting characters may be a beneficial way to nurture confidence in her own ability to handle the scary changes involved in growing up until she is able to integrate reality with imagination on her own (Bettelheim 1989). But for an adult, the fairy-tale splitting that enables a resolution to complexity and ambivalence by setting a part of oneself or of another aside, generally serves only to reinforce the dominance of a particular discriminatory discourse or narrative, and to mask or delay the real work an individual or a culture has to do to achieve true integration of the possible, utopian, or threatening with the real, known, and secure.

Although these two movies, to their credit, do not completely erase the possibility that Grace and Chris will continue to grow and develop, or even rebel, both movies end by splitting their protagonists in two, one part independent, adventurous, and open to change, and the other again caught in the embrace of potentially limiting relationships and the status quo. As *Saving Grace* comes to a close, even though Grace has undergone a remarkable change since the opening scenes, has written a best-selling account of her adventures that won a prestigious book award, and is planning a second novel, she is cast at the same time as a lost and lonely princess who is "rescued" by marriage to Jacques, a prince charming who renders her financial problems moot and provides her with criminally-tinged and overzealous male protection from any too-inquisitive reporters who might question how closely her fiction mirrors real life. And at the end of *Calendar Girls*, despite the fact that Chris has gained new confidence in the power of her ideas and has come home to applause and admiration after having raised $286,000 for the hospital through sales of the calendar,[8] an appeal from Annie that echoes the enduring idea that individual freedom for women is somehow "selfish" (Kessler-Harris 2001) nudges Chris to decide that her adventures have caused problems for her son and husband and she returns to her rightful place, caring for them. Neither ending attempts to resolve the inherent contradiction posed by independent, successful older women in a culture that too often refuses to see or hear them. These films simply sidestep the problem by splitting them in two and bringing the "good" part home.

The splitting put forth by the fairy tale is, thus, another manifestation of the concept of the split subject, an abstract and inherently alienated being that reflects the binary constructions on which our Western culture, politics, and institutions are based. In these binaries, as in fairy tales, a character associated with good is equated with the primary term while threats or changes to the good are projected onto a character or some aspect of a character representing the secondary or subordinate term. As Judith Butler argues in *Precarious Life*, this projection of evil onto another not only perpetuates inequality but can also result in the dehumanization of the other, an act that limits the cultural frame in which we understand

3. The Silence and Invisibility of Older Women

what it is to be human (Butler, J. 2006). Butler goes on to argue that we collectively use this limited frame to dehumanize an individual or group whose appearance, behavior, values, or way of life differs from or threatens our own, often rendering them "likened to ... animals" (Butler, J. 2006, 73), a strategy that many fairy tales take literally.

If we take Butler's ideas about the construction of the human/non-human or animal binary and apply them to the split subject, it becomes clear how useful the concept of the split subject is for constructing, enforcing, and perpetuating difference. Like any binary, the split subject creates the perception of a space or a time or an entity with a line drawn through it that marks one side as dominant and good, the other as subordinate, bad, and in need of control. In the case of the binary young/old, the dominant side is the privileged category young, the line is the chronological age at which one becomes a person of a distinct and inferior kind or ceases to be identified as a human being, and the subordinate side is the despised category old. If we overlay young/old with the masculine/feminine binary on which patriarchal power relations hinge, then with the culture/nature binary in which male mind takes precedence over female body, and finally with the split subject's subject/object binary through which attempts to conform to social and cultural norms are regulated by internal self-policing, it appears that older women are often perceived (and may perceive themselves) as less-than-human powerless bodies who can no longer live up to society's and culture's youthful norms and should remain, due to these deficiencies, silent and invisible — and controlled.

Thus, older women experience multiple types of discrimination and oppression because of their position in relation to the imaginary lines drawn by an abstract binary conception of the world rather than because they possess a particular set of essential attributes or internal characteristics that define them (Alcoff 1997). Although by no means a homogenous category, older women do share the experience of crossing the line in the context of economic and political assumptions that often relegate them to poverty, as we saw with Grace, cultural expectations that habitually consign their bodies to invisibility and their voices to irrelevance, as we saw with Chris, and social conditions that separate them from those of other ages and regularly dehumanize their existence. As a group united by history and circumstance rather than by essence, by discourses and the bodies of knowledge they produce rather than by truth, to the extent that the older women in this group become aware of the constructed nature of their experience, resist it, and work to change it, they pose a constant threat to the status quo.

Fairy-tale endings, rather than encourage older women to conceptualize the problems and conditions against which they struggle as external from self and as "inherently open to new meanings, reinterpretations, recontextualizations" (Grosz 1995b, 189), handle this threat by "othering" it, making older women's struggle to move beyond the identities prescribed for them private and invisible, keeping them in their "place." Furthermore, fairy-tale endings both dehumanize and infantilize older women by denying them the chance to do exactly what Bettelheim argues a fairy tale ultimately promises to do: achieve integration of the complex and ambivalent feelings and emotions that the split subject represents and works to contain (Bettelheim 1989). Only by growing up past the necessity for splits and binaries to a place where "the self is no longer in battle with itself" (O'Grady 2004, 104) and no longer defined by what it is not, will the frame of the human become large enough to accommodate a woman's entire life course.

Conclusion

Although the fairy-tale-like endings that *Saving Grace* and *Calendar Girls* proffer are unquestionably emotionally satisfying in that they simultaneously fulfill our desire for the underdog protagonists' personal success and grant our wish for their re-immersion in happy and secure relationships after sometimes harrowing adventures, we need to look at them with Barbara Walker's evil eye of sharp judgment to see if and how much the stories these movies tell challenge the gendered and ageist stereotypes that haunt older women's lives. Do these stories leave us with an altered view of older women's appearance, desires, and capabilities? Have these movies made us more cognizant of the structural and institutional causes of many of the problems older women face? When we leave our homes or the theater, do we hear older women's voices and see their bodies in a way that encourages us to include them in our lives? Are we more aware of the fact that our participation in older women's cultural devaluation makes us complicit in our own eventual descent into obsolescence and oppression?

These are difficult questions to answer because, as many comedies do, these films "want to have it both ways: joyous rebellion and a status quo securely in place" (Carson 1994, 214), older women who clearly exceed

3. The Silence and Invisibility of Older Women

their subordinate position, yet do so in a context of cultural forces that attempt to repress them. But hidden within the comedic and fast-paced action, these movies address two of the most serious problems that older women face: socially-constructed poverty and the silence that goes with it, and culturally-devalued bodies and the invisibility they bring. Therefore, the ways in which both protagonists break through the silence and invisibility that often characterize older women's lives and insist on doing things that will ultimately allow them to become vocal and visible are not only hilarious, but pose a serious challenge to the attitudes and behaviors that constrain older women's lives. This challenge is strengthened by the fact that the lead actresses themselves, both over 50 when the movies were made, are still busy and successful,[9] and by the generous presence of older actors playing character roles in *Saving Grace*. If we look past their stereotypical eccentricities, these characters, such as the two older ladies who mistake marijuana plants for tea and try to tend their store while high, and who enthusiastically take part in the pot-induced bacchanalia caused by Grace's decision to burn her mountain of marijuana buds, show older women still working, playing an active role in their community, and thoroughly enjoying life.

Yet neither film explores where Grace and Chris's new identities might lead, what career options their successes might offer, how they and their families and communities might adjust to the changes their newfound confidence and desires might occasion, or how much their later-life success might destabilize theories about the stages of life. With endings that mitigate the importance of their self-transformation and emphasize continuity, as does the last scene of *Calendar Girls* where Chris and her friends are shown back on the hill overlooking Knapely exercising as in the first, how will we imagine their futures? Will we follow the films' utopian bent and picture Grace writing more novels that encourage older women to dare to follow their dreams, Chris using her success to build a coalition of older women who challenge the stereotypes that devalue their appearance and their abilities? Or will the fairy-tale endings succeed in obscuring the important issues these movies address, leaving us to engage in the all-too-common magical thinking that underestimates the real difficulties older women face and that prevents us as a society from developing more equitable policies and programs to address the economic and social inequalities that only intensify with every decade a woman lives.

Hopefully, these movies will at least function as a counterstory to the fairy-tale-like narrative Freud recounted in "Anxiety and Instinctual Life" in 1933 and that, all too often, repeats itself even today. In Freud's story, when a woman "no longer young" was finally freed from the symptoms that had kept her from participating in society, she plunged into life, eager to develop her talents and enjoy some late-life success. But when each of her attempts resulted in failure due to the ageist attitudes of others and the structural age bars she encountered, her discouragement and internalized ageism got the better of her and she gave up, resigning herself to decline in silence and invisibility. Freud, who saw older women as threatening and less than human, believed that they should desire less than the young and approved of this outcome (Woodward 1991). Calling it a happy ending, he appealed to the power of the split subject to regulate behavior and attributed the woman's failure to an unconscious need to punish herself for stepping out of gender and age-related bounds. He ignored the real culprits: sexism, ageism (Mellencamp 1999), and the myriad binary distinctions that continue to allow these prejudices to operate unchecked.

An even happier result than functioning as a counterstory to Freud's dark vision would be one in which watching these films inspired older women (and all of us) to resist ageist stereotypes and internalize a different imagination themselves. This is precisely the outcome that 78-year-old psychologist Philip Zimbardo is betting on with his "Heroic Imagination Project." Based on an experiment he did over forty years ago that revealed the illusory nature of a boundary between a role someone plays and that person's "real" identity,[10] his program trains people to recognize the ways their environment shapes their imagination. He then exposes them to what he calls heroic narratives, stories of ordinary people who do extraordinary things, and encourages them to internalize an "heroic imagination" that will help them resist both external pressure to conform and internal doubts about their abilities (Zimbardo 2011). Knowingly or not, his project draws on both Butler's theory of performativity and Hacking's ideas about the looping effects of human kinds in order to show that deterministic ways of thinking about human behavior are wrong, and that new ways of imagining life can actually effect positive change.

Rather than bemoan the power of the split subject to police us into conformity, a program like Zimbardo's helps us redirect its energies towards resistance, and rather than decry the power of story, discourse, myth, and narrative to stereotype and constrain life, such training asks us to draw on their power to reimagine and reshape it. If every aging and older woman would avail herself of those energies and that power to free her life from the clutches of cultural devaluation and the silence and invis-

3. The Silence and Invisibility of Older Women

ibility it brings, no matter how small or seemingly inconsequential her success might seem, then Patricia Mellencamp's assertion that "the most interesting and powerful woman is the old woman ... the summation of all ... life" (Mellencamp 1999, 325) could very well come true. It might even be reflected back to us in the movies.

4

Intimacy and Desire in Later Life

> And, oh, if I had known —
> I'd do it all over again.
> Some things just get better and better
> And better than they've already been.
>
> — Greg Brown, *If I Had Known*

From her wheelchair in a home for the aged, eighty-year-old Frances looks in the direction of the camera with blind eyes and declares that she has finally met the great love of her life, the man she should have been with forever. Watching her adoringly, David, an elderly resident and man of letters who could choose from a plethora of available older women, clearly shows he reciprocates the feeling. When the camera moves to show Frances and Davy hugging, he with his hand on her "tush" and she repeating "Davy, dearie" with her head on his shoulder, Frances assures us that, although sex is limited in the nursing home due to cramped quarters, they make do. When together, she continues, it doesn't matter what other people think, they're in their own private world.

In these few scenes, Frances, one of the heroines of Deidre Fishel's 2003 documentary *Still Doing It: The Intimate Lives of Women Over 65*, charmingly shatters both the stereotype of the old woman as sexless and the taboo against speaking in public about the sex lives of the elderly. By revealing a life still full of desire, romance, and personal growth, Frances, along with the eight other women in this film, gives the viewer an opportunity to hear how older women feel about their bodies, their sexuality, their desire, and their loves, and to see images that celebrate, rather than denigrate, what love and romance in older age can be. To the extent that watching and listening to Frances and the other women in this documentary make us question our assumptions about desire and identity in old

4. Intimacy and Desire in Later Life

age, this movie, as reviewer for the *Village Voice* Amy Taubin noted, presents an irreverent challenge to the extreme ageism harbored by almost everyone in our youth-obsessed culture.

Yet, how much influence can one documentary film exert on the way the romantic relationships of the aging and the old are portrayed in popular cinema? To put it another way, as did one reviewer on efilmcritic.com, regardless of this film's uncanny ability to make us feel ashamed of ourselves for cringing when older people get romantic in public, after watching this movie, how many of us will fail to cringe anyway? What if, rather than continuing to cringe, we were to see *Still Doing It* as marking the moment when the shared meanings, discourses, narratives, and philosophical positions about aging and old age that we have absorbed and internalized rub up against real-life revelations that destabilize our surety in the "truth" about old age with which we have been presented? What if this film caused us to consider why we are cringing in the first place? What if, when it comes to sex and romance, we began to realize that "the social and cultural nature of norms for age-appropriate behavior ... [are] constructions themselves" (Swinnen 2012a, 9), born of economic, political, social, and cultural imperatives that often ignore the ability of the old to create "relationships and intimacy that build on the unique advantages of aging and the empowerment that may come with being disenfranchised" (Connids 2006, 147)? And finally, what if we considered what a film needs to do to entice, cajole, admonish, inveigle, or exhort us to stop cringing and start embracing the notion of older persons as romantic, desiring beings who, like Frances and Davy, are capable of intimate relationships that are as "intense, committed, emotional, caring, mutual, and sexual" as those of any other age (Connids 2006, 124)?

In this chapter, we will try to answer these questions by examining if, to what extent, and how some of the concerns and experiences expressed in *Still Doing It* have been incorporated into the characters and the stories we find in popular cinema.[1] In light of all we have learned about aging and ageism so far, we will look closely at the ways in which the movies *Something's Gotta Give*, *The Mother* and *Beginners*, and *The Best Exotic Marigold Hotel* portray older characters in romantic and sexual situations and ask: does a film encourage a view of older people as romantic and sexual beings? foster the understanding that much of what we observe about intimacy among older adults can be a function of their times or an outcome of current age relations in which the opportunities for intimacy are limited by age-based socially constructed barriers (Connids 2006)?

portray the narrative of decline as an artifact of youth bias rather than a physiological process? feature older actors and characters who have overcome their own ageist attitudes toward old bodies and behavior and now find them attractive and desirable? support the fact that we know nothing about another person's sexual life at any age unless that person chooses to tell us (Gullette 2011)? Hopefully, by attempting to answer these questions, we will come to the conclusion that a "culture that relishes older bodies" (Gullette 2011, 141) can help us to put perceived age-related losses into perspective by becoming aware of all that's retained and newly achieved as well. The answers we find may even allow us to stop cringing.

Resexing the Older Body

Something's Gotta Give (2003), a romantic comedy that tells the story of Harry Sanborn, an aging, rich, and determinedly single music executive who unexpectedly comes to appreciate the charms of Erica Barry, a divorced woman and successful playwright in her fifties, opens with Harry's voice intoning his philosophy of romantic involvement against a backdrop of multiple young and nubile female bodies parading into an exclusive club scene. "Ah, the sweet, uncomplicated satisfaction of the younger woman. That fleeting age when everything falls right into place. It's magic time and it can render any man anywhere absolutely helpless. Some say I'm an expert on the younger woman. Guess that's because I've been dating them for over forty years!" True to his word, the next scene shows him in his convertible with Marin Barry, a young beauty who happens to be Erica's daughter, on the way to her mother's beach house in the Hamptons for the weekend. Yet before they have a chance to consummate their desire, Harry is seized with chest pains, rushed to the hospital, and finds himself forced to take refuge in Erica's guest bedroom to recover from a mild heart attack while Marin and Harry's entourage of helpers return to their lives in the city.

Unnerved by the way her reaction to the recuperating Harry disrupts her resolve to remain aloof and in control of a post-divorce life free from the vagaries of romantic involvement, Erica begins to appreciate Harry's company despite her distaste for his lifestyle and reputation. And Harry, finding himself strangely attracted to her as well, begins to wonder whether his exclusive taste for younger women has been a tad too limiting. From this point on, we know that Harry and Erica will eventually fall in love. We're just not sure how they will work through the emotional and comedic

4. Intimacy and Desire in Later Life

complications that ensue, such as young Dr. Mercer's interest in Erica, Harry's reluctance to relinquish his non-monogamous lifestyle, Marin's willingness to date an older man versus her distress at the fact that her father's fiancée is her age, and Erica's decision to base her new hit play on some of the less than flattering real-life events of the time she spent with Harry.

Before the happy ending, in which Harry and Erica find themselves contentedly enmeshed in the role of adoring grandparents, we, as viewers, have been exposed to a surfeit of situations in which aging or age differences have played a part. From the gendered expectations that structure the different ways older men and older women are treated, through the health problems we presume older people will experience, to the inevitable jokes about sexual function, body parts, eyesight, and memory, we have been led on a journey of chronology (accompanied by the old standard *As Time Goes By*) that concludes with the realization that, as Fran, Burt Monroe's girlfriend from *The World's Fastest Indian* (discussed further in chapter 6), put it when seen emerging from his house one morning in her bathrobe, "dirty old men need love, too." So it's worth a more discriminating look at what we may have learned on this journey, and at whether or not this knowledge has led us to a keener appreciation of the ambiguities and uncertainties involved in the process of growing old in contemporary society or has simply left the narrative of decline a bit shinier but largely intact.

When during dinner at the beach house Zoe, Erica's voluble and animated sister who teaches Women's Studies at Columbia, recognizes Harry as the subject of an article called "The Escape Artist" and embarks on a rant about the differential treatment of single older men and single older women that ends in an explanation of our cultural characterization of Harry as "a catch" and Erica as someone who stays home and never dates, she is not only repeating the "truth" as the narrative of decline would have it, but opening up the plot to a consideration of the way gender and age inequality intertwine. Her conclusion that older women as a category "are about as fucked a group as can ever exist," despite the fact that they, like Erica, are often "productive" and "interesting," refers to the manner in which "relations of power within specific social and historical contexts configure relations between age, gender, sexuality, and the body" (Marshall and Katz 2005, 76). From this point on, much of the humor and many of the plot twists of the film rely on our cultural acquaintance with the paradoxical nature of both a medicalized view of aging that asks us to grow simultaneously "older and younger at the same time" (80) and a gendered view of aging that increasingly tethers older bodies to impossible-to-maintain and often unwanted youthful or mid-life norms—hegemonic masculinity and emphasized femininity.

According to Amir Shalev-Cohen in *Visions of Aging: Images of the Elderly in Film,* since "access to the existential condition of an aging mind has to be gained through aging" (Cohen-Shalev 2012, 11), much of old age lies outside of "the empathetic repertory of the non-old" (11) and must be accessed through metaphor. In *Something's Gotta Give,* these metaphors function by drawing on the shared meanings we have assigned to certain phrases and expressions, and serve as a kind of shorthand that gives those who consider themselves non-old a point of entry into the world inhabited by the older characters in this movie. For instance, when Harry tells Marin, "women of a certain age don't date *me,*" and later, when Zoe remembers that Harry was once engaged to Diane Sawyer and he responds that "women your age love her," without explicitly saying so, he is using these expressions both to further establish his reputation as a still desirable, virile, productive, and wealthy man, and to distance himself from both older women and other older men. Even after he realizes that he is attracted to Erica, his language continues to reflect this strategy of distancing when he insists he likes "to travel light," he's "not good at being monogamous," he doesn't "know how to be a boyfriend," and cannot bring himself to type the words, "I miss you," when chatting on his computer with Erica. In these examples, Harry's words closely conform to what age theorists Robert Meadows and Kate Davidson have identified as one of the strategies older men employ to cope with the friction between aging and dominant forms of masculinity (Meadows and Davidson 2006). Given that we as an audience probably unreflexively associate aging with a narrative of decline that feminizes and desexualizes aging men, Harry's language serves to help us understand that he considers himself to be an older man who is an exception to the rule of decline, or at least in better condition than other men his age.

Another strategy that Harry uses to maintain his connection to hegemonic masculinity is his faith in his ability to perform sexually in a way that conforms to the stereotype of a young, unattached male, and his eagerness to let us know it. Perhaps the scene in which he and Erica are caught in a thunderstorm while picnicking on the beach, run back to the house only to find the electricity has failed, and proceed to the bedroom to make love illustrates his use of this strategy best. When they kiss, Harry

4. Intimacy and Desire in Later Life

is pleased to let both Erica and the audience know that he can still be aroused without his usual dose of Viagra. And although he had previously apologized for accidentally seeing her nude in a way that implied it was not a pleasant experience to see a woman that age naked, he now eagerly cuts off her turtleneck and tells her she's beautiful. After their love making, when they both find themselves tearfully surprised at its intensity, Erica's surprise refers to the pleasure of the sex act itself, but Harry's is directed more at the fact that he managed to have sex three days after a heart attack and didn't die rather than at the emotion surrounding the sex or his reaction to his partner. His actions and reactions are both self-centered and designed to conform to what he believes to be the culturally accepted conduct of a hip and single young male.

From Androgyny to Andropause

Since it is by way of embodiment in a particular cultural context that aging and gender come to be experienced throughout a lifetime, if we return to Foucault's characterization of sexuality as a transfer point for relations of power and a point of support for strategies of bodily discipline and control (see chapter 1) and again expand it to include the intersection of age and sex, then we can better understand how the way aging is understood through science, politics, and morality becomes a problem of "truth" that often constrains the ability of the old to define themselves (Marshall and Katz 2005). As age-studies scholars Barbara Marshall and Stephen Katz have pointed out, before the advent of modern medicine, aging was neither a necessarily pathological process nor was it characterized by inevitable sexual decline. Although, since that time, women's aging has been consistently pathologized, by the nineteenth century, with the first treatise on what was called the male climacteric, behavioral, emotional, and physiological changes began to problematize the onset of old age for the male, as well. At first, the issue of waning sexuality and loss of youthful markers of identity were seen as a positive development "leading to the natural, stable, and beneficial conditions under which older ... men could fulfill their appropriately mature roles as asexual subjects" (Marshall and Katz 2005, 76). Given that the sexes were assumed to become more androgynous, adjustment to this convergence was posited as a moral problem that required tacit acceptance of the passage of time in the body rather than as a purely biological problem.

Nevertheless, the idea of the male climacteric also marked the beginning of the use of expertise to shape the aging process "in ways that articulated it with the moral and technological ideologies of the time" (Marshall and Katz 2005, 167) and thus legitimized medical intervention. By the early twentieth century, the previously positive changes associated with the climacteric were viewed as an old-fashioned "pathological adaptive response rooted in ignorance or fear" (173), and the newer idea that an active sexual life was a necessary part of healthy aging had turned into a popular crisis that demanded the development of rejuvenation therapies and the invention of anti-aging technologies. Solutions to this perceived crisis were now sought in the very science that had codified the aging body within a discourse of senescence in the first place, leading to the marketing of regimens of rejuvenation, such as animal gland grafts and surgical procedures to redirect the semen into the body, along with the promotion of a discourse of optimism that promised recovery and renewal through scientific progress.

With the advent of synthetic testosterone in 1935, sex itself became chemical and testosterone therapy to counteract the deficiencies faced by the aging male began to be seen not only as the key to the retention of physical sexual performance but also to the maintenance of youthful vigor and enterprise. The merging of sexual function with behavioral and moral attributes such as vigor and enterprise marked the beginning of what Marshall and Katz describe as a contest between an emphasis on the importance of changes related to work, status, and cultural expectation *in* life and the significance of the belief that changes *of* life were primarily hormonal. This contest, which included a change in the term used to describe sexual problems from impotence to erectile dysfunction, eventually resulted in the creation of the idea of a male midlife crisis, similar to menopause in women, signified by the hormonal deficiency syndrome of andropause.[2] By the late twentieth century, andropause was described as a clinically treatable disorder characterized by a mix of physiological and psychological symptoms such as decrease in libido, lack of energy, sadness, and even falling asleep after dinner (Marshall and Katz 2005)! Thus, the maintenance of an active sex life, obtained by chemically warding off the diminution of sexual desire and performance previously interpreted as a normal and even beneficial part of growing older, came to be equated with both a healthy biological life and a wholesome social and cultural lifestyle.

Products such as Viagra, a staple prop for displays of humor in current popular films with aging male characters, therefore promise to remedy not only the array of sexual dysfunctions and anxieties created by our scientific discourse on aging, but to lead to a healthier and more vigorous style of living as well. Ironically, by displacing the former discourse of sexual convergence and androgyny that potentially could have led to less gender discrimination, such products and promises have strengthened the hold that sexual stereotypes exert on us across the life course. Marshall and Katz argue that this "resexing of aging bodies intensifies the sense in which performing gender becomes a lifelong project" (Marshall and Katz 2005, 91) that both reinforces heterosexual normativity and discourages gender equality and social diversity for the sake of ideals of performance and for profit. For an aging male such as Harry, it is easy to see why exposure to this discourse could lead him to firmly anchor his sense of masculinity in sexual functionality and stereotypical gendered difference no matter the changes age might bring. Yet, as Foucault argued in his writings on sexuality, this stance often places a subject and the reality of his lived experience in a struggle against the orders of power and truth that both shape him and demand that he discipline himself according to their dictates (Marshall and Katz 2005, 184).

If we look more carefully at Harry's language and behavior, we can see that he is experiencing some of the difficulties that occur with attempts to continue to perform the cultural ideal of gender in a situation where the expectations are often at odds with an older person's lived experience. Although cloaked in humorous situations, instances such as Harry's reluctance to include Viagra in his list of medications at the hospital, his insistence that he requires only four hours of sleep a night, and the fact that he reluctantly uses reading glasses to see the time or read instructions, all point to his need to deny some of the realities of life that are coded as age-related deterioration in order to maintain his masculine sense of self. His struggle is particularly evident in the scene where he and Erica are on the beach and, as she leaves, he is left staring forlornly at the flight of stairs he must be able to climb before he's allowed to resume sexual intercourse. The low camera angle of the shot up the steps lets us in on Harry's perception of these stairs as a gigantic obstacle looming over the recovery of both his sexual prowess and his sense of self that is dependent upon it. When self and masculinity are tied in this way to an ability to "perform," it's not difficult to imagine a situation in which failure to climb those stairs could represent the loss of something much greater than a particular physical capability. As far as Harry's character goes, despite the incongruence between expectation and experience, his identity remains constructed according to a narrative in which many of the changes that may occur with aging are interpreted only in comparison with ideals of youth and defined solely in terms of decline and loss.

Growing Older and Younger at Once

The imperative to grow older and younger at the same time also ties Erica to an ideal of emphasized femininity that becomes increasingly difficult to maintain over time and, as discussed in the previous chapter, tends to obscure other aspects of a woman's character that may emerge with age. From one of the earliest scenes, when Erica and Zoe unexpectedly return home only to discover Harry in the kitchen with his head stuck in the refrigerator and, grabbing a knife, Erica threatens to call the police, the language Harry uses to describe her leans toward the masculine. Painting her as "formidable," "a tower of strength," "flinty," "impervious," "macho," and remarking that he wishes he were half the man she is serve to convey his disapproval of the way she looks and separates herself from others. Although these characterizations could be taken as complimenting her on the way she is able to support herself, something that both Grace and Chris ardently desired, they also can be seen as a linguistic device for drawing attention to the way that the "social loneliness" (Jacoby 2011, 138)—or the lack of informal interaction with others common to many older women's lives that Zoe spoke of—has masculinized her. Later, when they are shopping in a French delicatessen, the way the camera frames an unflattering shot of the two stereotypically "old" women Erica notices then quickly shifts to a view of Marin's supple young form and Harry's lascivious reaction to it, makes visible the internal struggle Erica is undergoing over her appearance and her conduct, and the unreasonable way they are judged.

Possibly in reaction to these remarks and her experience in the shop, and clearly in response to Harry's provocative inquiry asking her if wearing turtlenecks all summer never makes her hot, Erica readily accepts Dr. Julian Mercer's unexpected invitation to dinner, appearing for her "date" in a black, form fitting, V-neck dress.[3] Although far too worldly to show obvious disapproval when a young woman such as her daughter or her ex-husband's fiancée are interested in an older man, despite Julian's insistence that their 20-some-year age difference doesn't matter, that he finds her sexy and beautiful, and that he never met a girl his age that affected him like this, Erica's internalization of the cultural narrative that equates female

4. Intimacy and Desire in Later Life

bodily aging with loss of attractiveness and desirability kick in as her mind denies the truthfulness of his assertions while her body revels in his attentions. We can see the ambiguity of this split at work again as Erica's relationship with Harry develops. For instance, older women can applaud the way she puts menopause in a favorable light as the perfect method of birth control and, after she and Harry make love during the storm, her statement, "Oh my God, I do like sex!" can be seen as an affirmation of "the benefits of being postmenstrual," including "better sexual communication, ... increased orgasms, wonderful sex..." (Gullette 2011, 92). Yet, the brief scenes of Erica nude or in her bra can have an ambivalent effect, either boosting the confidence of older women in the acceptability of their appearance, especially if they are aware of actress Diane Keaton's insistence on looking authentic and her public opposition to plastic surgery, or causing them to despair because they lack the time and resources to keep their physical bodies in such good shape, or both. Nevertheless, compared to the three scenes where we are allowed to contemplate Harry's naked behind, as Roger Ebert noted in his online review, the almost subliminal shot of a nude Erica only reinforces the gendered double standard that declares the aging male body to be more acceptable than the female.

Erica's behavior in these scenes is a classic example of how an older woman can become a split subject (see chapter 3), viewing herself at once as both an object that is unworthy of romantic advances and a subject who resists a narrative that devalues her worth. This same ambivalence plays out in *Still Doing It*, when Betty, 73 at the time of filming, expresses a similar paradoxical relationship with herself while recounting how she met her current lover, a man 40 years her junior, four years ago. Though their online relationship had been going smoothly, when Betty finally mustered the courage to ask him to meet her in person, she feared he would quickly lose interest due to her appearance. Fortunately, he wanted to stay, insisting that it is his good fortune to have met Betty and to be able to enjoy her company while he can. Interestingly, he notes that, although initially Betty was inclined to try to point out what she saw as flaws in her body, it is her current acceptance of the appearance of her aging body, along with her ability to ignore disparaging remarks about the appropriateness of their relationship, that allow their partnership to work.

Looking at Erica's behavior and feelings about herself both with Julian and with Harry in light of Betty's experience, we can see that resistance to the cultural narrative that promotes menopause as a disease in which "bodily aging equals hormonal deficiency equals loss of femininity" (Marshall and Katz 2005, 83), and replacement of attempts to resex the body after menopause through often risky pharmaceutical means with acceptance of the older female body as still attractive and desirable, does have the potential to heal the split that so many women feel and that influences the way they behave both in real life and as characters in popular cinema.[4] Although not every older woman who accepts her body will want or have Betty's or Erica's experience, every woman could greatly benefit by reimaginging how she would like to see herself.

All the ambivalence that women feel could reflect what Margaret Gullette describes as the outcome of rituals of social comparison, such as looking at celebrities, watching other people's sex, and bonding with age peers in feeling substandard, that are so harmful, especially to women. Gullette's argument that whenever we substitute body image, such as a picture we see in a movie, for body experience, a picture we have of our everyday lives, and think the look we present to others counts more than the feel of being ourselves, we have succumbed to the ageist and sexist anxieties created by the narrative of decline, does ring true (Gullette 2011). But, although it can certainly be argued that watching popular movies can and does cause social comparison, popular film also has the ability to portray a more meaningful vision of aging, one that goes beyond what we actually see to an inner mental picture that could lead to better expectations and practical life strategies as we age. As Cohen-Shalev argues, cinematic images have the potential "to partially bridge the schism between aging as subjective experience ... [and] aging as a social phenomenon" (Cohen-Shalev 2012, 2). When we see Erica and Harry's faces, they are real; their appearance and expressions convey so much of the actors' real-life experience, humor, and knowledge to their characters that, when the film was criticized for confusing autobiography with fiction, the consensus was that the blurring of fact and fiction was one of the pleasures of the movie. Thus, cinema not only mirrors a cultural understanding of growing older, but serves as a creative outlet in which to learn how others have resisted the narrative of decline and with which to explore other ways to age.

Despite the many ways in which *Something's Gotta Give* conforms to the perspective of growing older contained in the narrative of decline and keeps youthful gendered differences largely intact, it does present the viewer with older characters who are creative and successful and who, in spite of their initial resistance to stepping away from the attempt to maintain hegemonic masculinity and the belief that older women should insulate themselves from the vagaries of love, do allow unexpected love and

4. Intimacy and Desire in Later Life

romance to alter the trajectory of their lives. In spite of all their tears, their soul-searching, and the rather childish and vindictive way Erica's play makes fun of and dispatches the character modeled on Harry, they do learn to see some aspects of the world from the other's perspective. As Harry says while standing alone on the bridge in Paris, "I finally get to be the girl." So although the final scene showing Harry and Erica married and having dinner with Marin, her husband and new baby, is overly sentimentalized, without dialogue, and lacking in substance, much as the sequence of scenes which depicted Carl and Ellie's life together in *Up*, it does present us with an image of later-life happiness and contentment that, despite its fairy-tale feel, is not so different from the true-to-life picture we have of Frances and David in *Still Doing It*. Such a picture is well worth keeping in mind.

Towards an Economy of Touch

Conversely, Freddie who is 75 at the time of filming *Still Doing It*, tells us that when her husband died she tried to suppress her sexual feelings. Surprised at the persistence of her desire, she says she wanted to find a way to meet other men but has found it difficult. Lowering her eyes as if confessing a failure, she admits that she was never very good at pursuing them anyway. Then, looking straight into the camera in one of the most touching moments of the film, she says, "Nobody really looks at me any more. It's a terrible thing that older women, who should be revered, are treated so badly." "But," she adds, her tenacity and enduring zest for life showing through, "life is full of surprises."

One of these surprises is the movie *The Mother* (2003), a British film that squarely addresses some of the anxieties and the desires of the aging that are rarely dealt with in the movies. Eschewing the overwrought sentimentality and facile palliatives that populate so many films that purportedly deal with aging, *The Mother* takes an uncomfortable look at the way Western families ignore the needs of their elders, often wishing them simply to disappear. This hard-headed look at aging comes in the form of the story of May, a rather ordinary looking woman in her 60's, whose husband Toots has a heart attack and dies while they are visiting their children, Bobby and Paula, and their grandchildren in London. Suddenly freed from a lifetime of looking after others, of taking care of their needs before her own as she did in the first few scenes with Toots, May finds herself at loose ends for the first time. When her son drives her home after the funeral, she walks in, looks at the slippers Toots had left on the floor, leafs through old photos of her children when young, and decides she can't stay. "If I sit down," she says, "I'll never get up again. I'll be like all the other old girls around here. I'm not going to a home ... I'd rather kill myself." When Bobby chides her for being difficult and urges her to sit and watch TV, she defiantly responds, "Why not? Why shouldn't I be difficult?"

Once back in London, May shuffles back and forth between Bobby's house and Paula's apartment. Seen as an intrusion by Bobby's wife, and by Paula as someone to care for her son and to blame for her own emotional difficulties, May wanders through London, ending up literally as lost as she feels. Her inner state of confusion is revealed to us by the way this scene is filmed, her distorted, troubled image cast back to us in "a mélange of reflections" (Kaplan 2012, 27). Yet this experience, rather than making her even more timorous, marks the beginning of her sense of liberation. When Paula asks her to talk to Darren, the handsome and perpetually adolescent builder who is working on Bobby's conservatory, about his intentions towards her, May agrees.

Having witnessed an episode of roisterous and argumentative sex between Paula and Darren a few nights earlier, May forthrightly asks him what he's doing with Paula. Surprised by her honesty, Darren befriends her, eating the tasty meals she prepares for him with pleasure, taking her out to lunch, and listening to her express her desire to finally do the things she loves as she sighs, "Dear God, let us be alive before we die." Before long, May is dressing to please Darren, buying him presents and, even though she still describes herself as "a shapeless old lump," ultimately daring to ask him to accompany her to the spare room. For May, their sexual adventures together are life changing, allowing her to express herself in ways she had never been able to before, and to imagine a kind of life for herself that had never seemed possible.

Yet, while sitting at Bobby's dining room table to discuss finances and what to do with mother, Bobby and Paula discover May's rather explicit drawings of her sexual encounters with Darren. From this point on, May's already tenuous relationship with them and her secret affair with Darren both start to crumble. Cold and unable to empathize at all with their mother's awakening sexuality and desire for life, Bobby and Paula ask her to leave, even offering to help her find counseling; and, incapable of rising above the unending frustration he feels with his life circumstances, Darren explodes in an episode of violence that shatters any lingering hopes May might have had of going away with him.

4. Intimacy and Desire in Later Life

Her suitcase packed, May walks slowly out of Bobby's house, neither her children nor her grandchildren giving her anything more than a cursory wave or "Bye," and takes the train home. Once there, she spends one night in her old room. In the morning, rather than resign herself to the dreary and predictable old age her children have in mind, she packs her bag with a few clothes and her books on drawing and walks out smiling, finally ready to face all the surprises life has to offer.

Unconscious Ageism

As Ann Kaplan states in her article, "The Unconscious of Age: Performances in Psychoanalysis, Film, and Popular Culture," *The Mother* is one of the few popular films about aging that dares to explore what she calls the "unconscious of age." For Kaplan, this term encompasses not only the ageist biases and stereotypes that linger in both theoretical and clinical psychoanalytical perspectives, but the unconscious personal conflicts that may reemerge in an older individual over time, and even the cultural response to movies that refuse to adhere to viewer expectations concerning the staging of age. Kaplan argues that only by better understanding the "inner psychic, lives of older people" (Kaplan 2012, 17), by exploring their affective states as well as their more obvious material conditions, can we move beyond a public discourse full of negative emotional and practical assessments of their bodies, needs, and even their very social presence.

Beginning with Freud who, as noted in chapter 3, did much of his creative work in his later years yet doubted that the old could benefit from psychoanalysis due to their lack of flexibility and creativity, Kaplan traces how the perception that the unconscious of the old was rigid and "bound by time" (Kaplan 2012, 18) evolved through the work of Erik Erikson on the different stages and tasks in life to the recognition by professor of psychiatry Harold Blum that the way we live our lives and how we experience life itself can change personality at any age. By the 1970s and 1980s, Kaplan notes, psychoanalyst Pearl King incorporated these revelations into a psychotherapy designed for older people that saw life as a dynamic, ongoing process, and recognized the that common pressures of aging, such as fears associated with retirement, bodily changes, loss of a partner, or dependence, could bring on crises that might reactivate problems or neuroses from an earlier time. King's recognition that older people could be functioning in several different time scales at once, Kaplan writes, meant that older patients could work through the ways in which they might have transferred past meanings to events in the present, learn to understand the resultant emotions and accept the changes or losses that may have sparked these feelings, and move on to look for present advantages and opportunities.

Yet in spite of significant changes in discourse and practice regarding aging and old age, unconscious biases, narratives, and stereotypes remain, as in the concept of "'transcending old age,' which retains the notion that old age requires 'transcending' in the first place" (Kaplan 2012, 22). These biases result in part from the ways in which we "other" the old to prevent the destabilizing recognition of our common vulnerabilities and responsibilities to and for each other. But they also emerge from the way we frame aging, how we image and imagine the inner lives of the old.

> If the elderly freely mingle with us in person and on the screen, and if their performances challenge how we unconsciously think they should behave, then we cannot so easily forget. Anxiety will result: strong feelings such as disgust may emerge. On the other hand, some might argue that not having the elderly highly visible (if one could control that) would lessen the likelihood of disgust. I believe that familiarity through seeing the elderly in life and on the screen is likely, over time, to enable younger others to overcome negative feelings [Kaplan 2012, 22].

In this passage, Kaplan acknowledges that the frame — political, economic, social, artistic — can create a productive tension between a particular depiction of age and an expectation about age. To the extent that that frame encourages us to empathize with the problems and experiences of older people, it can help us overcome any sense of separation we may feel between "us" and "them;" but if the frame exacerbates differences, it can magnify any sense of alienation we may already feel from the world of the old. With the literal framing of old age that occurs in film, however, a particular frame can also create a space between reality and fantasy where this tension and these anxieties can be safely worked on without fear of suffering the repercussions that that same framing might occasion in everyday life. If the framing of aging is too realistic or probes too deeply into its ambiguities and contradictions, profits may be compromised and the film may be rejected; if it is too stereotypical, it may be potentially harmful to the development of a fuller understanding of old age. Therefore, a film that provides access to the internal fears and desires of an older woman such as May, and that challenges our ideas and values with non-stereotypical images without either turning us off with the harsh realities it

4. Intimacy and Desire in Later Life

depicts or assuaging our fears with a picture that simply consolidates the already prevalent "mask of aging," is rare and can have a deep impact on our world.

That *The Mother* succeeds in creating a space of productive tension where we can confront our fears and anxieties about aging is clear in the reviews that were written about it. Ranging from interpreting the film as a damning portrayal of the callousness of Western humanity to characterizing it as a perceptive look at the fragility of our common humanity, the majority of the reviewers nevertheless conclude that films like this will influence cinema in general to become less ageist. Therefore, it's worth a closer examination of exactly how *The Mother* crosses the categorical boundaries we have placed around aging and old age, both through the outer storyline and the inner stories of the characters, in a way that actually alters how we perceive and react to the expression of sexuality by older people.

Framing Age

The first scene of *The Mother* is of a woman in bed, eyes wide open, lying next to an older man. The next scene shows her dressing him, tying his shoes, and helping him outside as they embark on a journey to visit their family in the city. Although there is something in the expression on the woman's face that intimates a coming change, because the camera focuses on the difficulties the man is having breathing and keeping up, the predominant mood is one of despair. Remaining nameless until they arrive at their son's house where they become May and Toots, they are presented as part of the homogenous mass of the unremarkable elderly, from whom little is expected and to whom even less is offered. While the family bustles around getting ready for school and work, their granddaughter, who receives her gift with the careless abandon of the over indulged, points out the wrinkles on May's face. And when they find themselves alone—left behind—in the house with Darren, May wanders out into the backyard alone, invisible to the others while the camera focuses on Toots and Darren bonding over cricket.

Thus far, aging has been framed in a stereotypical way as passive, empty, and lonely. From the bland colors and obvious marks of aging that contribute to May's invisibility as an older woman and the shortness of breath and stumbling steps that construct Toots as unable to keep up and in decline, to the way that the dialogue is overlapping and unintelligible, the audience is maneuvered into a position in which what we see defines what we feel. Our affective state regarding May and Toots, and most likely the elderly in general, is so far based on vision alone. But to whom does this vision of aging as decline belong? As Donna Haraway points out in "Situated Knowledges," there is no disembodied vision. Despite the supposed transparent gaze of the camera, all vision, all framing, including any technological mediation through which it may be filtered, is partial and subjective, a view from an embodied somewhere. And since any view from a position of finite embodiment is limited, no affective state, or economy, based on vision can be objective — tell the whole story or represent the entire truth (Haraway 1991b).

Fortunately, this film does not allow us to remain comfortably ensconced in the visual narrative of aging as decline for long. As May walks out onto the lawn, it suddenly becomes quiet and "we are in a space with May alone" (Kaplan 2012, 24). Instead of the camera being still and recording the chaotic activity passing in front of it, the camera moves with May, allowing us to see from her perspective and to begin to feel the need for change awakening in her. That change is imminent becomes even clearer when we observe how May comports herself after Toot's death. Though confused, maybe shocked, by her own behavior, her refusal to acquiesce to her family's sudden desire to infantilize and control her, and her determination to begin living her own life signals a turning point in the way aging is framed. As Cynthia Fuchs wrote in a review entitled "Difficult," the camera now begins to reflect May's shifting sensibilities, revealing her point of view as she looks across traffic or in windows and doorways, literally framing her in panes and mirrors as she steps forward into her own life.

Beginning with these scenes, the frame of aging that relies on the visually based unconscious of age underlying a negative and stereotypical depiction of aging as primarily loss and deterioration shifts to a frame that concentrates on May's subjective experience of aging. That this way of "seeing" aging is also partial and embodied is less important than the fact that, with it, we have moved from experiencing age as a state based on vision and epistemological knowing to experiencing age through affect, a state based on ontological knowledge that highlights " touch, texture, sensation, smell, feeling, and affect over what is assumed to be legible through the visible" (Puar 2011, 90). This move displaces us from a frame that invites surveillance and separation to a frame that invites resemblance and connection due to the inclusion of vital information beyond

4. Intimacy and Desire in Later Life

the visual—from "looks like" to "feels like" (Puar 2011). Although this frame could be used to discriminate against people on the basis of vague intimations or feelings, as has happened with racial profiling, it can also be used to create affective connections that might be difficult to forge based on vision alone, such as those that ignore or downplay differences in age.

Patricia Clough and Craig Willse describe this move as taking us from a concept of populations, or what Foucault described as groupings of human beings as subjects of rights and responsibilities engaged in discourses about knowledges and the nature of truth, to the idea of publics, or groups of human beings who are united by common characteristics, features, or parts (Clough and Willse 2011). In contrast to populations, whose identity rests on empirical facts and statistics, publics are formed at the level of affect and sensation, "drawn into images and commentary that are full of passions ... that allow affective states to take on a facticity without employing a logic of evidence" (Clough and Willse 2011, 53). Publics, such as the category "baby boomers," a group united less by any visual or empirical likeness and more by affective states, such as fear about their economic impact on society as they age or, conversely, by hope as to their potentially liberating effect on our perception of the aging and the old, come and go in time. Yet, while active, they can destabilize the relationship of belonging that characterizes larger populations, redefining, as Hacking explained, both the criteria for inclusion or exclusion and the way those within a certain category are perceived.

In the case of May, her refusal to remain cloistered in the normative aging and old population opens up our ideas of what constitutes the category of the aging and the old to include affective states— desires and feelings and the publics that manifest them — that were previously excluded. When her awakening sexual desire draws her to Darren who, as a misfit himself, is the only person in her life to display any compassion concerning her feelings of loneliness and isolation, seen from a perspective of affect that emphasizes feelings and passions over vision, her powerful desire for him begins to seem normal despite the fact that he is not quite half her age. Just as Darren is able to move beyond the othering of the old in which he had participated when May first arrived due to the discovery of their shared interests in art and life, the way in which May's age and sexuality are presented, even though they directly challenge prevailing notions of what is appropriate age-based behavior, also gives us as an audience a chance to move past the idea that sexual desire in the old is grotesque and to see it as a shared characteristic of being human (Kaplan 2012).

As the intimacy between May and Darren grows, her internal change is reflected externally in her face and her bodily appearance. Her skin appears less wrinkled and full of vitality, and her wardrobe becomes more colorful and attractive. By the time she asks Darren to accompany her to the spare room, the sexual tension between them has become palpable. As they undress and get into bed, Darren asks her to touch him and she admits to him that she thought no one would ever touch her again except the undertaker. With the image of their lovemaking deliberately blurred as May comes to orgasm again and again, we are transported from experiencing this scene through the limited frame of vision with its predetermined categorical exclusions to a frame that prompts us to participate in her pleasure through the medium of touch.

From the Visual to the Tactile

In *Embodying the Monster: Encounters with the Vulnerable Self*, bioethicist and feminist scholar Margrit Shildrick describes the transporting of someone from a visual frame to a tactile frame, or to what Deleuze and Guattari call a haptic frame in which the visual and tactile frames combine so that the eye participates in the function of touch (Puar 2011), as the move from the detachment and control of the so-called disembodied gaze to a sensuous engagement with the world and with others (Shildrick 2002). Basing her ideas on the inherent instability and vulnerability of the body, Shildrick posits that the Western desire for mastery over change and individuality can only be maintained by creating categories of exclusion for those with non-normative bodies that are degraded or lacking, such as the deformed, the disabled, the old, or what Haraway calls the monsters that have "always defined the limits of community in Western imaginations" (Haraway 1991a, 180). Yet, since no body can ever completely comply with the norms attributed to the abstract ideal of a "clean and proper body" (Shildrick 2002, 46) despite the ever increasing medicalization of bodily change and difference, the boundaries around these categories of exclusion are never secure and must be continually remade and reinforced. Whenever breached, a sudden recognition of our own vulnerability to "contamination" from the other causes both a corporeal and an ontological anxiety that is reflected in the way we treat others—in our ethical relationship with others and with the world — and in the way we evaluate our-

4. Intimacy and Desire in Later Life

selves—in our ethical relationship with the other inside us that we try to control through the split self.

According to Shildrick, this anxiety and fear of contamination is in reality a disavowal of the dynamics of growth, of becoming. From "the circuit of bodily exchanges that characterize the early maternal/infant bond" (Shildrick 2002, 105) to the liminality of the aging body as the forces of the "outside" encroach upon and eventually claim its form, the corporeal self is continually made and remade through its vulnerability to others and to the world. Rather than shrink from the world and the other, objectifying them as objects to be used or owned, as in an economy based on vision, Shildrick argues that the ability to live and grow can only take place if we seek out bodily engagement with others and the world, as in an economy based on touch.

Although "in comparison with the visible, with its clarity and distance, the tactile—a sensation that both frustrates detachment and compromises objectivity by reason of its reversible nature—is thoroughly devalued" (Shildrick 2002, 109), it is touch that has the power to awaken an awareness of the other that goes beyond objectification. By tracing how the concept of touch has challenged the notion of the "clean and proper self" through theoretical work on the body, such as that of Irigaray, who wished to abolish the dichotomy of active and passive in the nearness of touch (Irigaray 1993), Lyotard, who argued for the notion of an ineradicable first touch from before the "I" came into being (Lyotard 1993), and Merleau-Ponty, who postulated that the subject is in a mutually constitutive relationship with its objects and, therefore, intertwined one with another through touch (Merleau-Ponty 1968), Shildrick shows how an economy of touch can disrupt the distinction between self and other that founds exclusions, can lead to an acceptance of all forms of bodiliness, and can demand the creation of an ethics that this acceptance would demand. (This idea will be discussed more thoroughly in the last two chapters).

When we consider the relationship between May and Darren framed in terms of an economy of touch, we can better understand that it is May's desire to live and grow—a desire that is too often thwarted by a cultural narrative that both excludes the old from becoming and constructs the aging female body as monstrous and outside of the bounds of the "clean and proper body"—that simultaneously nourishes her mind and body as much as it shocks and enrages her children. The moral dilemma that revolves around how to think about May's desire is reflected on the screen in the director's decision to show May's nude body only from the back and in softly blurred light during the first sex scene, and to avoid close-ups of her body in the following, more graphic, scenes of her sex with Darren. It matters to the message the film sends about the acceptability and desirability of older women's bodies if his decision was based on concerns about a sense of aesthetics for the sex scenes that would discourage the viewer from slipping back into an economy based on vision with all its negative assessments of the old body thus keeping May within the frame of a more sympathetic economy of touch, or if it was in response to his own unconscious age bias against full display of an older woman's sexually aroused body.

Age scholar Aagje Swinnen explores a similar dilemma in her examination of a 1998 photo series by photographer Erwin Olaf called *Mature*. This series, which consists of ten portraits of women between the ages of 61 and 89 posed in ways that approximate famous pin-up portraits of the 1950's, intends "to revalue the aesthetics of elderly women's bodies by picturing ... aged models as sexual human beings" (Swinnen 2012b, 183). Yet, Swinnen concludes that it is difficult to know whether Olaf's project actually succeeds in deconstructing negative stereotypes of older women's sexuality. Reviews were mixed, with some reviewers saying that making older women's bodies visible is a positive contribution that can finally "render their attractiveness both thinkable and discussable" (191), but others noted the difficulty of not unconsciously falling back into the idea that "sex is the privilege of youth while late-life sensuality merely provides proof of monstrosity" (184).

A second moral dilemma concerns the construal by many reviewers of May's actions as selfish and unbefitting a mother and grandmother. Their distaste for May's behavior can be seen in their description of her as cold, selfish, callous, and concerned with "me" as much as her grandchildren. The fact that they read her decisions as without generativity and damaging to the family yet neglect to ask if the younger characters' behavior — Paula's affair with a married man with a son and her perpetual tendency to blame others for her problems, and Bobby and his wife's lifestyle of consumption and their too busy schedule — might not be harmful to the family as well, could be due to the ageist notion that older people should be without desire and exist for others (Kaplan 2012). Superficial concerns over May's supposed selfishness ought to pale in comparison to a larger questioning of the overall morality of the way our society treats elderly women that this movie asks us to consider.

4. Intimacy and Desire in Later Life

In the context of this larger question of morality, when May eagerly seeks out and enjoys sex, we can see that it is because she has become a woman full of passion who is experiencing a physical and emotional closeness that fulfills her for the first time in her life. Her sexual conduct cannot be explained by characterizing her as full of lust, something our culture does when we call older women "cougars," or her sexual encounter with Bruce, the older man to whom Paula introduced her in a writing class, would not be so poignant and painful both for her to experience and for the audience to watch (Kaplan 2012). Nor can it be interpreted by portraying her as selfish and lacking in generativity, since "it is hard to be generative until one has fulfilled interests and desires" of one's own (Kaplan 2012, 31). She behaves this way because she needs to touch and be touched in order to fill in what was missing in her life, to confront and work through what she sees as her failures as a wife and mother, and to move on and live fully in the present. It is the touch of her lips on another's when she first gives Darren a kiss, the touch of mutually enjoyable sex, the feel of Darren's firm shoulders under the touch of her hands while she rubs them, even the sharp touch of Paula's hand on her face as she hits May for her perceived neglect, that gives May the confidence to go out and face the world on her own. It is the experience of touch — of touching and being touched, an experience that is both deeper and more intimate than the experience sight allows — that enables May to come alive again.

When May decides to leave her son's house, the camera shows us all the people who have been touched by her. While at the beginning of the film "she was on the margins," now "*she* is the central focus" (Kaplan 2012, 29). Her refusal to succumb to their expectations of passivity and dependency, to behave in a manner befitting her age, has touched others, hopefully not only on the screen but in the audience as well. To watch a film from the viewpoint of an economy of touch, therefore, has the power to make us reconsider both the way we respond to older people and the effect our fears and expectations about growing older may have on ourselves and on others. Looking again at both Frances, who due to her blindness has no choice but to experience love and desire through an economy of touch, and Freddie, whose complaint about not being looked at implicitly includes the lack of touch, we can see that it is only through touch, through the tangible physical and emotional connection with others that touch makes possible, that we can achieve a meaningful social existence.

Starting Over

Another surprising film that deals directly with the sexual desire of an older person and in which we can see the importance of an economy of touch is *Beginners* (2011). Like *The Mother*, it explores the sexual passion of and the difficulties faced by an older person who decides to start over and, in the process, reflects on themes having to do with relationships and families, the impact of death on life, and the sometimes ambivalent connections between love and loyalty. Loosely based on recent events in writer-director Mike Mills' life, *Beginners* opens with a shot of Oliver in a closet, cleaning out shirts and medications, making piles of trash and treasures, while packing up the remains of his father's life. Taking Arthur, his father's terrier, home with him that night, Oliver narrates for Arthur and the viewer the first in a series of images that weave together incidents in his life with both the historical context of his parents' lives and the relationship of all lives to the play of human history.

Through Oliver's narration in which various characters speak we discover that, although his parents had been married for forty-four years at the time of his mother's death, his father is and always was gay. Announcing that at 75 he has no interest in being "theoretically gay" any longer, Hal tells Oliver about his search for a lover and introduces Oliver and the audience to his boyfriend, Andy. We also find out that four years after coming out, Hal dies. From this point on, the movie is structured through alternating scenes of the present, in which Oliver struggles with what he sees as the effects of his parents' strained relationship on his own prospects for love and romance, and flashbacks that piece together his father's search for the love and joy that was missing in his formerly closeted life.

Comparable to the way that Freddie's experience of near invisibility presaged the way May felt at the beginning of her inner journey, Hal's sudden decision to reveal his homosexuality and dive into the gay life is prefigured by the experience of Ellen, another of the heroines of *Still Doing It*. Aware of her attraction to girls since she was a teenager, Ellen nevertheless married and had a family in an attempt to suppress what were considered abnormal desires whose social expression would have had dire consequences in the 1950's. Ultimately, unable to hide her true identity any longer, she divorced and came out, joining an active feminist movement and feeling alive for the first time in her life. Then, at age 68, she met Dolores, the person who "physically turned her life upside down" with

4. Intimacy and Desire in Later Life

desire, and with whom she finally enjoys happiness and humor, and "knows what it is to be comfortable in one's own skin."

Like the real Ellen, the semi-real character Hal became aware that he was gay as a teenager in the 1930's. By 1955, he was tired of hiding in bathrooms to have sex and of constantly being told he was suffering from an illness, so he married Oliver's mother, who said of his sexual orientation, "I'll fix that," while he thought, "Oh, God, I'll try anything." Unbeknownst to them, on their wedding day, one of the first gay rights groups was secretly meeting only a few blocks from where they said their vows. Yet his loyalty to his family and the love he admits he felt for Hal's mother — "I wasn't the greatest lover, but we made do" — kept him from coming out until after she died. When he does come out, he behaves as if he has to catch up all at once on the myriad changes the gay movement has brought about: going to a gay bar, joining gay book clubs, participating in gay pride day, writing political letters, handing out rainbows. As with May, his need to fill in what he sees as the missing pieces of his life compels him to live life without reservation.

By juxtaposing a brief history of gay rights in America with the course of Hal's life, *Beginners* renders both Hal's sense of quiet desperation and his eventual lunge at life far more sympathetic and comprehensible.[5] In *Gay and Lesbian Aging: Research and Future Directions*, Gilbert Herdt and Brian De Vries describe the marginalization and discrimination that drove homosexuals like Hal to choose to remain closeted as a denial of "sexual citizenship." Arguing that citizenship is "shaped by and/or denied to those who do not engage in normative and socially acceptable sexual behavior" (Herdt and De Vries 2003, xvi), they maintain that becoming a sexual citizen entails being or acting heterosexual regardless of one's actual sexual orientation. As with economic citizenship, something denied to many women due to their caregiving activities (see chapter 3), Herdt and De Vries posit that the notion of sexual citizenship makes visible the limits of the political and moral dimensions of personhood on which citizenship is based. Therefore, failure to carry out all the social duties and responsibilities of heteronormativity can result not only in the denial of full citizenship but in the denial of full personhood as well, making "the impact of living as a gay or lesbian under the sign of social heterosexuality ... profound and oppressive" (xvii).

Judith Butler describes the profound sense of oppression that results from the repudiation of homosexuality as the production of the abject, a term that comes from the Latin verbs to reject and to throw away, and refers to those who are without self-regard and dignity. Arguing that the production of the abject is necessary to designate which zones of social life are "'unlivable' and 'uninhabitable,'" Butler sees the abject as defining the limit of which bodies matter and, therefore, of which bodies can be accorded personhood (Butler, J. 1993, 3). Yet, Butler continues, even though the heterosexuality presumed necessary to full personhood is cultivated through prohibitions and threats, "sacrifice of desire under the force of prohibition" does not make homosexuality disappear, it simply "will incorporate that homosexuality as an identification with[in] masculinity," leaving the masculine haunted by the loss of unlived possibilities (Butler, J. 1995, 26). Given that there is no public recognition of a preemptive loss—a loss of the possible—that loss can neither be articulated nor externalized. Yet that loss remains, manifesting itself in what Butler describes as a sense of melancholy that may be expressed through rage or frustration with the self, as in Hal's desperate attempt to try a heterosexual marriage "cure," or that may burst out at the first clear chance of expression due to a change in circumstance or to a "reconceptualization of which bodies matter" over time (Butler, J. 1993, 4), as in Hal's sudden, almost theatrical, decision to come out.

No matter the mode of expression, when the cumulative effect of being gay across a lifetime, whether one has openly experienced discrimination or has experienced the stress of hiding one's identity, combines with the stress of the discrimination and oppression heaped on the aging and the old, the effects can be dramatic. For some, the confrontation with ageism can lead to "accelerated aging," a phenomenon in which the often extreme ageism encountered in gay experience leads gay middle-aged men to describe themselves as "old" at younger ages than do heterosexual men, an occurrence that strengthens the stereotype of the lonely, aging, homosexual (Herdt and De Vries 2003). But for others, it can lead to the decision to lead "uncharted lives," to construct new ways to express themselves and their creativity and to give meaning to aging and aging well (De Vries and Blando 2003).

For Hal, the latter is true. Christopher Plummer, who at 82 brought over seven decades of acting and living experience to the role of Hal and who won an Academy Award for best supporting actor, makes Hal elated and buoyant, a man, as reviewer David Edelstein said, joyously skipping along the surface of his life, a surface on which he was never before allowed to tread. Like May, who exuberantly leaps into her previously unexpressed sexuality without fully considering the possible consequences, Hal flings himself into the gay community with gleeful abandon. Even after the flashback where he calls Oliver from a bar with the disheartening news that "young gay men don't go for older gay men," he persists by placing an ad in the paper with the description, "Old single guy, attractive and horny ... if you are willing to try an older guy, that's me." And when he meets Andy, a quirky, non-monogamous, physical trainer who has always been attracted to older men, Hal's joy, like May's with Darren, becomes infectious.

Although *Beginners* lacks the sexually explicit scenes of *The Mother*, we do see numerous scenes of Hal and Andy kissing — in the house, at the hospital, on the floor — and their physical affection for each other is apparent in the way they laugh, dance, hug, and touch each other. Andy brings Hal flowers, recordings, even a live green caterpillar, and makes sure both that Oliver does not feel threatened by his homosexuality and that his right to see Hal at the hospital is respected. Hal calls Andy his number one boyfriend, telling Oliver, "I like Andy because he isn't like me. He's fun!" and asks his son to be happy for him when Andy moves in despite the fact the Andy has other boyfriends. Even when facing a diagnosis of stage four lung cancer, Hal resists revealing to Andy the gravity of his illness in order to make the most of the time remaining to them, and insists on continuing the (literal) party both in his hospital room and at home when his options for further treatment have disappeared. As Margaret Cruikshank suggests, behavior such as Hal's may be a manifestation of his "nonconforming spirit," a way of resisting the impulses, so prevalent in our society, to see an older person with an illness as "a manifestation of disorder rather than an individual who is ill" (Cruikshank 2003, 39) and to assume an older person is no longer a romantic or sexual being. We see this resistance at work again in the scene when Hal, in frustration, counts out and mechanically slugs down his medications. Here, he is engaging in behavior that bristles at our society's equation of medical care with drugs, and with the fact that most "mainstream doctors are not trained to be healers of the whole person" (61), a person who may, at any age, continue to desire sexual intimacy despite living under the shadow of a life-threatening condition.

For to be a whole person, to "be alive before we die," as May said, *is* Hal's most ardent desire. To celebrate the importance of love, friendship, and compassion despite "the fearsome reality of illness" (Cohen-Shalev 2012, 53) is Hal's last and most cherished project. Like Martha, the elderly protagonist of the film *A Woman's Tale* (1991) who is dying of cancer yet lives fully and on her own terms until her death, Hal makes the present tense his reason for living. In his analysis of Martha's behavior, Cohen-Shalev describes her conduct as "an existential project of making the 'now' of the last days of life into a fully lived reality" (55–56). In this sense, Hal is again like Martha, neither living for a future of which there is little left nor letting memories of the past take over and interfere with his project — the full intake of what his world may still offer. Hal's present-bound existence is not only the joyous expression of his previously covert sexuality, but an individualistic and pro-active engagement with the world, a reaching out to new people and activities that give him a reason for living. Like Martha's, Hal's fullness of identity emerges "in spite of, not as a result of" his past (58), giving the lie to the idea that life-review and coming to terms with what you were in the past is the final task of old age, a view the absence of portrayals of Hal in the flashbacks of Oliver's early life confirms.

Despite the brevity of Hal's immersion in the gay community, he succeeds both in strengthening his relationship with his son Oliver, who, in contrast to Bobby and Paula, supports, cares for, and loves his father to the last, and in assembling a chosen family of camaraderie and caring who enable him to not merely survive, but to engage in meaningful social interaction until the end. As do Martha and May, Hal chooses to resist the prescribed segregation of old age that spirits the elderly "away from the unmediated touch with the reality of beauty and love that the world provides freely" (Cohen-Shalev 2012, 60). Living by his own rules, Hal finds meaning in the immediacy of affect — of feelings, sensations, and intimate physical contact — in an economy of touch that also touches the viewer and asks her to consider an image of old age from within as the continuing creation of an "authentic" self, rather than the maintenance of a socially acceptable one (Cohen-Shalev 2012).

Though, at first glance, it may seem strange to look at the experiences and choices of May and Hal together, when we take into account that they are both living in a space where stereotypes of the old as inflexible and beyond desire, and myths of the aging body as undesirable, undesiring, and incapable of sexual expression, intertwine, it makes perfect sense. From the perspective of coming to a better understanding of the intersection of aging and old age with sexuality, love and romance, their inclusion in the category old often takes precedence over their separation into different categories according to sexual orientation. Since neither a heteronormative culture nor a gay culture elaborates on nor provides a range of

4. Intimacy and Desire in Later Life

age-related roles and identities, May and Hal's lives are not well reflected by any culture. Given that neither May nor Hal feels "on schedule" with respect to social age norms and life experience, their "life transitions deviating greatly from the expectable timetable" (Kertzner, Meyer, and Dolezal 2003, 101), the choices they make lack ready social comparisons. And inasmuch as neither allows social opprobrium to put him or her back into the cage of aging, their resistance and non-conformism allows them to create counterstories that give them room to grow, making them allies in demanding the right to freely express their desire.

In addition, the manner in which both May and Hal's stories bring the issue of love, relationships, and sexuality in older age to the fore almost demands that the viewer confront her own scruples and misgivings and exclaim, "Why not?" as did Oliver to his father's unexpected revelation, instead of "Why?" as did Bobby and Paula to their mother's surprising conduct. "Why not?" can expand the frame we put around aging and old age, revealing its inherent ambiguity in the concurrent desires to assert individuality and to construct meaningful social relationships within an economy of touch. Ultimately, this frame can touch us in a way that changes not only how we view growing older but how we live at any age. In the final scene of *Beginners*, when Oliver's girlfriend Anna asks him, "What happens now?" and he answers, "I don't know," Oliver is finally *beginning* to understand that both life and love require a daring, often disturbing coming out of "the closet," a leap into the unknown that exposes our vulnerability to the other and resists the safety and the security of closure.

Into Another Country

Aging has often been portrayed as a journey into the unknown, into another country of which we have no true comprehension until, with old age, we arrive. But seldom has this metaphor been taken so literally as in the film *The Best Exotic Marigold Hotel* (2012). An endearing comedy about seven English retirees who trade a dreary and unaffordable British future for a chance to spend their remaining years in an elegant yet substantially less expensive retirement hotel in Jaipur, India, this movie, like the others discussed in this chapter, summons us to an awareness of our own "unconscious of age" in relation to love, romance, and starting over in later life. Opening with brief sketches of the travelers, whose reasons for leaving England range from financial difficulties to immediate need of less costly medical care, and from the wish to reconnect with the lover of one's youth to the search for love and romance, *The Best Exotic Marigold Hotel* charts their growth and transformation from frustrated and marginalized elders into people who act to fulfill their desires, come to embrace change, and learn to thrive.

The premise of moving to a different country allows this film to situate the characters in an environment in which becoming rigid and resisting change is not an option. Thus, India, especially the city of Jaipur, as Roger Ebert noted in his review, becomes a supporting character. With its teeming streets, explosion of light, colors, and heat, and its riot of sounds, textures, and smells, the very location challenges the protagonists to viscerally experience success as the ability to cope and adapt — to the food, the climate, the people, and their emerging selves — rather than gauge success as the ability to remain the same (Graham and Stephenson 2010). Even the hotel, a building they discover is far from the luxurious retreat they had seen advertised online, prods them to accept the fact that change is a process they must learn to live with and through. In contrast to the sterile and confined architecture of the English retirement house that was being shown to Douglas and Jean in one of the first scenes, a depressing design that emphasized the losses of aging without room to accommodate the gains, the dilapidated architecture of the Indian hotel, with its lack of working telephones, reliable plumbing, and the odd door, is, in a sense, a reflection of the state of their lives—falling apart yet, at the same time, built on a solid foundation and ripe for renovation and reconstruction. Its unlatched windows and airy archways, open to hungry pigeons, stunning views of cranes flying through the sunset, and most of all to each other, evince their growing openness to the fullness of life that Western culture would so often deny them.

A consideration of the importance of where people retire and of how they shape their identities and community in a particular setting is part of what Stephen Katz calls the study of spatial gerontology. Spatial gerontology is concerned with the "conditions and contexts in which an individual's adaptation to aging is either facilitated or limited" by their environment (Katz 2005, 204), and with the interaction of the space in which an older individual lives with the subjective conditions within that environment and the person's subjective reaction to it.[6] Thus, although due to financial considerations the move to Jaipur for the characters in *The Best Exotic Marigold Hotel* was not entirely freely chosen, it nevertheless reflects their desire to spatialize their personal identity in a way that

4. Intimacy and Desire in Later Life

is not based on architectural, financial, symbolic, and emotional relations that remind them of their increasing isolation and marginalization as they age, but on relationships with things and places that allow them to make connections and grow. That the formation of a community based on their own perception of their wants and needs would happen in a hotel in India rather than in the depressing, medicalized environment that characterizes so many spaces constructed for retirement in the West, simply reflects their need for what Katz terms a more suitable "person-environment fit," one that better matches their abilities and desires with the demands and resources of the environment (Katz 2005). From this point of view, Jean's failure to adapt and her return to England is due less to a personal failing than to a poor "person-environment fit," whereas her husband's ability to flourish reflects his immersion in an environment that matches his needs.

In addition, the idea of "outsourcing" old age, a comic conceit that could have unintentionally subverted the humanity of the characters through their commodification, instead works in their favor. Rather than remain in the West, where "the advertising industry ...[and] its portrayal of the new anti-ageist, positive senior as an independent, healthy, sexy, flexi-retired citizen" routinely glosses over "the negative realities of poverty and inequality in old age," and ignores or even punishes those who are unable or refuse to conform to a consumerist style of life (Katz 2005, 191), such a move exposes them to a less demanding set of social and cultural expectations. Even Sonny, the young and effervescent owner of the building, whose dream is to make his hotel a success by attracting the elderly from all the "countries where they don't like old people" and who could have envisioned his venture as a way to profit at the expense of the financially strapped retirees, is portrayed as wishing to include the residents in his business plan. By taking account of their needs and desires and relying on their experience and abilities, as he does with Muriel, expertly played by Maggie Smith at 77, who saves both his hotel from financial ruin and herself from a lonely and isolated existence with her accounting acumen, Sonny's project integrates the reconstruction of the hotel with that of the residents' lives and identities and, thus, carries few of the negative connotations usually applied to outsourcing. As long as the West perceives the increase in the number of elderly as a social problem that can be solved by individual rather than collective means, assumes "that the economic dimension of aging supersedes all others" (Cruikshank 2003, 26), and ignores both the reciprocal benefits of care and the contributions of the elderly to society through not only their generativity but their creativity, it may be in the best interests of the old to outsource themselves. Within a culture that, in Sonny's words, is honored that "the elderly and the beautiful" have "chosen to spend their last days with us," the stories told about these English expatriates emphasize their choice to step out of both the stereotypes they have internalized and the external cultural concepts that have constrained their lives.

Evelyn, played by Judi Dench at 77, is a recent widow who is forced to sell her flat upon discovering that her husband has squandered all their savings. Initially depicted as a technologically inept older woman overwhelmed by her circumstances, she nevertheless finds the Marigold Hotel online and decides to go to India to make a fresh start rather than live with her son, who speaks to their lawyer in front of her as if she weren't there and is less than supportive of her efforts to take charge of her life. Her blog, which narrated aloud, provides both a timeline for the movie and a commentary on her adjustment to "a new and different world," provides the viewer with an insider's perspective on her transformation into a capable woman who finds both a satisfying job that takes advantage of her talents by teaching call-center workers to sound more "human," and on the development of her unexpected romance. That Evelyn's romantic involvement bears an uncanny resemblance to that of Ruth in *Still Doing It*, simply makes Evelyn's story more believable. Like Evelyn, who met Douglas by chance, Ruth met Harry when she was least expecting the renewal of love and romance. Happily describing how her relationship with him feels like first love despite her 67 years, she says she feels fortunate to have someone whose company she enjoys and with whom she can grow old, an apt description of the way the relationship between Evelyn and Douglas is presented.

Douglas, played by Bill Nighy, 62, is the patient half of a quarrelsome couple who came to India after losing their life savings investing in their daughter's start-up company. He revels in his exploration of a new culture, in stark contrast to his wife Jean with her fear and rejection of all things foreign. Finding himself attracted to Evelyn, who shares his interest in their surroundings, he nevertheless agrees to return to England with Jean. Yet, when they become hopelessly stuck in a traffic jam on the way to the airport, Jean admits that their marriage has been over for some time, only surviving due to his "kindness and loyalty," and leaves on her own. Returning to the hotel after an interesting night spent smoking "apple tobacco" in his taxi driver's brother's brothel, he sees Evelyn on her way

4. Intimacy and Desire in Later Life

to work and they make a date for afternoon tea. Though demonstrating typical English restraint in their behavior, their intellectual and physical pleasure in each other's company shines through.

Graham, acted by Tom Wilkinson, 64, is a retired judge who grew up in Jaipur and is returning for the first time since his youth, not to find new romance, since he admits he is now gay more in theory than in practice, but to reconnect with the young Indian lover he left behind. Disgraced when they were discovered asleep in each other's arms as children, he has since lived with the guilt of abandoning his friend and lover, and wants to see him one more time. Finally locating his whereabouts, Graham finds that his friend, though happily married for many years, has never forgotten his first love. After spending the night reminiscing, Graham is found dead from a heart condition, his serene expression reflecting the peace and closure he felt in returning to the place where he felt most loved.

The designs of Norman, played by Ronald Pickup, 72, and Madge, acted by Celia Imrie at 60, are focused less on the memory of past desire and decidedly more on the satisfaction of those in the present. Both Norman, introduced to us in England at a speed-dating event where he is serially humiliated due to his age, and Madge, whom we first see leaving her children's house where, refusing to babysit again, she is accused of having "lost it" for wanting to find yet another husband, actively seek the company of the opposite sex. Once in India, their resistance to the narrative of decline in which they find themselves trapped shows through when Norman tells us he "wants to feel young again, to feel needed" as much as he needs, and Madge admits she doesn't "want to grow older, to be condescended to, to be marginalized and ignored by society." Fortunately, their comic and ultimately unsuccessful attempts to impersonate well-to-do older characters who might appear more attractive than their real-life selves, and their mutual preoccupation with their outward appearance leads them into an unlikely friendship that results in Norman's happy and, unbeknownst to him, Viagra-less relationship with Carol, and in Madge's realization that, as far as the search for sex, love, and companionship goes, it's never over. As with Evelyn and Ruth, the striking resemblance between Madge's vacillation between periods self doubt and determination, and the experiences of Harriet in *Still Doing It*, a woman of 75 who fluctuates between despair at her appearance and a single-minded intent to find the next in a series of life-long sexual engagements, is uncanny.

These romantic relationships, though in a less sexually explicit and/or confrontational manner than those in *Something's Gotta Give*, *The Mother*, and *Beginners*, nevertheless represent a cinematic attempt to counter ageist attitudes that hold older adults to be asexual and that deny or ignore their enduring need for love, romance, and intimate contact. That the stories told involve narrative conventions that are familiar — Evelyn's creative solution to her financial predicament and her discovery of a more egalitarian love relationship (Grace), and her sense of being both figuratively and literally lost in an unfamiliar city (May); Douglas' feelings of loyalty to his wife despite their incompatibility (Hal), and his familiarity with marijuana, often considered the province of the young (Grace); the unquestioned acceptance of Graham's sexual orientation (Oliver), and Graham's return to the love and desire of his youth (Hal); Norman's efforts to maintain his connection to hegemonic masculinity and his discovery of companionship with a woman his own age (Harry); Madge's refusal to be content with the role of grandmother and her commitment to continue the search for love in the present (May) — should not be considered a failure of originality, but part of an emerging effort to present an increasingly authentic picture of old age and to reintegrate those figuratively exiled to another country back into the common cultural consciousness.

Conclusion

In one of her early blogs, Evelyn writes, "Old habits die easier than we think and new ones form.... The only real failure is the failure to try ... and the measure of success is in how we cope.... Nothing else matters." Although these sentiments may sound like empty platitudes or kitsch, the overall effect on those who watch films about older people who try, fail, and succeed in learning to cope with the challenges of forming romantic relationships in later life will be to gradually alter what Stuart Hall calls the shared cultural construction of common meanings through which we live and represent our lives (see chapter 1). Though fictional, these characters' "existential choice of present-bound caring engagement with the human world" surrounding them (Cohen-Shalev 2012, 60) is an important step in correcting what C.G. Prado in *Rethinking How We Age* terms the interpretive parsimony that makes us blind to new possibilities of illuminating the aging experience (Prado 1986). The fact that these narratives often reflect true-to-life experiences, such as those presented in the documentary *Still Doing It*, only strengthens the impulse to expand the narrative, and thus the lived boundaries, of old age.

The stories that *Something's Gotta Give, The Mother, Beginners,* and

4. Intimacy and Desire in Later Life

The Best Exotic Marigold Hotel tell also conform to the findings of Toni Calasanti and Jill Kiecolt in their study of relationships among older people: that older adults continue to desire intimate relations, embrace the need for partnership and love, and consider sex an important part of these relationships (Calasanti and Kiecolt 2007). Although these later-life relationships are diverse, often innovative, and may take different forms than those that occur earlier in life, due to influences such as memories of a former marriage or spouse, a wish to avoid traditional gender relations, fear of the potential burden of care work, or worries about preserving the inheritance of children, Calasanti and Kiecolt found that most adults want some kind of long-term romantic relationship. It can be traditional, like that of Erica and Harry in *Something's Gotta Give*, although it is the widower or never married man who is more likely to show interest in later-life marriage than the single older woman, who, according to Calasanti and Kiecolt, is quite often loath to lose her hard-won personal and financial independence. It can take the form of cohabitation, an alternative to marriage that is better suited to gender equity and control over personal resources, a choice that is reflected in the scene in *The Best Exotic Marigold Hotel* in which Carol is reading on the bed in their room while Norman is washing out and hanging up their socks. And although *Beginners* doesn't address the possibility of gay marriage for Hal and Andy, cohabitation appears to be their relationship of choice as well, one that is consistent with the finding that older gay men are increasingly likely to want, and to be happy in, committed long-term relationships in later life.

Like intimate relationships at any age, those with one or both partners in late adulthood are full of challenges that can promote physical and psychological resilience (Bliezner 2007) as well as provide a template by which younger people can structure their own relationships. In *Something's Gotta Give* and *Beginners*, a parent's willingness to fall in love is pictured as both a feat of daring that the younger generation admires and as a lesson in the impossibility of joy without the possibility of pain. After watching and listening to the experiences of Erica and Hal, both Marin, who takes her mother's advice about not hiding from love, and Oliver, who takes to heart the intensity of his father's love for Andy, begin to overcome their reluctance to open themselves up to love. Even in *The Best Exotic Marigold Hotel*, the interest Evelyn takes in Sonny and his girlfriend Sunaina's budding relationship encourages Sonny to go against his mother's wishes and tell Sunaina he loves and wants to marry her. Filmic examples of love in later life can strengthen the tie among generations by teaching the young something about the enduring power of love that may encourage them to change not only their own behavior but to modify any negative attitudes they may have about love, romance and sexuality in old age.

Although the films discussed in this chapter can rightly be criticized for a failure to seriously consider the deleterious effects of class differences and limited income on an aging individual's ability to resist the marginalization that ageist attitudes and policies generate (a topic that was only briefly dealt with in *The Best Exotic Marigold Hotel*); to address the structural and institutional difficulties that debilitating conditions of a deep and dependent old age can bring (an issue brought to light only by the difficulties of Frances and Davy in *Still Doing It*); and to document the cumulative effects of racial and ethnic differences on growing older (a matter touched on with the greater measure of disgrace that befell Graham's young Indian lover), their depictions of older individuals as potential intimate partners are nudging us in the right direction. And even though the criticism that Margaret Gullette levels against *Still Doing It* for presenting sex in a way that furthers the assumption "that if older women *don't* do it, or don't do it the young way, that [they've] fallen below the standard" (Gullette 2011, 124) can leave those (including men) who don't do it in that way, have chosen to forego sex, or decline to reveal their private sexual lives on the defensive is valid, her complaint applies more to the framing of the message than the message itself: that sexual intimacy and touch is still valued among the elderly.

As Cohen-Shalev says, there remains "a glaring paucity of believable, committed, and altogether worthwhile cinematic realizations of old age," most depictions "doing little justice to the complex and variable phenomenon" (Cohen-Shalev 2012, 4). Yet, though small, the number of movies that deal with the realities of aging in the same breath as an older person's need and desire for sex, love, and romance is steadily increasing. Despite the fact that Twentieth Century–Fox declined to produce *Something's Gotta Give* for fear that the lead characters were too old to be bankable, it became a surprise box office hit. And although it was difficult to obtain financing for *The Mother* "because the ways in which it blended age and sex was [sic] seen as too challenging and therefore not marketable" (Kaplan 2012, 33), it, too, was successful, though more in Europe than in the U.S. Of course, the sexual desire of older men has been an integral part of cinema from the start, but the desire of older women or of an older couple for each other, unless it is marked as abnormal or desexualized, is still a cinematic rarity. Many of the movies featuring older women, therefore, focus

4. Intimacy and Desire in Later Life

on thwarted desire, such as *A Month by the Lake* (1995), the story of a British spinster, played by 58-year-old Vanessa Redgrave, and her pursuit of an older gentleman who is taken in by the charms of a young nanny. Even though the movie is really about sexual needs and desires, due to the characters' classic British reticence and reserve, something we also see in the relationship between Evelyn and Douglas, and possibly to a cultural distaste for displaying older women's bodies, it never gets beyond the flirtatious tone that often characterizes interchanges between an older woman and a male character. On the other hand, *Ladies in Lavender* (2004), starring Maggie Smith and Judi Dench as Janet and Ursula, two elderly sisters who live an isolated and sometimes lonely life, presents the sexual desires and romantic fantasies of Ursula more openly. Yet, as an aging woman who has never married and probably never had sex, her desire for the young man whom she and her sister rescued is depicted as entirely inappropriate and out of bounds, foreclosing even the possibility of a fresh start. Another way the desire of older women is both misunderstood and understated can be observed in *The Iron Lady* (2011). This movie's portrayal of the older Margaret Thatcher as an unfulfilled, lonely, and distant woman whose interaction with her deceased husband is simply a sign of incipient dementia rather than an attempt to maintain an important connection in later life, directly contradicts the well-documented ability of "imaginary intimates" to provide a "source of intimacy in old age for those who feel that their appetite for intimacy was well-served by those relationships" (Connids 2006, 139).

In the end, despite their failings, these films present various degrees of nonconformism and defiance of ageist social convention in order to bring us stories of elderly people that describe both their inward desires and subjective states of mind along with the concrete, material changes these inner states may lead them to adopt in their lives. By using seasoned, veteran actors who can bring to their roles a personal perspective on aging, these movies can prompt us to a greater acceptance of bodily difference that deemphasizes our reflexive reliance on vision in favor of an economy of touch that underscores affect. Through the frame of affect, our culture's treatment of the body as simply instrumental, a container whose appearance must continually be worked on and "resexed" in order to mask the reality of aging, begins to matter less than the raw reality of desire and emotional and physical intimacy portrayed. Thus, movies about desire, love, and romance in later life can reveal both the pain and anguish caused by an ageist society, and the strength and determination of the aging and the old to create and maintain the ties of intimacy throughout all of life. As Evelyn says as she rides off on a motor scooter, her arms around Douglas and a smile across her face, "All we know about the future is that it will be different.... Perhaps what we fear is that it will be the same. So we must celebrate the changes."

5

The Cultural Work of Alzheimer's

Half erased, the attractive gray-haired woman stares at us from the cover of *Time* (October 25, 2010), the word "**ALZHEIMER'S**" slashed across her face in bold black print as if it were a warning label on a poison that, once ingested, would make you slowly disappear. Or cause you to fall apart or be mangled or ravaged, or become a shadow, a stranger, a ghost, a non-person. A silent, pathetic, mindless, futureless shell who, despite a softened brain and an eradicated essence, is forced to attend your own never-ending funeral even though you're not really there.

These are but a few of the images depicting those suffering from Alzheimer's disease that I encountered while researching this chapter. Each of them paints having Alzheimer's as living through a narrative of tragic decline and devastation from which there is no escape. And each of them draws its power to paint such a picture from our store of cultural and historical anxiety about getting old — our fear of becoming a burden, of being out of control, of entering the unknown, of enduring the shame of dependency, and ultimately of meaninglessness. These fears, clustered around the "nation's fourth leading killer," often encourage us to think of Alzheimer's as a metaphor for old age and death, to unreflexively portray Alzheimer's itself as the "American brain and body killer" (Cohen 1998, 125).[1]

Yet, to say that someone died of Alzheimer's is to erase the entire web of medical, social, cultural, and physiological practices that reduce an old and senile human body to the plaques and tangles of Alzheimer's. As Lawrence Cohen argues in *No Aging in India*, the move to understand the relationship between the progressive deterioration of brain function that occurs with Alzheimer's and the bodily processes that may precipitate other terminal diseases as one of direct cause and effect is to mistake the social and contingent responses to the afflicted old person with the "essential" nature of the disease (Cohen 1998). And, as Hacking makes clear, the equation of cultural response to an event or process with the event or process itself is a categorical error, one that, by confusing the person with the category constructed to contain her, replaces her individuality with stereotype and, in the case of Alzheimer's, marks her with stigma as well.

If to stereotype is to place someone in a category according to an oversimplified, standardized image or idea of that person's characteristics and behavior, to stigmatize is to further mark that person as shamefully undesirable and socially unacceptable. Although the last stages of life have always been stereotyped and sometimes stigmatized, the last years of life with Alzheimer's are beyond stereotype, "at the outer limit of stigmatization" (Ballenger 2006, 115). "Despite the best intentions of professionals in medicine and gerontology to destigmatize old age by recasting *senility* as *Alzheimer's disease*" (117) and their relative success in portraying it as "a problem in the brain, not of the mental or moral fortitude of the person suffering from it" (107), their discourse has merely reinforced the line between those with Alzheimer's and the rest of us. Across this boundary, an older person diagnosed with Alzheimer's must live with much more than the fact that something is medically wrong; she also must exist in that ambiguous region of uncertainty where the normal and the pathological meet, where ideas about what is human and what is not collide. Stigma, then, is directly related to the social consequences of exhibiting a certain group of symptoms or behaviors that are judged to deviate from even the falsely homogenizing "normality" of stereotype. And the social consequences of displaying the set of symptoms and behaviors associated with Alzheimer's are severe indeed, "calling into question the very personhood of those who exhibit them" (114) by subjecting them to the erasure depicted by the disappearing image of the woman on the cover of *Time*.

Since Alzheimer's continues to carry such a powerful stigma, one that can overshadow the entire experience of aging, some of the most important questions to ask when watching a film about Alzheimer's or a movie in which a character suffers from Alzheimer's are: To what extent are the people who have this disease stigmatized? How does the stigma attached to Alzheimer's intertwine with or build on stereotypes about growing older and old age? Does the story this movie tells try to capture the ambiguity and the complexity of the Alzheimer's experience or does it tell a narrative of simple decline? Are the views of both the person suffering from Alzheimer's and those of the people who care for her presented

5. The Cultural Work of Alzheimer's

in this film? Is Alzheimer's portrayed solely as a problem for science to solve, or are the social and cultural conditions under which Alzheimer's is diagnosed and lived explored as well? To what extent does this film present the growing incidence of Alzheimer's as a looming epidemic or crisis with tragic social and economic consequences as opposed to a disability to be managed or a manifestation of human difference?

In the past ten years, numerous films have taken up the subject of Alzheimer's, including *Away from Her* (2007), *The Savages* (2007), *Aurora Borealis* (2006), *Wellkamm to Verona* (2006), *The Notebook* (2004), *The Forgetting* (2001), and *Iris* (2001). Although almost all these films put forth impassioned pleas for increased funding for research into the causes of and cures for Alzheimer's, and urge copious amounts of compassion towards those with the disease and those who care for them, not all movies about Alzheimer's are created equal. As Anne Basting points out in *Forget Memory* (2009), even though movies about Alzheimer's run the gamut from those that present the experience as pure tragedy to those that depict people with Alzheimer's as still capable of communicating, engaging in emotional relationships, and living a meaningful life, most focus too tightly on the personal and economic tragedy of living with the disease rather than presenting the experience in a way that will reduce the fear and stigma that surround it and lead to a change in our attitudes and practices of care (Basting 2009). She argues that only by burrowing directly into that fear, confronting it and coming "to understand it more fully so that it won't interfere with living a full life ... or fully living with and loving people with dementia" (4), will we be able to change the tragic personal and social conditions, and therefore the images, that characterize having Alzheimer's.

Given that the images displayed in films about Alzheimer's form part of the shared meanings, or background noise, of our culture and, therefore, will influence how we think about, act towards, live with, and value those who have or may be diagnosed with the disease, it makes a great difference both what kinds of stories we tell and how critically we understand them. Yet these images can change when we learn to notice how a story that foregrounds stereotypes about aging and Alzheimer's works to multiply feelings of fear, as in *The Forgetting* (2004), or tends to simplify the variety and the complexity of the experience of living with dementia, as in *Iris* (2001). They also can change when a story makes us aware of the history of the disease and how it is continually reshaped by both humanistic and scientific perceptions of what constitutes a full and "successful" life, as we begin to see in *Away from Her* (2007). And most of all, the images we hold of those with Alzheimer's can change when a story helps us learn to expand rather than contract the boundaries we place around concepts of memory, self, and personhood, as is done in *Wellkamm to Verona* (2006). By viewing movies that deal with Alzheimer's with the expectation of encountering as wide a variety of stories as are told about those who are "normal," we can learn to move beyond stereotype and stigma and begin to believe that all human beings should be treated with dignity, love, and respect.

Senility, Dementia, Alzheimer's

The Forgetting: A Portrait of Alzheimer's (2004) is a documentary based on the book with almost the same name, *The Forgetting: Alzheimer's, Portrait of an Epidemic* (2001) by David Shenk. He was inspired to research the disease and write about it when he found himself feeling "horrified, terrified" after he observed a wife who no longer knew who her husband was. Although the book is nuanced, putting Alzheimer's into historical context and sharing the experiences of people who have the disease, the film presents Alzheimer's as pure and unmitigated tragedy (Basting 2009). By combining the story of the race to find an explanation of how the disease works and the quest to discover a cure with the personal decline narratives of how Alzheimer's affects the people who have it and their families, *The Forgetting* can easily leave a viewer feeling informed yet overwhelmed by her vulnerability to the disease's indiscriminate depredations. These emotions are intentionally strengthened by descriptions of the disease as "a slow and silent killer" that "robs you of who you are," and by social commentary that characterizes it as "mushrooming" into an epidemic that could "consume the entire federal budget by 2030." By the time we see one of the women the film examines, Isabel McKenna, lying almost comatose in her bed in the late stages of Alzheimer's and hear from her family that the chance to enjoy retirement years with her husband was stolen from her, we already agree that this disease must be stopped.

Yet, a careful look at the historical evolution of the current "epidemic" of Alzheimer's will show the film's metaphors and statistics to be slightly misleading. Lawrence Cohen locates the roots of what we now call Alzheimer's in the concept of senility, a term that was used to describe the "decay of the body, its reason, and its voice, its ability to be heard as a speaking subject" (Cohen 1998, xv). He further describes senility as a

5. The Cultural Work of Alzheimer's

process of material physiological change occurring in various sets of social practices that determine how differences of age come to matter, how we understand the body and its behavior through time. Senility, sometimes called dotage, Cohen explains, entered medical discourse as a juridical term during the Inquisition when doting and decrepit old women were accused of performing evil deeds and were subsequently burned as witches. Even though many letters from doctors of that period acknowledge that these poor and dependent old women could do no actual harm, their lack of control over their bodies and voices, and the gradual delegitimization of their excessive "claims on [their] neighbor's resources" (Cohen 1998, 74) and on family that came with changing definitions of community did reveal them to be incoherent, sometimes demented.

The association of old women with senility continued during the Renaissance with the idea of the climacteric, or points along the life course when the body was particularly susceptible to emotional excess and morbidity. The climacteric was especially concerned with the mental decline and bodily decay that old age could bring. Originally ungendered, it later split into male and female forms that gave credence to the belief that postmenopausal women were far more likely than men to suffer the mental deterioration that led to senility (Katz 1996). George Miller Beard drew on the concept of the climacteric as the beginning of age related deficiencies to popularize the diagnosis of neurasthenia, an ailment that, by stereotyping growing old as being necessarily out of step with the times, helped to legitimize the denigration of old age. In *Legal Responsibility in Old Age* (1874), Beard claimed that the brain and the moral faculties that depended on it declined more quickly than the rest of the body, resulting in the calamity of senile mental deterioration, the "start of the gradual, vegetative process of death" (Ballenger 2006, 107). Like today's stereotypes, Beard's descriptions represented the senile as dangerous and an obstruction to progress due to their inability to fulfill intellectual and moral tasks.

Charcot, who, as we have seen in chapter 3, studied institutionalized old women in Saltpetriere between 1862 and 1893, concluded, like Beard, that old age brought about the enfeebling of function. But unlike others, Charcot attempted to make a distinction between diseases *of* old age, some of which might bring about senility, and diseases *in* old age, which although they might exhibit symptoms similar to senility, could be treated and alleviated. By making this distinction, Charcot inadvertently bequeathed to medicine the continuing problem of calling a condition a disease for which it does not yet have a cure, producing disorder which the medical arts cannot control and provoking doubt about their authority (Katz 1996). Like Charcot, Ellie Metchnikoff, in *The Prolongation of Life* (1907), saw old age as a curious meeting of the pathological and the physiological, and pictured the old body as a "site of struggle between vital forces within tissues and cells" (Katz 1996, 83). Although he believed that decay eventually overwhelmed cell growth, ending in diseases of senility, he was more positive than many others about the ability of science to alleviate some of the suffering of the senile old.

But perhaps it was Leo Nascher who, in *Geriatrics: The Diseases of Old Age and Their Treatments* (1914), most clearly defined how the elderly were to be differentiated on the basis of their bodies, their mental capacities, and their behavioral attributes (Katz 1996). Returning to the idea of the climacteric to explain the difference between the normal and the pathological, he ended up constructing "a subaltern physiology" (Cohen 1998, 76) for the old body by framing its normality in terms of other kinds of subordinate bodies. For Nascher, "old people were normal in the same way women and children could be normal" (76). Linking geriatrics to pediatrics, he stereotyped the old (similar to the way Aristotle did) as being selfish, demanding constant attention, complaining of constant neglect, and being incapable of autonomous behavior like the very young; linking geriatrics to women, he described the old as feminized, weak, vain, and alternating between periods of confusion and rationality as did women. By describing senility, here used as a synonym for old age, as a second childhood, he positioned childish behavior and mental incapacity at the center of the study of old age. And by characterizing senility in gendered terms, he continued the tradition of using "female physiology ... to anchor construction of a (male) body" (78).

Thus, by the time Alois Alzheimer encountered the strange behavior of 51-year-old Auguste Deter in his clinic in 1901, heard her say that she had "lost herself," and observed the distinctive neuropathology of her sliced and silver-stained brain after her death in 1906, the division between normal and pathological disease in the old, the use of women's bodies to construct the mental deterioration of old age, and the identification of aging with senile dementia was well underway. Nevertheless, when Alzheimer saw the plaques and tangles under his microscope, despite its early onset and extreme presentation, he did not see Auguste Deter's condition as a distinct disease, but as part of an already existing category (Cohen 1998). It fell to Alzheimer's colleague, Emil Kraepelin, to leave the affective and delusional symptoms that Alzheimer had observed to one

5. The Cultural Work of Alzheimer's

side and to stress the cognitive irregularities, which were much more easily measured than emotions (Hacking 1999), in order to construct a distinct disease category and write it up as such. But, since seeing this case as a separate disease went against the prevailing medical consensus of the time, which was to expand senile dementia to include early onset cases, rather than propel Alzheimer's into the limelight, Kraepelin's omissions helped relegate it to the sidelines for half a century. During that time, arteriosclerotic dementia, which unlike Alzheimer's was amenable to treatment by vasodilatory drugs, emerged as the dominant explanation for senile dementia (Cohen 1998). Yet, the distinction between Alzheimer's, "a pathophysiologic term" focusing on a "set of cellular and subcellular processes" that result in "a certain neuroanatomical picture" (xv), and senile dementia, a term combining a nonmedical description of a social condition with a clinical description of a pathological state, continued to be problematic. By the 1940's, researchers often made the distinction on the basis of age rather than pathology, believing that for all practical purposes, the conditions were the same. Nevertheless, the distinction persisted officially into the 1970's (Ballenger 2006).

After World War II, when gerontology was becoming an increasingly important field of study, researchers such as anthropologist Leo Simmons took a different tack and began to argue that senility, though "a virtually universal phenomena ... was culturally contingent" (Ballenger 2006, 110) and, in modern societies, was the result of the lack of roles and opportunities for the aging and the old. The argument that senile dementia was a cultural artifact even led to the theory that the pathologies of contemporary society actually caused the constricted blood vessels of the old brain that led to dementia (Ballenger 2006), a theory that harkened back to explanations given for neurasthenia almost a century earlier. Although theories about the "social production of senility" did succeed in bringing about significant policy changes that improved the material circumstances of those over 65, it also rendered untenable the broad concept of senility that espoused inevitable physical and mental decline.

In the context of changing attitudes and policies towards the old, interest in Alzheimer's reemerged in the 1960's. Using new imaging technologies, researchers looked for a correlation between the number of plaques in the brain and the level of cognitive decline, a finding that would provide demonstrable evidence of the "existential excess of the old" (Cohen 1998, 82) first expressed during the time of the Inquisition. Researchers also discovered evidence that the brains of the elderly with dementia closely resembled those of children (Leibing 2006), as Nascher had earlier suggested. Yet, Robert Butler, an advocate for the elderly, saw the tendency to attribute all the problems of the old to decline and dementia as a way to rationalize neglect of their ills. He found the very term "senility" obnoxious, "a 'wastebasket term' applied to any person over 60 with a problem" (Ballenger 2006, 112) and, like Charcot and Nascher before him, stressed the necessity of distinguishing disease in old age from the aging process itself. As founding director of the National Institute on Aging (NIA) in 1974, he resurrected Kraepelin's construction of Alzheimer's disease as a distinct pathology and made research into its causes a priority. By insisting that researchers would find the difference between irreversible dementias such as Alzheimer's and dementias caused by conditions that could be treated, Butler played a pivotal role in causing the absorption of a diagnosis of senile dementia into a diagnosis of Alzheimer's. By the latter part of the twentieth century, Alzheimer's had not only become a medical idiom for dementia (Cohen 1998), but had come to be regarded as a specific disease of the brain that could be understood and cured only through basic scientific research.[2]

Finding the Line

Returning to *The Forgetting* with a clearer idea of the porosity of the boundaries separating senility from senile dementia from Alzheimer's, and of the progression, sometimes regression, of one term to another, it becomes easier to see how this film takes a particular stand when it "depicts science as our one great hope to end the pointless wasting of minds, lives, and money" that Alzheimer's causes (Basting 2009, 15). By positioning science, rather than culture, language, the economy, or other social practices, as potential savior of those with Alzheimer's, the division between normal and pathological aging is secured, ambiguity is eased, and, ironically, a sense of control, of being able "to create order from the disorderly aspects of living with dementia" (Cohen 1998, 61), returns with a definite diagnosis. As Basting argues in *Forget Memory*, this division is reinforced by filmmaker Elizabeth Arledge's choice to focus on three women who are in the later stages of the disease (although the behaviors associated with Alzheimer's are usually ungendered, it is interesting that all of the "victims" are women) and to intersperse old home movie clips, photographs, and family stories into the immediate story in order to make a sharp distinction between the person as she was and as she is now. This distinction

5. The Cultural Work of Alzheimer's

not only reinforces the normal/pathological binary created by the biomedicalization of dementia, but creates an entire array of binaries—light/dark, near/far, controlled/chaotic, here/gone—that are used to further describe these three women in subordinate terms. When the normal/pathological binary of Alzheimer's and the array of dualisms it engenders are added to those that already construct the old, especially older women, as a despised category (see chapter 3), then the struggle of the split self for control finally can be resolved by the substitution of the object or disease for the subject or person herself.

The process of substitution of object for subject is well illustrated in the scene in *The Forgetting* in which an older woman and her son come into a doctor's office so that she can be tested for incipient Alzheimer's. As the doctor asks her a series of questions, she nervously answers, worry that she will "fail" lining her face and fear of what she might find out erupting as inappropriate laughter. When the test is finished, instead of giving her the results, the doctor speaks to her son to tell him that his mother has crossed the line and is in the early stages of Alzheimer's, ignoring the woman sitting in front of her as if in the act of being diagnosed she were already beginning to disappear. Robert Gard vividly describes the fear and sense of loss this woman is experiencing in his book, *Beyond the Thin Line* (1992). Having watched a friend descend into dementia, Gard, who was 82 at the time, becomes obsessed with finding the line between "the normal and the pathological, between a coherent, stable self and the incoherent, chaotic dependency of dementia" (Ballenger 2006, 116). Yet, as he carefully scrutinizes his behavior, looking for the slightest lapse in memory or sign of confusion, he concludes that the line isn't really there. Like the line dividing youth from old age, the line separating normal from pathological is ambiguous and insubstantial, a cultural construct made through the performance and the "continual reenactment, through meetings ... articles, books, and videos of the status of Alzheimer's as a real and biological disease" (Cohen 1998, 7).

In *The Forgetting*, the selfhood that the woman taking the test is so fearful of losing has already vanished for the three "protagonists." These three women, far beyond the line, already lost to the darkness of the disease, share the cultural imaginary that informs the movie *Iris* (2001). Based on the memoir *Elegy for Iris* (1999), *Iris* tells the story of writer and philosopher Iris Murdoch's descent into "Alzhiemer's hell." Having been a woman for whom intellect and language were paramount, the movie presents the loss of her intellectual prowess and of her possible future literary contributions as a tragedy. Like *The Forgetting*, *Iris* sets this tragic tone by contrasting scenes of Iris when young, daring, brilliant, unconventional, and full of life, with the older Iris, watching children's cartoons, wandering lost in the rain, unable even to find words with which to think. Although Iris's deterioration is foregrounded, the story is told mainly through her husband John's struggle to make sense of the "dissonance between her life before and her life with Alzheimer's" (Basting 2009, 42). Even when he can no longer deny the changes in her that so often frustrate and anger him, he desperately clings to the idea that she will be "the exception," that somehow, despite the doctor's assertions that there are none and the everyday reality of the private, mysterious, and barely communicative world she now inhabits, the real Iris is somehow still there.

Picturing the Brain

Both *The Forgetting* and *Iris* rely on the evidence presented by brain scans to solidify a diagnosis of Alzheimer's and to reinforce visually the difference between a normal and a pathological brain, and conceptually between our world and the world of dementia. Since Alzheimer first saw a physical cause for mental symptoms on the slides he made from Deter's brain, science has been searching for visual evidence to corroborate clinical diagnoses of dementia. In *The Forgetting*, colorful representations of the sticky plaques and tangles that "block" and "choke" the neurons abound. We "see" synapses disappear, neurons die, and the brain shrink, while hearing how these physical changes prevent neurons from "talking" and new thoughts from forming, erase long- then short-term memories, cause unexpected alterations in emotion and personality, and eventually interfere with even the most basic functions necessary to life. We are told the story of the ten-year-long search for the Pittsburgh compound, a substance that could quickly cross the blood-brain barrier, stick to the plaques long enough to be scanned, then harmlessly leave the body. At last, the scientists cheer, objective evidence for the plaques that will enable them to actually observe the effectiveness of potential drug therapies!

Even though the story is riveting and the scientists truly care, neuroimaging, as Joseph Dumit explains in *Picturing Personhood* (2004), is neither as neutral nor as objective as the movie proclaims. In his study of brain scans, Dumit argues that the brain images that allow us to watch action and change within the body construct a visual map of brain types that become equated with kinds of people, "reinforcing ... assumptions of

5. The Cultural Work of Alzheimer's

difference and making them seem obvious and normal" (Dumit 2004, 6). Though we may recognize that the substitution of person for scan is a categorical mistake, the inevitable effect of these encounters with images is the provocation of uncertainty about our own normality and categorical identification. Thus, Dumit continues, brain scans make claims on us that tend to fix us on a scale in relation to normality, having a real "looping effect" on how we understand, construct, and position ourselves and others.

But, Dumit asks, what is normal and how is it constructed? Since there is no other way to verify the data that a scan produces, researchers must create a baseline definition of normal that involves the selection of "'ideal' subjects, or 'supernormals' who have no probable pathology" and have been free of symptoms for a number of years (Dumit 2004, 62). Dumit documents that Positron Emission Tomography (PET) brain studies generally choose white, right-handed male subjects, even though in doing so these studies risk that material differences due to age, gender, race, and other confounding variables will appear as abnormality. Once subjects have been chosen, temporary characteristics, such as ingestion of vitamins or medication and use of caffeine or nicotine, must be accounted for. Dumit notes that some labs even report that the time of day when the scan takes place can affect the results. In the end, the decision to exclude as many differences as feasible in the choice of supernormals masks the assumption, lurking in the concept of normal itself, that these differences probably do matter greatly.

Dumit further explains how areas such as small sample size (usually between 4 and 20 subjects), methods of controlling subjects' behavior during the test, design of a task that will correspond to discrete mental functions, development of a tracer that can stand in for and represent brain activity, the architecture of the scanner itself, and the construction of the dataset from the raw images can all affect the outcome and replicability of a particular study. In addition, each step involves replacing the biological brain with concepts about how the brain functions that assume it *is* measurable and "knowable as a set of combinatorial states" (Dumit 2004, 80). This conceptual object, or brainset, takes the place of the brain so that it can be compared to other brainsets in order to find significant differences in activity. Once differences are discovered between a normalized brainset and an "abnormal" one, the differences are "windowed," a practice that makes differences stand out clearly even though the brainsets may be quite similar, and colored, a process that can make any feature prominent although it may exaggerate or distort the information in the original image to do so. According to Michael Ter-Pogossian, the "father of PET," differences due to color schemes allow a brainset to "signify whatever you want it to signify" (94) thus making the brainset highly dynamic and extremely difficult to read out of context.

Once windowed and colored images are chosen for publication and become part of a textual argument, they are called brain types and may be presented as proof that the differences discussed in the text actually do exist in the brain. For example, in an experiment to measure the effects of aging on the brain involving subjects aged 18 to 78, extreme images, or those that looked the most different from each other, were used to "prove" that hyperfrontal metabolic activity gradually declines with age. But, looking at the graph showing the same data rather than at the images, it is obvious that, although the average level of activity did decline slightly with age, the variation in activity among brains of different ages is so great that there is no basis on which to decide in what age category any individual might belong. Nevertheless, the use of extreme images leaves the false impression that younger and older brains *are* easily distinguishable (Dumit 2004).

Perhaps the greatest danger involved in the use of extreme images to strengthen an argument or hypothesis can be found in their cultural effects. As these images travel from science articles into popular culture, their importance is amplified through simplification. Like cartoons, they become iconic rather than realistic, dealing in forms or ideas rather than in the physical world in which they originated, and are, therefore, "more subjective (personally invested in) and universal (generalizable to human nature)" (Dumit 2004, 147).[3] For laypeople, a brain image can become an expression of pathology that appears to show a disease itself rather than a small portion of activity in the brain of someone who may or may not have symptoms of a disease. This is another categorical mistake that further collapses the symptom into the referent. In the case of Alzheimer's, although a 2008 study using a technique that can take PET scans of the brains of live patients showed that 21 percent of patients whose brains exhibited the plaques and tangles associated with Alzheimer's displayed no outward signs of cognitive impairment (Sharples 2009), the tendency to equate brain type with person and to let brain type speak for the person *regardless of that person's actual behavior* remains strong. This tendency not only obscures the coproduction of brain scans by scientist and machine, both of which leave marks on an image that, by itself, is ambiguous and multivocal, but ignores how the images that represent certain physical properties of bodies become signs themselves, carriers of social meaning (Dumit 2004).

The substitution of brain type for person happens early in *The Forgetting* when Harry, the husband of one of the three "protagonists" with Alzheimer's, explains the origins of his wife Gladys's irrational behavior to their grandson by saying that it's the disease talking, not his grandma. By replacing Gladys with an image of Alzheimer's as it "exists" in the brain, Harry may be protecting the woman he loves from moral blame and his grandson from the loss of his grandmother's love, but he also is participating in the cultural narrative this image as sign tells and is promoting the concepts of human nature this image espouses. By reiterating the Alzheimer's story in this way, he is enabling the image to become a building block in the production of the world that produced it and of which it is a part (Dumit 2004).

Moments of Grace — Memory, Self, Forgetting

Although for Harry, Gladys, in one sense, has become the disease, his words that separate the disease from the grandmother for his grandson's sake betray his ongoing belief that she's still there. Like John's belief that the real Iris is just hiding, Harry's statement implies that the Gladys he knew, her self, somehow endures even in the Alzheimer's fog that cloaks it. In a way, his words manifest a subconscious understanding of the ambiguous nature of the claim that the visibility of the biological basis of mental illness has made insignificant the space between person and organ (Rose 2007). On some level, Harry understands that brain types not only express themselves as the person (as a substitute for the person herself), but in the person (as something she has rather than is) as well, leaving us with the paradox of the continuing existence of the person who's no longer there.

In the face of the devastating losses experienced by both those with Alzheimer's and those who love them, in what ways does the person erased by the disease continue to exist? Is there something more to a person than the self that is no longer there when the brain with Alzheimer's becomes the person? In *Iris*, when the first bound copy of the book Iris had recently, and with great difficulty, completed arrives in the post, she doesn't even know what it is, no less that she has written it. Yet later, when she haltingly says, "I wrote" and glances at the volumes that line their every wall, John excitedly finishes her sentence with "books." Again, near the end of the movie, when John finds Iris unhurt after she's fallen from their moving car and rolled down an embankment, laughing she looks at him and with recognition in her smile says, "I love you." These moments of clarity when the world of then and the world of now, the person as she was and as she is, come together in the temporary harmony called normal both give John hope and make him question the authority of diagnostic brain scans. At their next visit to the doctor, John asks, how can she be even momentarily lucid if her brain's been wiped clean of memory?

These moments also characterize the film *Away from Her* (2007), the story of the relationship between an older couple, Grant and Fiona, who struggle to keep their love alive through all the unexpected changes that Alzheimer's brings to both of them. Neither her diagnosis, nor her move into a nursing home, nor the development of a new intimate relationship between Fiona and another patient, Aubrey, and between Grant and Aubrey's wife, Marian, fully erases the love and commitment they continue to feel for each other. In *Away from Her*, Fiona calls these brief experiences of normality moments of grace, moments concerned with the now rather than with looking forward and planning for the future or dwelling on the past. She finds them in the beauty of a flower that in the oblivion of memory loss is newly yellow every time she looks, or in the unexpected blossoming of a relationship that fulfills her need for simple human touch and understanding shorn of the confusing expectations of a disappearing and uncertain past. *Away from Her* concludes with a moment of clarity strikingly similar to the one at the end of Iris. As if to confirm what the nurse Kristy has told Grant about the fractured and uneven nature of memory loss, in the final scene, Grant opens Fiona's door expecting to find her sullen and mired in silent depression only to encounter a woman who, recognizing him as her husband, hugs him lovingly as the screen fades to black.

Moments of clarity or grace, thus, refer to memory, which, in American culture, represents the key to the construction of a self (Basting 2009). Since Kraepelin reworked Alzheimer's first cases to focus more on cognitive losses than on delusional or affective symptoms, memory loss has become "metonymically identified with the wide range of behavioral and neuropsychological changes consequent with dementia" (Cohen 1998, 126). This metonymy creates a cloud of anxiety that hovers over each forgotten name and every unremembered word, intensifying with each passing year the fear that Alzheimer's may become the personification of our

5. The Cultural Work of Alzheimer's

own aging. In *Away from Her*, this fear is stoked by the way the actors talk about Alzheimer's before the film begins. As in *The Forgetting*, the "crisis" of Alzheimer's is invoked, made even more terrifying by the knowledge that someone is diagnosed every 72 seconds and that the genetic form of the disease can start as early as thirty. Yet, as the story unfolds, the social crisis of epidemic proportions condenses down to a personal crisis of memory loss embodied in the growing forgetfulness that nudges Fiona to say the words that implicitly connect self to memory, "I think I may be beginning to disappear."

But what is memory? Why is it so important? How does it work? And why do we equate memory with self? Basting defines memory as "how we store and retrieve our experiences" (Basting 2009, 13), a process that allows us to use earlier experience to learn and grow from new encounters. Memory also lets us organize our experiences across time through the creation of a narrative about connection and meaning. By creating stories out of life experiences, we simultaneously create a sense of self, something that ties experiences together that otherwise might have no intrinsic connection. Philosopher Alsadair MacIntyre argues that without narrative we would have no self, "that lives are *comprehensible* only in [the] narrative terms" (Small 2007, 94) that memory occasions.

Yet memory appears in many different forms. Divided into two main categories, long-term memory concerns past events, whereas short-term memory is of those more recent. Closely connected to short-term memory, working memory stays in our brains only a few seconds, just long enough to manipulate things or ideas for the present task. As parts of long-term memory, episodic memory stores information about people and events, semantic memory concerns general and text-book knowledge about the nature of places, people, and objects, and procedural memory encodes information about what to do with things. Implicit or subconscious memory deals with knowledge we may not be aware we possess, while explicit memory stores information about things we consciously know. External memory refers to devices, from hand-written notes to all types of computers, that free us from having to store certain information in our brains but, nevertheless, allow us to retrieve it. Although each type of memory is stored in a different way and region or regions of the brain, memories are never totally separate and have the ability to mix, mingle, and combine in often surprising ways. Long-term memories are perhaps the least constant, merging with another memory or incorporating what others tell us about that memory in a continuous process of revision.

The Becoming of Age

In addition, not just memories but memory itself changes over time, giving the concept of memory a history as well. In *History and Memory*, historian Jacques Le Goff divides the perception of memory in Western culture into five main stages, each encompassing a shift in the way we understand and make use of memory. He locates the first stage in the time before writing, when memory lived in and among our minds and we made extensive use of the natural world to embody both personal stories and collective history. The second stage came about when memory began to be externalized through writing and could be stored outside of our minds in museums, archives, and libraries. Marking the beginning of the contested practice we know as history, writing allowed those in power to better control how stories were remembered, making some people's memories more valuable than others. Medieval Christian ideas about the importance of memory in relation to God's teachings and the sin of forgetting frame the third stage. In this stage, the use of mnemotechnology (mnenonic aids to improve memory) increased greatly, as to forget God's word brought such severe consequences. The fourth stage saw the invention of the printing press, a technology that distanced memory even farther from the mind by allowing it to be compiled and stored in dictionaries and encyclopedias, and photography, a technology that expanded memory by making it literally visual. Le Goff identifies the fifth stage as the age of computers and memory prosthetics, devices which inundate us with information then hold out the promise of helping us manage and organize it (Le Goff 1992). With the increasing externalization of memory that has occurred over the course of Western culture, "we have moved from experiencing memory as a vital living thing existing inside of us and between us toward thinking of it as something outside of us that we purchase and maintain" (Basting 2009, 23).

Yet, by itself, human memory is not like our memory machines. We can't just go to some master index when we wish to retrieve a memory because that memory, unlike a machine's, is not static. We filter it "through who we have become and all the subsequent experiences we've had since the moment that piece of information entered out minds" (Basting 2009, 18). Rather than stable, human memory is alive, constantly created, stored, and recovered in relation to the people around us and the culture in which we live. People, events, smells, sound, and touch influence both how and if a memory is encoded, reclaimed, and given meaning. Human memory is, therefore, both biological in that it leaves marks on our brains, bodies, and lives, and social in that it relies on

5. The Cultural Work of Alzheimer's

others for its creation and retrieval. It is, as Judith Butler would say, not expressive but performative.

Memory is also intimately attached to forgetting, for, despite what is implied by the title *The Forgetting*, it would be impossible to function if we remembered with perfection.[4] Memory is subject to transience or weakening over time, absent-mindedness or the temporary inability to encode a memory, and blocking or being unable to recall a specific episode or bit of information. We also experience misattribution or assigning an incorrect source to a memory, suggestibility or attributing another's suggestion as our own experience, bias or allowing beliefs to influence a memory, and persistence or haunting by unpleasant and unwanted memories (Schacter 2002). All these kinds of forgetting keep us from being overwhelmed by too much information and allow us to form patterns that tie us to the events, places, and people who have made us who we are, made our self. And who we are, our self, in turn, influences which events, places, and people we will remember (Basting 2009).

Keeping in mind the history, nonlinearity, performativity, and complexity of memory, and the relation of memory to forgetting, to what aspect of memory are we referring in the equation of memory with self? Do we mean the memory that is embodied in objects and in the natural world, the kind sparked in Fiona by a yellow flower or a glimpse of her cross country skis on a visit to the cottage after her admission to the nursing home at Meadowlake? Do we mean the kind of memory that fears the shame attached to forgetting, the kind that we see in Fiona when she pushes Grant away because he confuses her with his attempts to make her remember? Or are we thinking about memory as fixed in what Saussure calls the "tyranny of writing" (Derrida 1976, 38), a tyranny that in Fiona's obsession with post-it notes all over the kitchen calls for a mastery she fears she is losing? Or are we considering the persistence of Fiona's long-term memories of Grant's earlier sexual indiscretions although she would prefer to forget them? Or the procedural memory that enables her to dance with her husband, as Iris did with her friend and former lover Janet, long after "the forgetting" has begun? Or of the way she creates, through misattribution or suggestibility, a memory of having met Aubrey in the hardware store where she insists he worked while they were young? Or of how strong are her short-term memories of Aubrey when, after his departure from Meadowlake, she gently and tearfully strokes the sketches he made of her that are taped to her wall?

And what concept of self do we conjure when we insist that to lose our memory is to lose our self? Do we imagine some essential and unchanging self, made in the image of Plato's forms, that we can recognize in the way Fiona retains her pre–Alzheimer's lady-like demeanor despite her new environment and relationships? Do we assume a self constructed and disciplined by what Foucault might call the discourses of "truth" according to Alzheimer's, one that adjusts to mirror the expectations built into the situation in which Fiona lives in the nursing home? Or do we consider the self as both contextually essential and socially constructed due to the interaction between idea and self, as Hacking posits, one that allows Fiona to maintain her own sense of self as essentially caring and thoughtful at a time when her experience of Alzheimer's makes it too complicated to keep intact relationships based on the past?

Any careful consideration of memory and self will position both as historically situated cultural concepts that derive their meaning as much from the environment in which they are deployed as from scans or disease categories or the narratives constructed around them. Although a culture that stigmatizes any type of dementia, especially when it occurs in concert with the ubiquitous ageist attitudes and behavior to which our culture subscribes, may desire to erase people with Alzheimer's, they do not disappear. Those with Alzheimer's love, hug, cry, play, fear, find and lose relationships, make new memories and forget others, and do so around, among, and beside us. And if we really look and listen, they can show us that the self is greater than its memories, that there are possibilities for growth, learning, and happiness in spite of the "tragic" losses. As Anne, a woman who suffers from early memory loss and the narrator of one of the performances of the play *To Whom I May Concern*, says, "I also try to forget. I know that may sound funny ... forgetting is at the heart of my problem. But I do try to forget about dementia. I don't want it to define me. I'm more than my memory. Let's have some fun" (Basting 2009, 93).[5]

A Self More Than Memory

But do movies ever depict those with Alzheimer's as having, and being, a self that is more than the sum of their memories? And do they ever have fun? Those with Alzheimer's both retain a self and enjoy it in *Wellkamm to Verona* (2006), a film that reconceptualizes Shakespeare's story of Romeo and Juliet to reflect the emotions and experiences of elderly residents with Alzheimer's who live in a Swedish nursing home called

5. The Cultural Work of Alzheimer's

Verona. Rather than emphasize the past by contrasting the person of then with the person now as do *The Forgetting* and *Iris*, or focus on loss while admitting the possibility for growth as does *Away from Her*, *Wellkamm to Verona* concentrates on the here and now, foregrounding the ability of those with Alzheimer's to make new lives and enter into new loves. Deliberately ignoring the dire statistics surrounding the disease that preface other movies, *Wellkamm to Verona* opens with an upbeat promotional video for the residential home that is reminiscent of a travel short. From the start, the boundary between us and them is called into question and we, as viewers, are invited to position ourselves as potential future residents of Verona rather than as outsiders.

The two main characters are Walter, former director of the Swedish Royal Theater who often forgets he is retired, and Virginia, an elderly enchantress whose present behavior as man-eating diva mirrors her mysterious past as an opera singer. When Walter falls for Virginia at first sight, partly in order to court her, he agrees to take up his role as director once more and stage a performance of Romeo and Juliet featuring the home's residents as actors. Supported by Asa, the unmarried and childless 30-year-old caretaker who empathizes with the residents' devalued social position, Walter organizes rehearsals in which he encourages his cast to tell the tale of Romeo and Juliet in their own words and to disregard the linearity of the narrative in order to concentrate on the emotional meaning behind the story. By teaching them to use their entire bodies to communicate through touch, gesture, and facial expression rather than to rely on language, Walter makes full use of whatever communication skills they may retain in spite of losses due to Alzheimer's.

As the rehearsals progress, Walter succeeds in winning the attentions of Virginia, Joseph falls in love with Helena, and two older women discover they were meant for each other, developments that echo the love of Romeo and Juliet. At the final performance in front of an audience of friends and family, rather than stick to a version of the storyline they had rehearsed, Walter and Virginia perform the essence of the story by publicly declaring their love, while Joseph and Helena do the same by getting married. By the time of the reception, the already ambiguous line differentiating the "real" world from that of the residents has completely disappeared. In a series of contradictory and fast-paced scenes, we see Walter riding a horse through the woods, then standing in the position of a rider with no horse beneath him; dying on the beach in the arms of Virginia as she kisses him one last time and shoves his body out to sea in a flaming burial canoe, then lying in his bed connected to a multitude of tubes while Virginia wades alone in the empty water. Although it is clear that Walter has died, another nod to *Romeo and Juliet*, nothing marks the transition from the actual to the imaginary, and we must decide for ourselves which vision to privilege and if it really matters (Swinnen 2009b).

If we choose to privilege the scene that shows Walter in bed, dying, and assume that his presence in the woods and on the beach is only a delusion, then we subscribe to a biomedical model that takes no account of the discursive context in which the person with Alzheimer's speaks and performs, and that dismisses his voice and actions a priori as without meaning. But if we choose to believe that the scenes that depict Walter riding and being kissed by Virginia on the beach are of equal importance, then the decision to interpret his speech and performance as meaningful can result in real communication. As Aagje Swinnen notes in "The Orchard Walls Are High.... And the Place Death," when the "intention to produce meaningful speech acts is ... present, but the instrument to realize this intention is defective," (Swinnen 2009b, 5), someone with Alzheimer's can appear as a semiotic subject based on the intention, not only on the success, of their nonverbal, theatrical communication *as long as* we do not confuse the instrument with its user (the disease with the person).

A further difficulty involved in giving meaningful voice to those with dementia results from the logocentrism of Western culture. According to Derrida, logocentrism is the view that speech is central to the construction of language. In logocentric theory, speech is the original signifier of meaning, expressing a quality of interiority and a presence that is closer to the original nature of language than writing, which is seen as derivative. In the case of difference due to culture, level of health, age or other social markers, Derrida continues, a logocentric attitude can promote ethnocentrism, or an othering of those whose facility with speech, and therefore with writing, is found to be lacking, and whose history does not conform to a linear and sequentially temporal norm. Looking at Alzheimer's sufferers as a category of people whose ability to express themselves through either speech or writing is compromised, and whose memory (history) is distinctly nonlinear and nonsuccessive, it is not difficult to see how we in the West could devalue both their selves and their efforts to communicate. In order to see or hear those with dementia, we need to undo logocentrism, as Derrida does in

5. The Cultural Work of Alzheimer's

Of Grammatology (1976), to recognize that neither speech nor writing is originary, and to accept the pluri-dimensionality and non-linearity that logocentrism has suppressed.[6] By questioning the equation of the mastery of language with the mastery of self, and by allowing for the existence of other ways of organizing one's history and self, the voices and the selves of people with Alzheimer's can begin to be audible and visible in a socially meaningful way.

If, as Derrida argues, there can be a self outside of or not contained by language then, rather than see the "ravages" of Alzheimer's simply in terms of loss, we could begin to see those changes as revelatory of an additional layer of the self (Shulman 2008). In his study of lytigo-bodig disease, a neurological disorder endemic to Guam that manifests itself in a progressive parkinsonian-like paralysis or reptilian stare punctuated by explosive reptilian-like motion (Sacks 1996), Oliver Sacks argues that the changes in a person's behavior due to this disease are more than loss and deficit and that they reveal a different layer of existence "that has been obstructed by normal neurological functioning" (Wilson 2004, 79). For Sacks, the reptilian stare and movements demonstrate vestiges of past evolutionary commonalities that are stored biologically in the human brain. Thus atavism, rather than signal "a degeneration to subhuman form" (82), uncovers a current connection that, like Derrida's call for pluridimensionality and non-linearity, shows the human, the self, to be more than either logocentrism or linear evolutionary theory allow. To look at those with Alzheimer's in light of the work of both Derrida and Sacks is to see that they have neither lost themselves nor become like children or animals, but are exhibiting characteristics that, although brought out by neurological disease, exist within all of us and that every one of us is capable of comprehending.

The Commonality of Care

This commonality or connection, though liberating in one sense, is also frightening for it dissolves the categorical binary distinctions that separate normal from abnormal, young from old, and those who are healthy from those with Alzheimer's. It reveals, as Donna Haraway argues, that what counts as human is shaped by relationships rather than by definition, and circumscribed by boundaries whose stability is fractured by liminal beings (Haraway 1991a). The demented elderly can be read as just such beings. Between normal and pathological, now and then, memory and forgetting, language and silence, these beings force us to become aware of our own vulnerability. But they also ask us to be responsible for how we account for and act towards their difference (Shildrick 2002). "By moving through our fears, we can find hope ... that embraces the person as he or she is rather than looking solely to the future (for a cure) or the past (exalting who the person was)" (Basting 2009, 67). And by seeing liminal beings as having something to offer those who work with or care for them, they can provide models for our own old age and teach us about the enduring drive for love, meaning, and recognition.

Embracing our commonalities also has profound implications for the kind of care those with Alzheimer's receive. In *The Forgetting*, the biomedical model prevails, generally viewing the body as subject to pathologies that can be seen, that correlate with discrete dysfunctions, and that need to be targeted with drugs or other medical intervention. This reductionist view creates a patient out of a human being, separating the person from her body and leaving little conceptual space for the physical, social, psychological, and environmental processes that affect the health of people with dementia (George, Williams and Southern, 2010). It also focuses more on the pain of the caregivers and family than on the "despair experienced by the affected person when dealing with the dramatic changes in ... herself" (Leibing 2006, 250). Although in *Iris*, John holds a slightly different view of personhood, as evidenced by the way he tries to care for Iris himself and by the flashback in which he contests her assertion that "we can only think with words" by saying that "there are other ways to understand each other besides language," the reductionist view of Alzheimer's that erases the person and highlights the distress of others still suffuses the movie.

In *Away from Her*, there is a definite move away from the biomedical model towards person-centered care when Grant decides to validate Fiona's perception of the world by refusing to challenge her relationship with Aubrey. Yet, although the movie does a better job of balancing the distress experienced by both parties and of exploring their coping mechanisms, most of the film, particularly the way institutional need trumps that of the patient, as in the Meadowlake policy stating that Fiona can receive no visitors for the first thirty days in order to get her acclimated, still subscribes to the biomedical notions that brain equals person equals disease and that care equals control. As we can see in these three movies,

5. The Cultural Work of Alzheimer's

looking at a person through the biomedical lens can lead to biosocial death or the determination that disease has robbed that person of the ability to participate further in society. As Giorgio Agamben explains, by positioning a person between life and death, the biomedical model can strip her of political life (bios), leaving only the bare life (zoe or natural life) of her body to be cared for (Agamben 1998). Thus, "one who inhabits such a black hole in society [becomes] a 'living dead' person" whose life is without value (Leibing 2006, 249).

Only in *Wellkamm to Verona* are Alzheimer's "victims" humanized through person-centered care and, even though living in a nursing home, still considered part of society. Their experience of the disease is foregrounded over that of family and caregivers, their emotions and capacities are emphasized, their memories are perceived as interactive rather than individual, and their view of reality is validated "by finding relevance and meaning in their experiences, perceptions, and narratives rather than devaluing or ignoring them" (George, Williams, Southern 2011, 349).[7] One of the best examples of validation occurs when Walter's daughter, a policewoman that he no longer recognizes as his kin, is driving him back to Verona after one of his many forays into town to "go to work." Showing him a scan of his degenerating brain in order to convince him of the reality of his illness and of the necessity of staying in Verona, Walter looks at the picture and, instead of perceiving evidence of disease, laughs and tells her that he sees a clown. Paradoxically, the very disease that alters his view of reality ends up protecting him from his daughter's cruel act when she gives up and allows his version of reality to prevail (Swinnen 2009b). Rather than position Alzheimer's sufferers as the living dead as some biomedical models do, the person-centered care depicted in *Wellkamm to Verona* subscribes more closely to Charles Taylor's idea that every person is endowed with universal human potential, no matter her biological condition or her ability to realize it, and that that potential alone gives a life value (Taylor 1994).

Using person-centered care to validate the reality of those with dementia, whether or not we agree with their version of reality, also can be seen as part of the narrative turn in the study of aging, and is a process closely related to the creation of a counterstory (see chapter 2). The narrative turn asks us to examine a person's story "within the terms of the story itself, independent of its [objective] truth content" (McLean 2006, 157). Rather than define coherence as the existence of a logical time sequence and a consistent theme, coherence in the stories of those with Alzheimer's is defined in terms of a persistent, subjective, and emotional truth value. By creating a fictional or metaphoric self, the truth value of these stories enables the person telling them to give meaning to her life by connecting experiences that may have fragmented or dissolved a prior sense of self into a new identity. Both Fiona's relationship with Aubrey and the relationships that come into being in Verona are based on the subjective selves created in stories the characters tell themselves about their present lives and circumstances. As Athena McLean writes in "Coherence without Facticity in Dementia," to disconfirm a person's story "on the basis of its lack ... of correspondence to external indicators of 'truth'" (175), as the biomedical model often does, is to risk both elevating some voices over others and disempowering and invalidating an already fragile self. Thus, the narrative turn is an extension of MacIntyre's suggestion that narrative is crucial to the construction of the self, even when that narrative and the self it produces may be based on a memory compromised by dementia.

Although these two approaches, biomedical reductionism understood as neutral, natural, universal, and objectifying, and person-centered care perceived as subjective and as an attempt to communicate with the interior person, are based on differing epistemic cultures, are generally seen as oppositional, and have even set off "personhood wars" when methods of treatment have clashed in certain medical settings, Annette Leibing argues that both responses are necessary. She posits that, although the medicalization of dementia can result in the diminution of the person, and even though the central sign of Alzheimer's, loss of cognition, still has no effective treatment, many drug therapies do slow the progression of "behavioral and psychological signs and symptoms in dementia " (Leibing 2006, 256), giving the patient more time with close to normal function. Medical technologies that externalize and enhance memory such as the senescam, a small camera that hangs around a patient's neck taking photos every 30 seconds to provide a record of events and memory cues that can be revisited as often as desired (Harrell 2010), may help to keep episodic memory functioning longer as well. In combination with the person-centered care that treats those with Alzheimer's as still valuable persons, understands care as reciprocal, and encourages engagement in creative activities that deemphasize the past and allow use of voice and body in ways that communicate beyond words,[8] the biomedical approach can be extremely valuable.

5. *The Cultural Work of Alzheimer's*

Conclusion

Movies, then, are important cultural markers of how we envision Alzheimer's disease itself and those who live and die with it. As in *The Forgetting*, they can inspire dread and encourage stigmatization, making us wish to distance ourselves from those with the condition or, as in *Wellkamm to Verona*, they can enjoin us to reflect on alternative meanings of old age, love, memory, self, and dementia. When watching movies about Alzheimer's or with characters who suffer from it, it matters that we understand that the history of Alzheimer's, like that of those with the disease, is neither straightforward nor linear, but culturally and contextually situated and in a constant process of change. It matters that we comprehend that the equation of memory with self erases not the person with Alzheimer's but the fact that memory and self are not natural categories but are interactive and relational, stretching well beyond the borders of our skin, and in a process of continual revision in order to make sense out of often fragmented personal experience. It matters whether we treat those with Alzheimer's in a way that objectifies and depersonalizes them, accentuating their difference and calling their very personhood into question, or whether we are willing to discover and accept whatever the person has become and will become, even if that defies all our previous expectations. And it matters if we, like Suzanne Osten, director of *Wellkamm to Verona*, deliberately foreground the creative potential of those with Alzheimer's in a way that uses humor, emphasizes their continuing need for love and respect, and keeps us aware of our common fears and vulnerabilities.

We therefore need to notice where on the scale from pure erasure to total acceptance of the elderly with Alzheimer's a particular film stands. Ironically, *Do You Remember Love?* (1987), one of the first movies to deal with the changes that Alzheimer's can incur, is one that deals with the tragic losses experienced by an exceptionally intelligent woman (as in *Iris*) and the challenges these losses present to her family in a more straightforward manner than many later films. Although *The Notebook* (2004) also deals with tragic loss, this time of a great and enduring love (similar to *Away from Her*), it, in contrast, offers an overly sentimentalized depiction of the experience of Alzheimer's. *The Savages* (2007), a film that shows the uneven and irrational decline of a father with Alzheimer's, is (like *The Forgetting*) more concerned with the effect of the disease on the children and their relationships rather than on the father himself. But *Sunset Story*

(2003), a documentary about the still radical and politically involved residents of Sunset Hall, manages to portray aging, even with dementia, in a way that explodes stereotypes and validates the reality of the old (as does *Wellkamm to Verona*). As Basting notes, our fascination about and fear of memory loss is also reflected and piqued in the plethora of films about amnesia, even though, unfortunately, these films seldom deal with the old. Movies concerning amnesia, like those about Alzheimer's, depict memory loss on a scale from tragic and unbearable as in *Memento* (2000), to comic and frustrating as in *Groundhog Day* (1993), to a disability that can be managed as in *Finding Nemo* (2003). Although not about dementia, when watched critically, these films can help us understand the anxieties about identity that the specter of Alzheimer's disease can arouse, accept the fluid nature of memory and self, and envision the possibilities for a full life in spite of the reality of memory loss (Basting 2009).

The cultural work of Alzheimer's, in part accomplished through the stories told about it in film, thus resides in how the existence of dementia and its associated memory loss is made intelligible through images, words, metaphors, practices, and personal experiences— how Alzheimer's is embodied in different ways at different times and places. As Cohen explains in *No Aging in India,* the representation of the old body through Alzheimer's and the memory loss it causes is neither obvious nor universal. In some schools of philosophy in India, memory is neither seen as a key to the self nor as an accurate record of experience, but as a "re-presentation of objects to consciousness" that can represent "its object differently from the initial presentation" and may involve "secondary cognition and not be an immediate source of knowledge" (Cohen 1998, 142). Memory is, in this philosophical rendering, always a copy that deceives us into thinking that the phenomenal world and the self we know within it is all there is. The paradox of memory is, in this view, that only by forgetting can we remember the essential, transcendent, and connected self that memory prevents us from seeing. "Memory traps us within the illusion of the bounded and contingent self, yet memory explodes this self when ... [it] points us to something beyond the self" (144). According to the tenets of this philosophy, Cohen explains, the old who can't forget themselves are foolish whereas those who do forget themselves are good and wise.

A life that is open to the vulnerability of forgetting is, therefore, not necessarily tragic but "a potential force for moral good" (Small 2007, 86) if it uses the dependency of an old age with Alzheimer's as a way to connect to our common lifelong vulnerability as embodied creatures. This vision

5. The Cultural Work of Alzheimer's

of old age and dementia is not defined by reason, but is made possible by the decay of reason and the loss of capability that Alzheimer's can bring. As hinted at first in *Away from Her* and more forcefully in *Wellkamm to Verona*, such a vision can do much more than improve the care and treatment of the elderly with Alzheimer's. It can change the narratives we construct around aging, self, memory, loss, and even the becoming of life itself.

6

Age as Becoming

In contrast to the in-your-face realism that can leave film viewers in a state of panic about the risks and ridicule that may accompany growing older, or the fairy-tale thinking that can relegate the structural and personal difficulties that older people face to the unspoken background of assumed "naturalness," some movies allow the ambiguity, vulnerability, and creativity — the ongoing becoming — of the old to take center stage. By placing older characters in situations that highlight the way their desires and dreams can continue to transform their lives, these movies offer an implicit challenge to the assumptions of decline, stereotypes of incompetence, and feelings of aversion that mass media images of the old generally convey. Rather than present aging as a relentless march of accumulating losses that gradually erodes one's right to personhood, dignity, and respect, such films can turn growing older into "a 'work of art,' something to be achieved" where "losses are turned, reworked, and impression-managed into a variety of gains" (Graham 2010, 179).

Movies that allow elders to retain their agency and selfhood despite any changes that aging has occasioned can encourage us to collapse the distinction between essentialism and social construction, to see all of life as an open-ended and unpredictable process of becoming embedded in the world rather than a gradual unfolding of an imminent form or an inevitable submission to constraining historical disciplinary norms. They call on us to think about the way we understand time, and space, even matter, and to reconsider to what extent the way we measure age contributes to its very constitution. Such movies also challenge "the idea that the purpose of [cinematic] art is imitation" (Rodowick 1997, 18), recasting their purpose as an active and creative manipulation or restructuring of reality that reveals the temporal and unstable nature of what we call truth (Rodowick 1997). Linking life, as an ongoing process of individuation, to art, films such as *Strangers in Good Company* (1991), *The Straight Story*

6. Age as Becoming

(1999), *The World's Fastest Indian* (2006), and *Howl's Moving Castle* (2004) demonstrate how images of life as becoming can call a new future into existence. By reworking the resources of the past and the present in a way that creates something new, filmic art can lead us to take "a virtual leap into new worlds to come" (Grosz 2011, 191) that intimate different ways of understanding and being in the world.

Thus, when watching a film that makes us question the stability, self-identity, and predictability of life, notions that so often lead to negative characterizations of the aging and the old, we need to ask more penetrating questions. Does this film portray the future as an active and open dimension of life, even for the old? To what extent does this movie allow the older characters to retain dignity, agency, and choice? Does this film explore the conflict a character may feel between the pressure to conform to ageist cultural norms and the desire to continue to transform oneself and become other? Are the adjustments a character may make to manage the age-related difficulties she may experience portrayed as successful adaptations or as evidence of deterioration? Are "slower" attributes such as kindness, compassion, listening, and time for reflection valued as much as action in haste? Do others recognize and facilitate the ways in which an older character may continue to grow and contribute to the community? And finally, maybe most importantly, does this film lead us to envision and actually work towards a different kind of future for those we love and for ourselves as we age? Only when the answer to this last question becomes yes, when the barrier between a cinematic image or representation and what we call reality is breached, can we begin to alter the meanings, discourses, narrative, and myths that work to devalue and darken the last years of our lives.

The Porosity of Representation and Reality

A swirling white mist fills the screen. As it lingers, far longer than most movies would allow, we strain to see the indistinct figures that quiver and fade within it, then slowly begin to materialize. Gradually a group of older women takes shape, at first made recognizable more from the quality of their voices than from their form. Laughing as they amble into view along a dirt road in the wilderness, it seems as if they were just beamed onto a brand new planet or transported into a Narnia-like realm where it's possible that magic could still happen. According to Mary Meigs, author of *In the Company of Strangers* (1991), a book about

The Becoming of Age

the experience of making the movie *Strangers in Good Company* (1991), magic abounds.

When seven women aged sixty-five to eighty-eight, Mary, Alice, Beth, Catherine, Cissy, Constance, and Winnie, are chosen to "act" as themselves in a "semi-documentary" (Meigs 1991, 9) that has neither conventional plot nor action, Meigs describes the result as "the magification of every living and growing thing" (38), including themselves. The outline of the story is simple: stranded when the bus they had rented to find Constance's childhood summer home breaks down in the Canadian wilderness, the women find refuge in an abandoned farmhouse, and use their store of knowledge, skill, patience, and humor not only to survive, but to reveal themselves to each other in a way that allows them to become fast friends both on and off the set. Yet the atmosphere of magic that this story creates is considerably more complex. What kind of magic are we talking about? And how does it come about?

Throughout her book, Meigs variously characterizes the magic they feel as a kind of blind faith in their ability to push themselves "beyond [their] known limits" (Meigs 1991, 25), as an atmosphere "of downy non-judgement" (34) in which nothing reminds them that they "are old except direct comparison with ... [the film] crew members who are young" (77), and as a place that exists "out of time and logic ... a magic space where old women have room to exist" (10) and can become "how [they] want to be" (149). Implicitly or explicitly, all of Mieg's descriptions portray an alteration in their perception of time, and hinge on the ways in which the experience of making this film graces them with a period of time relatively free from society's ubiquitous imposition of chronological comparison. Ironically, this freedom from the constant reminders of age not only suffuses *Strangers in Good Company* with the hope and life precluded by ageism, but also restores the women's ability to alter their own relationship between past, present, and future, giving them the opportunity to flourish and continue to grow and become off as well as on the set. In this magical atmosphere, rather than simply being old women who are acting in a film, they come to see themselves as "film stars [only] disguised as old women" (34), and they begin to wonder just where the line between representation and reality is drawn.

Meig's observations about the way this film "magically" modifies how these seven older women experience and understand themselves in time address many of the same concerns that Gilles Deleuze deals with in his philosophy of cinema. In two of his later works, *The Movement Image*

6. Age as Becoming

(1983) and *The Time Image* (1985), Deleuze seeks to explain the entanglement of inhuman matter (including forces, concepts, and sensations) with human life (duration or time in space) by exploring what he calls the special relationship that the (forceful, conceptual, and sensational) images of cinema have to our contemporary perception of time and of ourselves. Arguing that since time can never be known in and of itself but only in relation to an image of something else, Deleuze maintains that, since the advent of cinema, contemporary culture has become fundamentally audiovisual, a culture in which we both understand and represent ourselves in step with cinematic renditions of time and space. In other words, Deleuze asserts that the way in which cinema presents the passage of time reflects culturally contingent strategies for both imagining and imaging ourselves and our place in the world. In *Gilles Deleuze's Time Machine* (1997), D. N. Rodowick further argues that the way in which Deleuze's books on cinema interrogate filmic representations of time presents both a profound critique of contemporary "concepts of identity and subjectivity" and a challenge to "questions of hierarchy ... [and the] identity politics" such categorical understandings of the world engender (Rodowick 1997, xiv). Rodowick, thus, sees Deleuze's books as an exploration of the "philosophical relation between image and thought" (xvi) in "service to life — the affirmation of life as the creation of the new — and to resisting those forces that inhibit in life the appearance of the new, the unforeseen, and the unexpected" (xvii).

In *The Matrix of Visual Culture* (2003), Patricia Pisters expands Rodowick's examination of the connections between Deleuze's film theories and his philosophy of time to explore the relevance of his work to interpretations of contemporary popular cinema. Starting with Deleuze's argument that we now live in a metacinematic universe, Pisters investigates how this kind of universe challenges "the borders of selfhood (or subjectivity) ... in time" (Pisters 2003, 20). Defining a metacinematic universe as one in which our constant exposure to images that are stored on film, to new images that are constantly generated by film, and to the way that both types of images mutually influence one another, Pisters argues that such a universe liberates us from the sequential view of time that tends to fix identity and constrain the becoming that is life. In this metacinematic universe, she continues, we have come to understand our own past, present, and future through a "camera consciousness," or a kind of perception akin to the ability of a camera to freely move or change viewpoints in time (2). Since this camera consciousness allows us to jump between nonchronological layers of time, our understanding of the present no longer relies only on bodily and cognitive experiences or traditional interpretations of time, but on the never-ending stream of non-sequential, non-linear, and often remixed or reorganized images to which we are continually exposed as well.

According to Deleuze, Pisters explains, in a metacinematic universe structured by camera consciousness, this stream of images does not *represent* the world, but literally *shapes* us and the world around us. Existing concurrently on what Deleuze describes as a "plane of immanence" (Pisters 2003, 4), both filmic and real-life images of the past and the future, or what Deleuze calls virtual images, and those of the present, or what he terms actual images, are equally real.[1] And since all virtual and actual images are readily accessible to us through our camera consciousness, we are able to rearrange them, interact and play with them, and use them to construct a life (Pisters 2003). When we look at *Strangers in Good Company* through the lens of Deleuze's concept of the equality of virtual and actual images, the women in this film are not *representing* themselves through one kind of image when on screen and *being* themselves with another kind of image when off screen, but are becoming, creating themselves anew in the "crystallization" (4) that takes place between the two. In this sense, according to Deleuze in *The Time-Image*, cinema and the images it produces are never a reflection of a real-life world set apart from and prior to its representation, but are an integral part of the very construction of the world and its subjects (Deleuze 1989).

An Indirect Image of Time

Deleuze's ideas about the simultaneous existence of virtual and actual images and the creation of the new through their constant interpenetration presents a challenge to traditional film theory and its reliance on the concept of film as a representation of reality. According to Deleuze, when film is seen as a representation of reality, difference can be signified only in relation to an already existing identity (Deleuze 1986) by making a comparison through identification, opposition, analogy, or resemblance, like the comparison the women make between themselves and the young film crew. Since comparison generally expresses identity in binary form, such as young/old, male/female, or good/evil, representationalism is a restrictive image of thought that negates both pure difference, or differences in themselves, and the concept of becoming, or constant growth and change,

6. Age as Becoming

in order to maintain a stable concept of the world, the subject, and the image. Representationalism is thus based on a Newtonian, static or spatialized universe in which the "I" who judges difference in relation to identity is transcendent, before and beyond perception and experience, and ontologically separate from the object it judges. It is also Cartesian, a "consequence of the Cartesian division between 'internal' and 'external'" (Barad 2007, 48), mind and body, that presumes our representations are more accessible to us than the objects they represent, and Lacanian in the assumption that subjects both on and off screen are motivated to construct their subjectivity through a desire for identification with an other who possesses what they lack rather than through becoming other (Pisters 2003).

In *The Movement Image*, Deleuze argues that representational thinking informs the way the greater part of cinema has been produced and viewed from its inception up through World War II. Projecting the largely deterministic universe that mainstream culture espoused at that time, cinematic events structured by representational thinking are linked by a chronology in which the past leads inevitably to the present and the future emerges predictably out of the present. Time is subordinated to movement, which cinema halts then reconstitutes as linear and successive by extracting and stringing together segments of motion in a representative fashion, resulting in what Deleuze calls an indirect image of time. Movement-image cinema thus imposes an order on life in which truth is unchanging, identity is preexisting, the whole is always the sum of its parts, and movement is linked by rational, predictable, and successive intervals (Rodowick 1997).

Looking at *Strangers in Good Company* in terms of a representation in which action is the master of time, the passage of time, rather than offering the possibility of the new, is spatialized in "frozen ... poses, aligned on a linear and irreversible continuum" (Rodowick 1997, 21). Time is envisioned as a straight line on which events occur, placing events in time (or on time) rather than seeing events as constituting time. This representational or indirect image of time as linear, abstract, and predictable underlies fixed constructions such as the stages of life and inflexible narratives like aging as decline, deterioration, and lack. It also provides a continual stream of static and pervasively negative images of who and what the old are, images to which the old have ready access through their camera consciousness, that can increase anxiety, contribute to incapacity, and lead to social inertia, a situation in which the perception of having access to a

The Becoming of Age

steadily decreasing amount of linear time is felt as social pressure and results in an inability to entertain new ideas or to struggle against perceived limits (Brennan 1999).[2]

We can see the effects of this indirect image of time on the construction of old age in *Strangers in Good Company* in the scenes that stress the physical limitations that the women's medical conditions impose on them, such as when they pass a cup of water around so that they can take medications for high blood pressure, water retention, heart trouble, and the aches and pains of arthritis, or when the women agree that Catherine, despite her arthritic feet, is the only one who has any chance of walking out for help. Rather than encourage confidence in their ability to act, innovate, and survive, these scenes create fear for their safety, a concern reflected in Cissy's terror of becoming destitute and unwanted as she grows older, and in the dread Constance expresses at the thought of dying in a hospital or a nursing home. Representational images like these also naturalize problems and fears that are rooted in the cultural and the social, and impose chronological limits (what Meigs described as known limits) on character and spectator alike, crushing the creative nature of existence under a medicalized view of aging that is built on conformity to the image of the same and on the inherent predictability of life.

The reality of social pressure as a debilitating force and its connection to movement-image cinema is particularly well illustrated in the scene in which Michelle, the young bus driver who has sprained her ankle and thus is even more incapacitated than the older women, encourages eighty-year-old Beth to take off her wig and give herself a chance to look "natural." When Beth refuses, admitting that she's afraid to look like an old lady with a wrinkled neck and thinning hair, and comments that she doesn't have much time left anyway, implying that it's not worth the effort to change now in any case, the consequences of imagining and imaging ourselves in a world ruled by Newton's static and linear universe, Descartes' splitting of mind from body, and Lacan's construction of desire as lack congeal. For Beth to reimagine herself now would force her up against the "truth" of old age and the forms of subjectification that command "you will be One" and that One will be marked, "once and for all, with a known and recognizable identity" (Rodowick 1997, 201). Representational thinking boldly declares Beth to be an old lady only disguised as a film star, a judgment with which she herself may concur through internalization of the decline narrative, even though film star and old lady are obviously the same.

6. Age as Becoming

Thus, to view *Strangers in Good Company* in the tradition of movement-image cinema with its indirect conception of time as linear, orderly, knowable, and predictable — spatialized — makes it difficult to move beyond the negative and disparaging representations of old age that emphasize limits and make derogatory pronouncements about what those within the category can accomplish. It leads both viewer and character to interpret the meaning of a movie in a way that is particularly detrimental to the construction of old age and leaves both spectator and actor with a store of negative images on which to draw as they, themselves, grow older. Since this perspective is unlikely to be the source of the empowering magic to which Meigs so often refers, rather than succumb to this anesthetizing image, we need to look at the movie from another point of view.

A Direct Image of Time

Deleuze accomplishes this perspectival shift when, instead of thinking in terms of representations, he proposes a more open, immanent way of thinking he calls rhizomatics. Rhizomatic thinking leaves behind the transcendental, static "I" and its binary judgments and opens up the concept of life as perpetual becoming. Contrary to representationalism, knowing, in the immanent tradition, "does not come from standing at a distance and representing the world but rather from *a direct material engagement with the world*" (Barad 2007, 49), a world of which we are a part and an engagement with it that involves mind and body as a whole. Deleuze's rhizomatic thinking, like Karen Barad's later theory of agential realism (see chapter one), characterizes matter and meaning, time and space, as neither determinate nor unchanging, but as mutually constituted through dynamic and ongoing intra-actions in which individuals, whether objects or living beings, emerge through specific discursive and material practices. Identity is, therefore, neither essential and pre-existing nor constituted through comparison with another, but is in "constant formation, always changing through multiple encounters" with the world and with others, and always open to the emergence of "unexpected possibilities" (Pisters 2003, 22). Signification is not a discovery but a process in which "each era thinks itself by producing its particular image of thought" (Rodowick 1997, 7). Desire is not based on a fundamental lack of original wholeness, as Lacan argued, but on what Spinoza characterized as a wish to live and preserve our lives by making connections with people and things that will affirm our power to act and give us joy (Pisters 2003).

In *The Time Image*, Deleuze argues that since World War II, the immanent tradition has begun to replace representationalism in cinema so that movement, rather than constructing time, has become subordinated to time. Instead of projecting a deterministic universe, time-image film, reflecting a culture influenced by ideas such as deconstruction, chaos theory, and quantum physics, presents a more probabilistic world. With what Deleuze calls a direct image of time, the temporal relationship between events is nonlinear and undecidable beforehand and the future remains open rather than being determined by the present and the past. Identity is not based on being but on a becoming that is constantly changing due to the thinking and the action that time and change provoke (Grosz 2005). And rather than subscribe to a notion of truth that is based on repetition as the eternal return of the same and that "poses change and differentiation as deception" (Rodowick 1997, 137), the direct image of time "puts truth into crisis" by picturing repetition as "recurrence and differentiation" (137). Since life is temporal and durational, "which means that within it, there can never be any real repetition but only continual invention insofar as the living carry the past along with the present" (Grosz 2011, 31), recurrence refers to the return that affirms the ongoing existence of a being and differentiation to the process of that being becoming other through time. Direct time-image cinema, thus, presents images that are expressive of the creative possibilities of life rather than representative of an abstract, ideal life.

When we look at movies in terms of immanent or rhizomatic thinking, time is no longer subordinated to movement but is an element in itself. With no straight line to constrain it, time becomes series of "irrational intervals that produce a dissociation rather than an association of images" (Rodowick 1997, 143), and that stress the differentiation that is the essence of all that exists. Direct time-image film does not consist of an uninterrupted chain of images linking action and reaction, each slave to the next (Deleuze 1989), but creates a sequence of images "whose aberrant movements unveil the force of time as change" (Rodowick 1997, 136). This concept of time positions truth as temporal rather than fixed, freeing both protagonist and viewer to create something new. Direct time-image cinema can empower the old to push beyond the limits imposed on them by negative discourses and narratives, and to reject the judgment that construes old age as an ending when the world is always and ever only a

6. Age as Becoming

becoming. In *Strangers in Good Company*, if we conceive of the situation in which the stranded women find themselves as the force of time as change generating problems for them to solve that will ensure "that they ... transform themselves" (Grosz 2005, 49), then Catherine's attempts to fix the bus engine with an emery board, Alice's conversion of a pair of pantyhose into a fish net, the making of an herbal poultice for Michelle's injured ankle, and even Constance's decision to throw away her pills take on new meaning.

Understood in the context of direct time-image cinema, this repair, these inventions, and this decision become creative acts that bring memory (virtual images) to bear on perception (actual images) in a way that reveals the complicity of mind and matter, virtual and actual. Catherine, Alice, and Constance all search out virtual memories in order to make their actual perception of the situation or problem meaningful. In this process, present perception, affecting the actual body in space, combines with memory, stored virtually in nonchronological layers of past in the mind, to bring "ever more complex and numerous points in time into relation with each other" (Rodowick 1997, 88). Each time a virtual image is called up in order to relate to an actual perception, an object, concept, or idea, is "de-formed and created anew, widening and deepening the mental picture it inspires" (90).

For example, when the series of images of the women's younger selves flash across the screen or when they share parts of their life stories with one another, they are not just making present connections, but are changing themselves through the act of revising both past and present in their becoming. One evening in the old farmhouse, when Mary is writing before sleep, she comments on how quiet it is and mentions how silence can sometimes be frightening. Cissy responds by telling how the nighttime silence was burst by the sounds the bombs made while she was in an underground shelter in England during World War II. As they listen to each other's stories, their present perception of quiet searches out virtual memories in order to make the actual perception of quiet more meaningful, and the notion of what constitutes quiet evolves for both of them. Thus, body and perception, brain and memory, interpenetrate to fuse matter and meaning, substance and significance, present and past into something unexpected and new (Pisters 2003 and Barad 207).

This interpenetration leads Deleuze to assert that there is no difference between matter and image, object and perception (Deleuze 1986). They are identical not because the object or concept somehow pre-exists the perception of it, but because perception creates the object by taking from the whole only what interests it or what serves its needs (Rodowick 1997). As Barad explains, objects are not already there (Barad 2007); they are formed by "contingent and partial picturings of matter ... samplings of a continuous flow" of everything that exists on the plane of immanence (Rodowick 2007, 35). For Deleuze, the continual reorganization of actual and virtual images, whether from a movie or from "real-life," around "a central nucleus of bodily interest and activity" is what life is (Grosz 2005, 98). And human consciousness of life, according to Deleuze, comes about during the interval between perception as interest and reaction as activity, an interval that gives the body time to select, organize, and integrate remembered (virtual) information into perception (actual) information before choosing how to respond (Rodowick 1997). For Deleuze, life and our consciousness of it are not special substances different in nature from matter; they are the result of the amalgamation of mind and matter. And the primary function of the brain is not to be a repository of ideas, freedom, and creativity, but to insert a delay between the stimuli produced by all the actual and virtual images to which the brain has access through our camera consciousness and our reaction to them, granting us freedom from predetermination and making an open future inevitable.

Elaborating on Deleuze's ideas, philosopher Alva Noe in *Out of Our Heads* (2009), argues that the brain is not an information-processing organ that constructs a mental representation of the world, but is more like a traffic cop whose job is to coordinate our bodily dealings with the environment and the others within it. "It is thus only in the context of ... embodied existence, situated in an environment, dynamically interacting with objects and situations, that the function of the brain can be understood" (Noe 2009a, 65). Perceptual consciousness is not in our heads, but is a learned relationship to and a skillful integration with both objects and the environment, shaped and structured by our body's ability to adjust our relation to the world around us.[3] We are not world representers, but are "dynamically spread-out world-involving beings" (82) in whom matter and life entwine by dynamizing the forces of matter in order to suffuse the actual material present with the virtuality of the past (Grosz 2011). It is this entwining of life and matter, enabled by the delay or hesitation in which we have freedom of choice, argues Deleuze, that constitutes time itself, the generation of the future through the reactivation of the virtuality of the past in the actuality of the present (Grosz 2005).

6. Age as Becoming

The Magic of Time

Time, looked at in this way, is neither a succession of equally metered moments nor a uniform background against which movement or stillness can be measured. It is neither linear nor absolute. It does not leave a mark and then march on, but is produced through the uneven and often discontinuous enfolding of historical practices and agencies in the sedimented mattering of the world. Matter, including our bodies, carries within it the evidence of the intra-active practices through which it is produced thus giving time a history which can be read in the differential and ongoing becoming of the world (Barad 2007). Contrary to what many of the discourses and narratives surrounding aging would have us believe, time is neither a cage that imprisons us nor a finite quantity of linear moments that will run out more or less on schedule. It is not something within which we exist, but is constituted by the very fact of our existence.

Time, as understood by Deleuze, does not trap us but is more like a kind of magic that can free us to live, continually opening up possibilities for becoming by giving us chance after chance to combine our past with our present in all sorts of new and unexpected ways. And cinema, "because it gives material form to varieties of ... time, and change" (Rodowick 1997, 140) by providing us with images of other ways of being and becoming, can aid in the affirmation of these virtual possibilities. When Miegs writes that the magic they feel during and after filming allows them to push beyond their limits in a nonjudgmental atmosphere that gives old women room to exist; when she says that they benefit from conditions on a set that "denies the passing of clock-time" (Meigs 1991, 77); when she describes the "lining up of self- and film images" (78) that forces them to let go of all their preconceived ideas about who they are and how they look, she is referring to the experience of becoming that a direct image of time can bestow.

Unlike indirect time or movement-image cinema, where the body is always acting, reacting, and gaining its perspective in a world organized by the totality of Newtonian predictability and Cartesian separation, direct time-image cinema returns to us an undecidable body for which "becoming-other in thought is the prelude to becoming other" (Rodowick 1997, 168). Direct time-image cinema, therefore, points us to another world, a science-fiction-like world that can, as Deleuze says, "affirm life and its untimely forces of creation" (xviii). When Meigs writes that the film is still "living in us" (Meigs 1991, 169), her words demonstrate an innate understanding of the porosity of representation and reality that Deleuze is talking about. She comprehends that filmic and real-life images together conspire to unlock the life hidden away in old women (Meigs 1991), to allow them to move beyond static representations of old age into the freedom of an open future of becoming.

"Nothing happens," says Winnie. "We are what happens. The film is about seven ... old women ... happening," answers Mary (Meigs 1991, 78). And Mary is right. When looked at as time-image cinema, *Strangers in Good Company* is ultimately "a film about life" (86), about the resistance of life to the forces that would exhaust and deplete it, forces that often render the lives of the old not worth living. As these seven old women laugh, dance, sing, dream of new love, and splash in the lake together, as they share their food and chores, their worries and fears, their hopes and dreams with each other, as they accept and celebrate their differences as Englishwomen, black, Mohawk, Roman Catholic nun, lesbian, and French Canadian, and become bound to each other both in the film and in life, they embody the power of the direct image of time to invent a new reality and to create joy. They demonstrate that old age, with its vast store of memories (or virtual images), often used to characterize the old as behind the times and unchanging, and with its physical and cognitive limitations and disabilities (or actual conditions that provoke change), often drawn on to represent the old as slow and unimaginative, are in reality precisely the circumstances that can make the old even more creative in their ability to combine the virtual and the actual in order to grow and survive.

After the movie became a success,[4] Meigs writes that Beth, then eighty-two, who during filming was afraid to remove her wig and show her wrinkles, was "reborn," finally "become the actress of her dream" (Meigs 1991, 167). Flying to New York and London, appearing on TV, seemingly ageless and inexhaustible with all disguises and preconceived notions of who she was gone, Beth became a shining example of the creative possibilities of life provided by the crystallization of filmic and real-life images. By refusing to differentiate between representation and reality, and by daring to combine the virtual with the actual in a new and unpredictable way, out of the swirling mists of a conventional and predictable old age, Beth made film star and old woman truly one. And in the process, proved that magic, as a becoming through time, really does happen.

6. Age as Becoming

Mind and Matter, Man and Machine

Perhaps the fundamental creative entanglement of mind and matter that leads to growth and becoming can be more clearly understood by looking at *The Straight Story* (1999), a film based on the true story of Alvin Straight who, at 73, drove 240 miles on his riding mower with a top speed of 5 miles per hour to see his brother, Lyle, who had had a stroke. Setting a mood similar to that of the first scenes of *Strangers in Good Company*, *The Straight Story* opens with shots of peaceful farm country under a jet black sky full of twinkling stars. As the camera lingers on the night-time heavens and orchestral strings evoke the music of the spheres, the stars seem to invite us to consider all the possible worlds out there, all the ways that life may exist in combinations of the virtual and the actual beyond our present, meager, human understanding. By the time the camera focuses in on an overweight woman sunning herself on the lawn in a lower middle-class neighborhood, the thud we hear from the modest house next door wrenches us out of our Star-Trekian reverie back to the "reality" of earth.

The thud turns out to be Alvin, who having not shown up to meet his friends at the local bar, is discovered by a friend, his sunbathing neighbor, and his daughter Rose, lying on his kitchen floor, unable to get up. Allaying their fears, Alvin calmly says, "I just need a little help getting up," and reluctantly agrees to be driven by his friend, who, from the way the movie pictures him operating the car, obviously should not be driving anymore, to see the doctor. In the next few scenes, we learn that Alvin has bad hips, incipient emphysema, eye problems due to diabetes, and an inadequate diet. We also learn that he adamantly refuses to use a walker, get an operation, undergo testing, or pay for X-rays. Leaving the doctor's office under the threat of serious health-related consequences if he doesn't change his behavior, Alvin grudgingly agrees to use two canes instead of one, and goes back home to light a cigar and tell Rose that the doctor said he'll live to be at least 100.

That evening while sitting on the porch watching a thunder storm, the news that Lyle, from whom Alvin has been estranged for ten years, is in bad shape arrives contemporaneous with a bolt of lightning. By the next day, despite the fact that neither he nor Rose can drive and the fact that there is no bus to Zion where Lyle lives, Alvin has decided that he is going to see Lyle and that he's going to make the trip on his own. Enlisting Rose's help, who although she is considered somewhat mentally

The Becoming of Age

retarded nevertheless is uncannily perceptive to her father's needs and moods, Alvin declares, "I'm not dead yet!" and begins to make plans for his trip. Thus, within a few minutes, this movie has set the scene for a confrontation between the biomedical view of aging that interprets physical changes strictly in terms of decline and loss, and a personal view of growing older that sets limits on the biomedical view's ability to circumscribe life.

Elaborating on the theme of resistance to medicalized aging, in part by demonstrations of a continuing relationship with hegemonic masculinity, the next section of the movie is structured in a way similar to some parts of *Gran Torino*, though at a slower and quieter pace. While building a plywood trailer to haul behind his riding mower, Alvin, like Walt, shows his facility with tools and the value of the mechanical knowledge and experience he gained as a long-distance truck driver in his ability to envision and construct what he needs. When his first mower-trailer breaks down not too far from town and he has to have it towed back only to start over with a newer machine, all under the doubtful gaze of his four old friends, he quietly takes out his anger at the situation by shooting the failed mower with his hunting rifle. Yet, in contrast to Walt, who boiled over at the gift of a grabber because of the spirit in which it was given, Alvin accepts his need for help due to his physical limitations by talking the hardware store clerk out of his favorite grabber for only $10.00 while simultaneously deflecting the numerous questions of his nosey old friends as to why he needs it. In the end, both Alvin and Walt resist being solely defined by concepts of dependency, frailty, or incompetence that rob them of their sense of masculinity, creativity and self respect by learning to picture the adaptations they make to their changing bodies as improvisational reinventions of an ever-expanding self despite any reservations their friends or families may express (Cruikshank 2003).

Yet, at this point *The Straight Story* veers off in a direction more analogous to *Up* than to *Gran Torino*. Instead of mutely accepting the "truth" of the narrative of aging as a series of increasingly devastating losses, an attitude that doubtless contributed to Walt's choice to die, Alvin sets about reworking the meaning of his "losses" and the inevitability of his supposed enfeebled power and agency that reminds us of Carl. Echoing what Janice Graham and Peter Stephenson found in *Contesting Aging and Loss* (2010), an ethnographic study of elders all over the world, Alvin implicitly grasps that the very notion that he is in decline presents him with a far larger problem than any difficulties his physical infirmities and loss of social and

6. Age as Becoming

economic privilege might cause. Like the elders in the ethnographic study, and like those in the Pixar short "George and AJ" who creatively defy all attempts to control them, Alvin is loath to define success as the luck to remain healthy and autonomous, instead seeing it as "an artful adjustment to changing circumstances ... in the face of the challenges that aging has brought" (Graham and Stephenson 2010, xi).

In coming up with the idea of a trailer attached to his mower as a way to get to Zion,[5] building it, making the journey, handling the difficulties, and enjoying the pleasures along the way, Alvin is proving false the equation of a medical prognosis of age-related disability with a prognosis on the expected quality of his life. As Aimee Mullins, a now successful athlete, model, and actress who was born with malformed feet and without the fibula bone in her legs, writes in "The Opportunity of Adversity," "There's an important difference ... between the objective medical fact of my being an amputee and the subjective societal opinion of whether or not I'm disabled. And, truthfully, the only real and consistent disability I've had to confront is the world ... thinking that I could be described by [the] definitions" of disability found in the thesaurus, such as "helpless, useless, wrecked ... worn-out ... senile, decrepit ... done-for ... counted-out ... and weak" (Mullins 2010). Mullins understands that adjusting to adversity is not overcoming it, not emerging from it unmarked, as if success consisted of circumnavigating the vagaries of life through either pretense or by chance, but adapting to it through changing ourselves in a way that allows us to maintain both our sense of self-worth and our value to the community.

Like the women in *Strangers in Good Company*, Alvin is making manifest the malleability of time by integrating the virtual from his vast store of knowledge with his actual circumstances to make something new: to create a life and a future of his own. But he is doing more than affirming the creative possibilities of the force of time, he is also making clear the idea that life is not a force divisible from matter, but extends materiality into a new and unknown future by delaying, rearranging, or otherwise altering various material effects. Returning to Deleuze's concept of direct time-image cinema in which time is the hesitation that allows the forces of creation to affirm life, Alvin's actions not only reveal the openness of life to the dynamism of time, but the openness of matter to the dynamism of life, as well. Just as a different conception of time can allow the virtuality of the past to become actual, so does an alternate concept of space enable matter to express its endless virtualities.

The Virtuality of Matter

In order to understand the potentiality of matter to transform itself, it is necessary to go back to Darwin's concept of evolutionary emergence as an ongoing dance between life and matter. According to Elizabeth Grosz, Darwin envisioned life as a relationship between the active nature of individual variation and sexual selection, and the passive nature of natural selection. Bergson elaborated on this concept with the idea that life exceeds itself by enabling matter to evolve by combining the virtual stored in the past with actual matter in the present. Delueze further refined Bergson's ideas by conceptualizing life as an impersonal force that runs along the porous boundary between the organic and the inorganic, a force "that characterizes events, even nonliving events, as much as it does life" (Grosz 2011, 27). Life, for Darwin, Bergson, and Deleuze, orients itself *out* to matter, space, and objects, and *in* to consciousness, time, and subjects, in an attempt to extend matter beyond the self and its present form. What we perceive as the resistance of matter to transformation or the seeming spatiality and stability of the inorganic world—that which makes it amenable to orderly and predictable scientific and mathematical calculations—results from what Bergson has called the mistaken assumption that matter is located on a spatial plane. Matter is never located spatially, argues Bergson, but instead is suffused with a space that is composed of constant movements, making space a map not of locations and points but of trajectories through time.[6] To see matter as spatial is to reduce it to the geometric or mechanical, the bearer of self-identity, the model of immobility (Grosz 2011) and, as Karen Barad argues in her theory of agential realism, to cut matter off from its intra-active entanglement with life (Barad 2007).

Inextricably entangled, the organic and the inorganic, mind and matter, time and space are never opposites, but are "different degrees of duration.... Life is matter extended into the virtual; matter is life compressed into dormancy" (Grosz 2011, 32). Life expands itself by rendering prosthetic the material; at the same time, the prosthetic object, taken out of its context in the material, is endowed with new qualities and capacities so that, as "the living transform nonliving objects, ... these objects in turn transform the parameters and possibilities of life" (Grosz 2005, 151). This ambiguity between mind and matter, time and space, "challenges ... the individualistic and mechanistic conception of the nature of embodiment" (Barad 2007, 155), rendering the construction of bodily boundaries inherently ambiguous. This ambiguity becomes visible when we try to pin down

6. Age as Becoming

the difference between the twelve pairs of "literal" prosthetic legs that Aimee Mullins owns, each fashioned to give her different capabilities, height, or "superpowers" as she calls them, and the not-so-literal (to those of us habituated to making binary distinctions between organic and inorganic) but equally prosthetic device of Alvin's mower-trailer.[7] The porosity or leakiness or ambiguity between the two sides of a supposedly self-evident binary distinction is what Deleuze wishes to make visible when he asks us to view movies from a perspective that nudges us to problematize the boundary between representation and reality. He wants us to question the distinction between life and non-life, to ask whether the material world is prosthesis for the living, whether we are merely prosthetic augmentations of the material world — its way of expressing itself and becoming — or whether we and the objects we relegate to the material world can be separated into two different categories at all (Grosz 2005).

When Alvin's mower loses its brakes on a steep hill and he narrowly avoids a devastating crash, finally coming to rest near a field where a family is watching firemen practicing their craft, the nature of the entanglement of Alvin and his rig becomes startlingly clear. In a melding of man and machine no less separable at that moment and in that place than a pacemaker or knee implant is separable from its "owner," our human position as part "of the world-body space in its dynamic structuration" (Barad 2007, 185) is difficult to deny. And when Alvin shares memories of his experiences in World War II with another old man he has met after the near disaster, it also becomes clear that he is not just reliving his past so much as synthesizing a part of his past in which death was a constant companion with the present experience of near death in order to learn, "to be better equipped to face the probabilities of future experience" (Parisi and Goodman 2011, 172–3). The unfolding of the past into present experience in order to "unravel a new future" (174) can also be seen in Alvin's conversation with a scared and pregnant teenager when he indirectly urges her to return home by telling her the story about teaching his child to recognize the strength of family ties by comparing them to the strength of a bundle of sticks, or in the oblique comments he makes to the bickering Olsen twins who repair his mower about the irreplaceability of a brother.

The intertwining of life and matter in man and machine, and the time-scrambling of past, present, and future that complicates any concept of linear, chronological time is also well illustrated in the film *The World's Fastest Indian* (2006). Based on another true story, that of Burt Munro, a 60-something New Zealander who was obsessed with coaxing unprece-

The Becoming of Age

dented speed out of his 1920 Indian motorcycle, this movie tells the story of Burt's unlikely trip to Bonneville Salt Flats where he intends to compete in the time trials for streamlined motorcycles under 1000cc. Like Alvin, Burt is presented as an older man with medical problems such as angina that, according to his doctor's medicalized view, should end his motorcycling adventures for good. Also like Alvin, who had to account for every cent of his Social Security check to travel to Zion, Burt is a man for whom traveling so far is only made possible by working as a cook on the ship to America. Yet, in defiance of the age-related advice and expectations of many, Burt, like Alvin, makes a trip that is full of a series of unlikely relationships with interesting characters who both transform him and help him grow and, in turn, are transformed by his forthright optimism and belief in the necessity of following one's dreams at any age.

After a rough reception at Bonneville Speed Flats, where both his condition and that of his motorcycle causes their initial dismissal as being "too old" and too decrepit to compete, Burt wins them over with his determination, sincerity, and intimate connection to and knowledge about his motorcycle, and ends up breaking the speed record for his class, a record that still stands today. The scene in which Burt breaks the record, then falls on his side, sliding and spinning on the salt until he silently stops, lends itself particularly well to a Deleuzian perspective on the movie. As he lies motionless on the sand, his leg burned by the heat from the engine, his goggles blown off in an attempt to stabilize the wobbling motion he encountered, and his old woolen shirt and Snoopy-like helmet all that separate him from the rough ground, we, as viewers enmeshed in the narrative of decline, may find ourselves preparing for news of his demise. Instead, he opens his eyes, laughingly yells, "I did it!" and ends up returning nine more times to Bonneville!

Like that of Alvin, Burt's determination to construct his own life by bringing the virtual (his desires and dreams) into the actual (his present condition as an older, low-income man in a culture where old age is devalued) in order to transform his future, and his ability to use the material world prosthetically in the sense that he and his beloved Indian become one, is both inspiring and unsettling. Inspiring in that it may well encourage viewers to resist the stifling depiction of old age as irredeemable loss, and unsettling in that it may cause us to question the fundamental bases, both philosophical and scientific, on which our construction of time and space, and thus of age itself, rests. Like the swirling mist of *Strangers in Good Company* and the silent star-filled skies and wind-swept fields of

6. Age as Becoming

The Straight Story, the comment made by one of his new friends at Bonneville as Burt races toward the record in the mute presence of the ancient salt flats, "He's gone back, back to whatever planet he came from cause he sure as hell ain't from this one!" points us toward an otherworldliness that suggests there's much more to old age than meets the eye.

The Indeterminacy of Age

This sense of otherworldliness is made explicit in *Howl's Moving Castle* (2004), an animated film based on the 1986 British novel of the same name by Diana Wynne Jones that critiques dominant narratives of age by exploring the powers and the pleasures of women's aging. Like *Strangers in Good Company*, *Howl's Moving Castle* sets a magical tone by opening with shots of a thick, soupy fog; but unlike the mist in *Strangers in Good Company*, which dissipates to disclose a world that looks just like "ours," this fog gradually clears to reveal a fantastical building walking on what look like chicken legs up a mountainside dotted with quietly grazing sheep. And, like *Strangers in Good Company*, *Howl's Moving Castle* draws us into a world inhabited by certain kinds of magic; but unlike *Strangers in Good Company*, in which much of the magic consists of internal alterations of the perception of the nature of time and its relation to possibilities in space, *Howl's Moving Castle* immerses us in a magical world in which alterations in time and space are literally animated or made to come to life, defying and challenging us to find in their wild fluctuations any meaning that might relate back to our "reality."

The tale begins as Sophie, the eldest and plainest of three daughters, leaves her drab job as a milliner to venture outside and is saved from the unwanted attentions of some obnoxious soldiers by the mysterious wizard Howl. Upon returning to the hat shop, the Witch of the Waste, who fancies Howl for herself, sees Sophie as a rival for his affections and turns Sophie into an old woman with a spell about which Sophie is forbidden to speak. Leaving her home, job, and family in shame and confusion, Sophie flees to the Waste where she takes refuge in Howl's castle. While there, she acts as a housekeeper for Howl, befriending Calcifer, the falling star who is indebted to Howl for saving his life and powers the castle in return with his magical fire, Merkl, Howl's young apprentice and helper, and Turniphead, the scarecrow who seems to have taken a fancy to Sophie and slavishly follows her around. Making a bargain with Calcifer in which he promises to undo her enchantment if she frees him from his compact with

Howl, Sophie cares for and defends Howl, the castle, and its inhabitants through wars and plots and betrayals, the disenchantment of the Witch of the Waste, and the near destruction of the castle, until she is able to return Howl's heart to him, break the spells on Calcifer and Turniphead, and happily fly away in a newly constructed castle with Howl and their new "family."

Although the story draws on many fairy-tale conventions, such as enchantments, stolen hearts, princes, witches, wizards, demons, and happy endings, it differs from the usual plot in that the heroine undertakes her adventures as an old woman or crone. Although the American Heritage Dictionary defines crone as "a withered, witchlike old woman" and shows the word to be etymylogically derived from terms meaning a dead body or carrion, someone who would definitely be othered and probably dispatched with in a typical fairy tale, in the context of the movie, crone takes on the more positive meaning that Ursula LeGuin attributed to it in "The Space Crone." In LeGuin's story, the last years of a woman's life are celebrated as endowing her with strength and wisdom and a position from which she is no longer afraid to critique society and to offer her vision of a better world. Due to this different embodiment of crone, *Howl's Moving Castle* also diverges from fairy tale conventions in that the heroine's route toward the happy ending is enmeshed in a critique of the modern world — its destructive and irrational wars, its callous attitude toward the natural environment, and, of course, its ageism — that evolves from a radically distinct way of seeing the world (Scott 2005). That this critique never makes room for any simple integration of the conflicting states, feelings, and emotions Sophie experiences, something most fairy tales explicitly attempt to accomplish, also differentiates it from the conventional story.

Therefore, despite the fact that, after her enchantment, Sophie exhibits many of the conventional physical markers of age — a bent back, shapeless body, big nose, gray hair, wrinkled hands, and a hoarse, creaky voice — rather than succumb to despair, ironically, she recognizes that her transformation into an old woman better reflects the reality of her narrow and colorless existence in the hat shop. As Aagje Swinnen argues in her analyses of the relationship of the novel to the movie, though young in years, Sophie realizes that she has been an "old maid" and "old at heart" (Swinnen 2009a, 171) for some time. So, after an initial fright when she first looks in the mirror, she accepts her condition, concluding that she still is "in pretty good shape," a bit stiff but not weak, and sets out to leave the city saying that no one's "getting the best of this old lady" yet.

6. Age as Becoming

By not connecting the markers of old age to frailty and ill health, this story allows Sophie to leave a society that has no room for the "unproductive" elderly and challenges the narrative of aging that denies moral and creative powers to those who are older. It sets Sophie free, enabling her "to make conscious choices" and achieve "permanent personal growth" (Swinnen 2009a, 172). Like Carl and Grace and Chris, the women stranded in the Canadian wilderness, May and Hal, and Alvin and Burt, Sophie utilizes the disparaging characterizations of the old that can leave them excluded and all but invisible to transform the way she herself perceives old age and its infirmities from a kind of chronological and biological truth into an opportunity for the practice of freedom as becoming.

Because the world in which Sophie experiences her freedom is unlike ours in that, within it, both beings and objects, life and unlife, can quickly shapeshift and transform themselves in ways that reflect their inward states in their outward appearance, such as when Howl becomes a winged bird of prey or his castle bulges up with power or breaks down in defeat, Sophie's age is similarly subject to sudden shifts. Rather than picture her enchantment as answering to the typical fantastical "metamorphosis of young into old and back again," her "age is visualized as a sliding scale, continuously varying and free from a simple narrative logic" (Swinnen 2009a, 179). Her outward appearance, therefore, reflects her inner experience of the non-linearity of subjective time, causing time to appear variable, multiple, and ultimately unpredictable. When Howl sees her as a young woman while she sleeps or when she momentarily reverts to a younger visage after crash landing her airship into the castle while escaping from the war, the changeability of her appearance points unequivocally to the constructed nature of time.

Time and Space in Chronotypes

Howls' Moving Castle, thus, takes us on a voyage away from the modern world's philosophical and scientific stance on time as an a priori on which the "increasingly exact mechanisms of temporal coordination" rest (Bender and Wellbery 1991, 2), and treats time as an indeterminate construction based on the exigencies of a particular narrative. That time could be a narrative construction was addressed by M. M. Bakhtin in the 1937 essay, "Forms of Time and of the Chronotope in the Novel." In this essay, Bakhtin coined the term chronotope, a combination of chronos or time and topos or space, to describe the models or patterns, such as our own construction of time as an orderly succession of equivalent units, through which time assumes practical or conceptual significance. Referring to chronotopes as mental constructions in which plot and characters merge time and space into an inseparable unity that reflects a world view, Bakhtin argued that these patterns always mirror particular historical, biographical, and social time-space configurations. Since chronotopes are, therefore, an ideological concept, their use both determines and reflects the image of man in culture and in the narratives that culture constructs to explain, justify, and maintain its existence (Bakhtin 1981).

In *Chronotypes*, a variation on Bakhtin's chronotope that expands its use beyond narrative theory to encompass the nonlinearity of time and the dynamism of place (matter), John Bender and David Wellbery argue that, since the late eighteenth century, the defining quality of the world has become a "*temporalization* of experience — [the] notion of time as the framework within which life forms are embedded and carry on their existence" (Bender and Wellbery 1991, 1). Seen as the scaffolding on which everything from geological history to the contemporary life course is constructed, time has become a productive medium that generates experience rather than a locational marker, a theory of time that suppresses inner time and subordinates other meanings of time in favor of a Newtonian view of time as absolute, true, mathematical, and without relation to anything external (Bender and Wellbery 1991). But as the Newtonian grid becomes increasingly destabilized by emerging scientific and philosophical theories that emphasize relativity and interrelatedness, the notion of narrative as a linear and predictable organizing principle also becomes problematic as "we confront a future inhabited by multiple times" (4).

Once we entertain the notion that time is not a universal given but is fabricated in an ongoing process of temporal, intra-actional, historical, improvisational, and culturally relevant chronotypes, then it is easy to understand how time is never a neutral medium external to social and cultural relations, but an integral part of the meanings, discourses, and narratives that structure our lives. Time, therefore, can be an object of contention. The relational theory of time addresses this situation by defining the temporal order as "constituted by means of ... relations between the events and processes to be so ordered" (Van Fraassen 1991, 24) as interpreted by those within the web of power with the influence to propagate and enforce the hegemonic discourses by which a society and worldview is categorized and regulated. Positing that the construction of time in the real world is not essentially different from the constitution of time in the

6. Age as Becoming

narrated world, the relational theory of time problematizes theories of causality as inherently conjectural and ambiguous, and asserts that the imaginary reality proposed by a text is no less determinate than what we call the real world.[8] The view of both fiction and reality as equally indeterminate does not negate personal experience — whether "I can ... touch *this* flesh, *these* stones, *this* wood" (37) — but it does preclude belief in a necessity in how things must be. It states that there is neither a definitive text, a definitive reality, nor a definitive meaning for either, since text, reality, and meaning are continually created anew in each intra-action with the world and its creatures.

Returning to Deleuze and his conception of the real as "dynamic, temporally sensitive forms of becoming" (Grosz 2011, 41) that intertwine what we might call representations and real life in one reality, we can see that, for Deleuze, the real is neither an empiricist reduction of the world to what is observable nor an idealist understanding of the world as coinciding with our representation of it. For him, the real is becoming as the expression of difference within a thing, being, or quality that actualizes the virtual in duration, a becoming that cinema can instigate or inspire by the way it rearranges and manipulates time and space to create a different reality. If chronotypes are spatiotemporal structures where stories take place, then cinematic chronotypes can make real the non-linear nature of time through temporal displacements of elements of a life or a society, and spatial displacements of objects and matter to a nowhere place outside conventional time and space (Smethurst 2000).

This is precisely what happens in *Howl's Moving Castle*. Both the places (matter) and the beings within it (life) visually exemplify the dynamism of time and space by speeding up, reversing, and otherwise playing with the becoming and unbecoming of the world in a way that emphasizes its unpredictable mutability. This dynamism calls into question the scientific laws that govern Western reality, including the construction of the Western life course, and bring to the fore the possibility that the nature of physical reality may exceed its everyday perception in fantastic ways. The five minutes of invisibility that Sophie and her airship are given in order to escape the demons who are chasing her makes us think differently about the discovery that an object coated with metamaterials, a substance that has a negative index of refraction, can bend certain wavelengths of light around it rather than bounce them back to our eyes, constructing a cloak of invisibility around that object (Kahalios 2011). And the changing location of the castle, which depends on where a dial by a particular door is set, a feature that often corresponds to the unknowable evil intentions of distant demons, or the ability of the castle to be in two places at once makes the existence of instantaneous communication between distant objects in the quantum world and the ability of some quantum particles to be in two places at the same instant (Al Khalili 2004) less unbelievable. These examples problematize the accepted "fact" that the laws that operate in the arcane world of theoretical science are simply irrelevant to the quotidian (Kirby 2011), making us aware that science, and the limits it sets on what both objects and beings can become, is an ongoing enterprise.

The dynamism of time and space embodied in the chronotypes that characterize this movie also unsettle the social and cultural constructions of time that underlie the Western life course and that are used to justify its negative attitudes toward old age. This dynamism enables the appearance of bodies to change, not only in response to the casting of spells or, in the case of the witch and the scarecrow, to the breaking of enchantments, but in concert with momentary emotional states, such as in the scene where Howl begins to melt when his changing hair color makes him feel too ugly to live. This dynamism also highlights the performative nature of choice, as when Markl disguises himself as an elderly wizard in order to sell spells, and the variability of the meanings attached to age, as witnessed by our diverse reactions of approval, disbelief, or criticism to the endurance exhibited by Sophie when cleaning and repairing the castle, or the strength she has when racing the witch up the stairs of the palace, or the intelligence she draws on to escape from the sorceress Suliman. By showing age to be both a fluctuating experience and a chosen performance, an action and a reaction to the environment and the others within it, and a becoming marked throughout the movie by constant yet almost imperceptible alterations in Sophie's countenance and movements, this story manages to undermine the concept of a biological or chronological basis for old age, to critique its medicalization and gerontologization, to deconstruct the binary opposition of young/old that so limits the possibilities of thinking, living, and becoming into old age, and to distance its lived experience from the physical laws that claim to govern it.

By the time the spell on Sophie is finally broken, "her thirst for action" (Swinnen 2009a, 180) and the continual disruption of our age-related expectations have made us forget about her age. Both she and we have detached the trajectory of her life from its categorical expectations and attached the story's happy ending to the possibility that age doesn't matter — that youth and age may exist contemporaneously in all of us. As she and Howl kiss, though her face and body have become youthful again, she retains her gray hair, a pleasant suggestion to Howl of starlight, a sharp rebuke to all of us who still harbor irrational fears about the physical markers of growing older, and a necessary reminder to everyone of the way that past and present, mind and matter, time and space, cinematic representations and "reality" intertwine to create the becoming that is life.

Conclusion

Films that present life as becoming implicitly ally themselves with emerging critical theories of aging that seek emancipation from "normative assumptions about aging, particularly as they are imposed by various agents of social control" (Graham and Stephenson 2010, 177). The stories these movies tell and the characters they create, therefore, present a challenge to the myriad ways contemporary ageism works. They make us think about ageism as not only oppression — the systemic, often unintentional, constraints imposed on a category of people by institutional, bureaucratic, and collective assumptions and reactions to them resulting in their inability to develop and express themselves fully — and domination — the institutional conditions that inhibit a category of people from determining their actions or the conditions of their actions— but as interference with the differential becoming of the world itself (Young 1990 and Barad 2007).

These movies let us see how older people exceed the limitations imposed on them by their categorical affiliation, and even their own internalized ageism, in order to remain an integral part of the becoming of the world — how life exceeds the model (Kirby 2011). In *Strangers in Good Company*, the women call on a lifetime of virtualities in order to improvise and survive in the actual present and, in the process, give both themselves and the audience an opportunity to see time as a creative force that inspires becoming rather than the ominous ticking of a universal mechanical clock. In *The Straight Story* and *The World's Fastest Indian*, Alvin and Burt expand the possibilities of their physically "diminished" lives by showing how becoming is not just a capacity of the human, but involves a reciprocal relationship with matter that results in a mutual transformation. In *Howl's Moving Castle*, the manner in which Sophie responds to her enchantment and her unpredictable world, makes clear that the chronotype or time/space configuration that underlies any narrative is itself temporal and subject to change.

Other movies that feature older people who refuse to live by the rules of the chronotype of universal temporalization, such as *Young @ Heart* (2008), a documentary based on the experiences of a chorus composed of mostly octogenarian singers, also shows how life exceeds the model. When these older people choose to challenge themselves to become rock and punk performers despite the existence of infirmities or the intrusion of death, they not only reinsert themselves into the stream of becoming that is life, but break down many of the generational barriers that worked to exclude them in the first place. And the classic *Harold and Maude* (1971), a movie in which 79-year-old- Maude teaches the self-imprisoned, unhappy, and depressed, young man Harold to see life as the freedom to become by defying life course-related expectations (at least until her eightieth birthday when she, too succumbs to the effects of the narrative of decline), is also a testament to the idea that "life overcomes itself through the activities it performs on objects and itself" (Grosz 2011, 53).

Looking at these films closely, we may find that the traits we admire most in their characters, what draws us to them, are there not in spite of their age but because of it, that their lives and relationships are "richer and more meaningful for the trials and tribulations [they] have gone through to maintain them" (Graham and Stephenson 2010, 178). We might conclude that the wisdom and experience afforded them by the continual self-overcoming that time and space demand has the potential to make them not only determined and resourceful, but caring, compassionate, and kind, good listeners with time for unhurried reflection who will often act in the common interests of their community (Graham and Stephenson 2010). For example, the sense of community that the women create in *Strangers in Good Company* is marked by kindness and respect, by time for really listening to each other's stories despite the exigencies of survival, and by a concern for the well-being of the whole that overrides mere self interest. And the atmosphere of kindness and compassion that characterizes both *The Straight Story* and *The World's Fastest Indian* is brought about in part by the non-judgmental acceptance of difference we see in the discrepancy between Alvin's estimation of Rose's ability to care for herself and others and that of the state, and by the considerate way that Burt treats Tina both before and after becoming aware of her sexual orientation. Again, the

6. Age as Becoming

thoughtful manner in which Sophie cares for the "helpless" Witch of the Waste after she has lost her powers manages to impart a sense of family to a story that, without the wisdom that Sophie derived from being an old woman herself, might have been marked by selfishness and revenge. Although these traits are certainly not universally present in the old any more than is the rampant self-interest that supports the stereotype of the elderly as "greedy geezers," the potential to see the world as an entangled process of becoming rather than as a series of individualized and disconnected endeavors certainly increases with the experience of repeated self-overcoming that accompanies age.

Finally, these films may also help us answer the question posed at the beginning of this chapter and in chapter one that asks, to what extent does the way we measure age contribute to its constitution? Taking a cue from the quantum phenomenon of decoherence, which posits that when a quantum system such as a single atom, existing in a superposition, or being in two or more places or states at the same time, is "caught" and separated from its entanglement with the world by a macroscopic object through an act of measurement (what Barad calls a cut), it decoheres, meaning its wavefunction collapses and it becomes a distinct particle in a particular location (Al Khalili 2004), we might think of becoming in somewhat the same way. Although this is certainly not an accurate analogy, nevertheless if life can be seen as somewhat like a superposition in that it is neither linear nor fixed but full of possibilities, then decoherence suggests that finding ourselves older and "caught" in a culture in which old age is persistently and deliberately measured, described, and devalued can, in some sense, cut us off from the continuum of life, eroding our ability to engage with what Barad calls "spacetimematter" in a way that disables our continuing becoming and that can even hasten death, as Becca Levy found in her study on the effects of exposure to ageist images (see chapter one). Yet, just as a wavefunction that has collapsed into a determinate particle does not cease to be a part of the "mattering" of the world, in another sense, death may be simply another step in the process of becoming and unbecoming that *is* our entanglement in the world, what Noe calls our dynamic expansion and extension into the world that always has made it difficult to tell where we stop and where the rest of the world begins (Noe 2009a). Maybe we could begin to see life and death as differential aspects of becoming that inhere in the ability of nonliving matter to express its virtualities through transformation by the living, and in the ability of life to actualize its virtualities through using nonliving materiality to undo what it was and become other (Grosz 2011). And just possibly, as Deleuze believed, the utopian force of cinema to call forth a new and different reality can truly change the way we measure, construct, react to, and live our lives, making us forget about age in the becoming that is life.

Chapter Notes

Chapter 1

1. Dr. Becca Levy, a professor at the Yale School of Public Health, studies how images of aging in the media and elsewhere influence older people's perceptions of their own reality. In a 2002 study of attitudes about aging, she found that those who viewed aging as a positive experience lived an average of 7.5 years longer than those who viewed aging in a negative way. The positive image had a greater impact on longevity than not smoking or maintaining a healthy weight.

2. Cumulative advantage/disadvantage theory links the processes of individual and cohort aging by showing that there is a systemic tendency for interindividual divergence in areas such as money, health, or status over time. Since CAD is not a property of individuals but of collectivities for which an identifiable set of members exists, it brings into focus questions concerning the extent to which age-related differences and variability result from systemic processes rather than from individual choices.

3. Jim Al-Khalili explains quantum nonlocality and entanglement and discusses some of the philosophical implications of these ideas more thoroughly in Chapters 4 and 6 of his book, *Quantum*.

4. The Activities of Daily Living is a standardized framework used to make measurable the physical abilities considered necessary to maintain an independent life. Yet, as Stephen Katz elaborates in Chapter 7 of *Cultural Aging*, its influence "reaches beyond individual assessment to encompass housing, finances, and service provisions" and "connects the worlds of elderly people to the largesse of expertise" (Katz 2005, 129) in order to organize and manage the everyday life of the old.

Chapter 2

1. Erik Erikson first published his eight-stage theory of human development in his 1950 book, *Childhood and Society*. He and his wife, Joan, expanded and revised this psychosocial-crisis theory in later books and it is still regarded as a powerful tool for understanding personal development today.

2. Biopower is a term used by Michel Foucault to refer to disciplinary and regulatory technologies used by modern states to control and optimize the life of both individual bodies and entire populations.

3. Translated as *The Coming of Age*, *La Vieillesse* (1970), written by Simone de Beauvoir at the age of 62, is a report on the predicament of the old in the modern world. Indicting society's cruelty and indifference to the aged, Beauvoir's work is a passionate attempt to illuminate the existential core of the condition of the aged.

4. Strategic essentialism is a term

coined by the Indian theorist Gayatri Chakravorty Spivak. It refers to a strategy that marginalized groups can use to present themselves as temporarily essentialized, despite the existence of significant differences, in order to make political demands that will improve their position in society.

5. Generativity, a term used in Erik Erikson's seventh stage called Generativity v. Stagnation, is concerned with the extent to which adults act to further the best interests of their own children and coming generations. An ideal of giving to future generations, generativity reflects Erikson's basic humanitarian philosophy.

6. In *The Constitution of Society* (1984), Anthony Giddens proposed a three-tiered theory of subjectivity to account for manifestations of group oppression. The first tier, discursive consciousness, refers to aspects of action and situation that are explicit and easily verbalizable, including beliefs about the relative value of other social groups. The second, practical consciousness, refers to aspects of action and situation that are on the fringe of consciousness, have become habitual, and can influence our opinions of and actions towards others in a way that often contradicts those beliefs we adhere to in discursive consciousness. The third, a basic security system, refers to the security and sense of autonomy required for coherent social action.

Chapter 3

1. According to Rina Rosselon in her blog on representations of older women in feature films, any female over 35, the maximum age of women in leading roles, is considered an older woman.

2. Social feminists, such as Jane Addams, believed that women must enter the public sphere because it was in need of their humane perspective. They also argued that women's distinctive interests and altruistic moral bent must be reflected in government decisions. Social feminism is classified as a part of cultural feminism.

3. In *Feminist Economics Today*, Marianne Ferber and Julie Nelson link the social construction of gender to the social construction of the discipline of economics. They argue that classical economics with its masculine assumptions of separate selves and self-interest ignores human dependence, mutuality, and altruism. They posit that an economics based on the provisioning of human life rather than on rational choice and markets could erase the masculine bias of the discipline.

4. In chapter two of *Jacques Lacan: A Feminist Introduction*, Elizabeth Grosz traces the development of the idea of the split subject through both Freud and Lacan's theories about the structure of the ego, and discusses the way in which these ideas problematize the Western universal subject.

5. Sex therapist and teacher, Gina Ogden's Integrating Sexuality and Spirituality Survey (ISIS), in which she interviewed 3,810 respondents, ages 18–86, over 10 years, actually finds that sexual satisfaction increases with age. She reports that women over fifty experience more sharing, laughter, and less angst in sexual relationships than younger women, a finding that challenges both medical and pharmaceutical biases.

6. Louise Nevelson was an American sculptor who, in a series of autobiographical reflections conducted while she was in her mid 70's and still creating, insisted that a woman derives her sense of self from both her social context and the way she styles herself. Whether an older woman sees herself as a little old lady or as a still powerful woman, then, depends on how she creates both her work and

Notes—Chapter 4

her self, for they are reflections of each other.

7. For a more thorough discussion of the merits of and problems associated with neoliberalism's agenda to privatize collective social policy, see *The New Politics of Old Age Policy* edited by Robert B. Hudson, and "The Government of Detail: The Case of Social Policy on Aging" by Stephen Katz and Bryan Green in *Cultural Aging*.

8. As of a few years ago, sales of the WI calendar had raised over $750,000 for the hospital.

9. Brenda Blethyn, born February 20, 1946, worked in an administrative career until she enrolled in acting school in her early 30's. She acts in theater, TV, and film, and has received Academy Award, SAG, Emmy, and Golden Globe nominations and awards. Helen Mirren, born July 7, 1945, has been a stage and screen actress since 1965. Now Dame Helen Mirren, she has won Golden Globe and Academy Awards among others, has been nominated for an Oscar, and has hosted Saturday Night Live.

10. At Stanford University in 1971, Philip Zimbardo created a simulated prison in which he paid some student volunteers to play guards and others to be prisoners. He had to end the experiment when some of the young men playing guards became sadistic and violent, endangering those playing prisoners. The results of his experiment, that people tend to conform even when that means doing terrible things, are still used to explain unexpected and cruel behavior today.

Chapter 4

1. Although no documentary can fully represent the views of all older women on sex, love, and romance, especially since only those willing to talk openly about their feelings and experiences will be seen and heard, nevertheless, I believe that these women's comments on how ageist beliefs and practices have affected both their ideas about themselves and their treatment by others provide an important template with which to evaluate the ways that cinema portrays aging and older characters and their stories.

2. In their article in *Age Matters*, "From Androgyny to Androgens," Barbara Marshall and Stephen Katz chart the development of the idea of a male menopause occurring at midlife into the problematical deficiency syndrome, andropause. Partially due to the success of the HRT industry with women, andropause was posited as an age-related clinical disorder that could be treated with testosterone therapy. Despite the fact that the symptoms occurring with this disorder are vague and could be caused by many other conditions, that testosterone levels vary greatly among healthy men, and that little research has been done on the effects of drug interaction, diet, stress, or illness on testosterone levels, the idea of a pharmaceutical fix that would correct the perceived hormonal imbalance caused by aging persists.

3. In 2006, screenwriter, director, and author Nora Ephron published a book of essays entitled *I Feel Bad About My Neck: And Other Thoughts on Being a Woman* that looked at aging in a humorous-girlfriend-confidant manner. In her essay about the neck, rather than contest the way an aging woman's changing physical appearance is interpreted as decline, she advised women to cover their necks by age 43 because, although their faces may be a lie, the appearance of their necks always tells the truth about their age.

4. In 2002, a Women's Health Initiative study of estrogen/progestin replacement therapy had to be cancelled because of the risks it posed to women of devel-

oping cancers and heart disease. Later studies found that such therapy also increased the risk of developing dementias and breast cancer. Yet, despite the presence of an FDA warning in ads for estrogen, the pharmaceutical industry continues to promote new hormonal creams and gels as if they had been thoroughly tested and were safe.

5. In the Introduction to *Gay and Lesbian Aging: Research and Future Directions*, the section entitled "Milestones of Gay and Lesbian Community Empowerment" provides a brief, yet cogent, description of the gay and lesbian social movement in the United States that stresses the importance of historical context to the expectations and beliefs of different cohorts.

6. A more thorough discussion of the implications of the study of spatial gerontology for understanding where people retire and how they create cultural spaces for retirement can be found in chapter 11, "Spaces of Age, Snowbirds, and the Gerontology of Mobility," in *Cultural Aging* by Stephen Katz.

Chapter 5

1. In this chapter, when I refer to Alzheimer's disease, I am talking about late-onset Alzheimer's that accounts for some 98 percent of the cases and generally occurs after age 60, rather than the relatively rare early-onset familial genetic type that occurs between ages 35 and 60.

2. From this point on in this chapter, I am using the medical terms *dementia* and *Alzheimer's disease* interchangeably.

3. In *Picturing Personhood*, pages 142–147, "Towards a Semiotics of Popular Brain Images," Dumit explains how PET images can often overturn the authority of the text they were meant to elaborate. The structural reversal of the relationship of image to text can "catch" people whose disease states or conditions are represented by these images in a particular form of identification within a simplified reality, obviating the need to consider qualifying information presented in the text and often leading to discrimination based on the authority of the image alone.

4. There are several kinds of superior memory, such as hyperthymesia, or the ability to remember autobiographical details, and eidetic or photographic memory, or the ability to recall images, sounds, and objects with precision. There are also accomplished mnemonists who use mnemonic techniques to remember lengthy lists of random information, and autistic savants who may possess an extraordinary memory in a particular area. Many of those possessing superior memory describe it as a burden as much as a gift and say that it can cause problems in daily life.

5. In chapter 10 of *Forget Memory*, Anne Davis Basting writes about the healing effects of "To Whom I May Concern," both a play and a technique for creating and presenting a theatrical performance using as actors those with early memory loss and employing their words as dialogue.

6. Derrida argues that logocentrism was an attempt to suppress all nonlinear writing, such as phonetic writing, and the mythogram, a writing that spells its symbols pluri-dimensionally, in order to impose a linear concept of time on all history. Linearization, or the relation of final presence to original presence in a straight line, thus disrupted the unity of symbolic thought in areas such as art, religion, and economy, and became "the intrinsic determining concept of all ontology from Aristotle to Hegel" (Derrida 1976, 86). That the line is only one way to think about history is also addressed in *Provincializing Europe: Postcolonial*

Thought and Historical Difference (2000) by Dipesh Chakrabarty.

7. Validation therapy, developed by Naomi Feil, affirms the phenomenological experiences of people with dementia. Caregivers using validation therapy are trained to use empathy and communication to support the emotional reality of the demented by remaining attuned to whatever verbal and embodied expressions of self they may demonstrate, resulting in less stress and happier patients and caregivers.

8. Part three of *Forget Memory* (2009) by Anne Davis Basting describes many of the programs that are helping those with Alzheimer's disease continue to function and to remain a useful part of society.

Chapter 6

1. Deleuze describes the plane of immanence as an unqualified embeddedness in a field without divisions or distinctions. Within it, there are only networks of forces and connections and becomings, relations of movement and rest and speed and slowness. It is a plane of composition and active production where the virtual and the actual intertwine. Since it flattens out all things, it precedes individuation and stratification; there can be no subject or object, no universals, and no transcendence. In *Immanence: A Life*, Deleuze writes that pure immanence is *a life*, and nothing else.

2. In "Social Physics: Inertia, Energy, and Aging," (in *Figuring Age* by Kathleen Woodward, 1999), Teresa Brennan argues that the effects of social pressure to conform appear as physical differences in the way we age. Since life is about change and becoming different, the constant demand to conform to age-related norms can bring us closer to death by impeding our ability to take on fresh ideas and grow. Like Deleuze, Brennan sees the power of images to be real material forces in the way we construct our lives.

3. Alva Noe argues that the idea that the brain is the thing inside of us that makes us conscious is not a new idea exemplified by brain scans but a simple substitution of a physical object, the brain, for the nonphysical stuff inside of us, our essence, that Descartes believed gave us consciousness. According to Noe, consciousness is neither located inside of us nor fundamentally neural, but is a work of improvisational relationships achieved in the processes of living in and with and in response to our environment, including the human and nonhuman others within it.

4. *Strangers in Good Company* not only won critical acclaim, but also won the 1991 Genie Award for best editing. In addition, Alice Diablo and Cissy Meddings were nominated for the 1991 Genie Award for Best Actress, Winifred Holden and Catherine Roche were nominated for the 1991 Genie Award for Best Supporting Actress, and the movie was nominated for the 1991 Genie Award for Best Picture.

5. Although Zion is the actual name of Alvin's destination, it also carries utopian connotations of both peace of mind and harmonious relations in one's present life that could refer to his desired reconciliation with his brother, and of a safe, spiritual homeland in heaven that could partially explain his insistence on the necessity of such a reunion now.

6. In chapter 2 of *Quantum: A Guide for the Perplexed*, Jim Al Khalili explains how a physical body is not only a localized object, as we perceive it in everyday experience, but a wave at the same time. Since the matter waves associated with various objects become smaller the larger the object in question, the wavelength of most of the objects we encounter in everyday life would be trillions of times

smaller than atomic dimensions. So, although they exist, these waves are too tiny to be easily detected since they are at a scale where, for now, the idea of space almost loses meaning.

7. In *Meeting the Universe Halfway*, Karen Barad illustrates challenges to the presumed givenness of bodily boundaries by citing an example Niels Bohr used to address the question of complementarity. According to Bohr, a person in a dark room can grasp a stick firmly and use it to find his way around the room, treating the stick as an extension of his body, or he can hold the stick in a way that allows him to assess its features, making the stick into an object for him to observe. Thus, the differentiation between stick and body is not self-evident but, once it is made, it cannot be other for that specific practice.

8. In the first chapter of *Chronotypes*, Bastiaan Van Fraassen argues that, as there is neither a privileged reader of a text since each new reader may discover a meaning or structure unnoticed by previous readers, nor a privileged observer of reality since each new observer may discern a fresh structure, order, or perspective, the fact that something is obscured from sight, does not make it unreal. This fact simply confirms the ultimate indeterminacy and inseparability of both text and reality, the fictional and the real world.

Bibliography

Achenbaum, W. Andrew. 2010. "Gene D. Cohen, MD, PhD: Creative Gero-Psychiatrist and Visionary Public Intellectual." *Journal of Aging, Humanities, and the Arts* 4, no. 4 (October-December): 238–250.
Agamben, Giorgio. 1998. *HomoSacer: Sovereign Power and Bare Life.* Translated by Daniel Heller Rozen. Stanford: Stanford University Press.
Alcoff, Linda. 1997. "Cultural Feminism versus Post Structuralism." In *The Second Wave.* Edited by Linda Nicholson. New York: Routledge.
Al-Khalili, Jim. 2004. *Quantum: A Guide for the Perplexed.* London: Weidenfeld and Nicolson.
Bakhtin, Mikhail. 1982. *The Dialogic Imagination.* Austin: University of Texas Press.
Ballenger, Jesse F. 2006. "The Biomedical Deconstruction of Senility and the Persistent Stigmatization of Old Age in the United States." In *Thinking About Dementia.* Edited by Annette Leibing and Lawrence Cohen. New Jersey: Rutgers University Press.
Barad, Karen. 2007. *Meeting the Universe Halfway.* Durham: Duke University Press.
Barber, Stephen M. 2004. "Exit Woolf." In *Feminism and the Final Foucault.* Edited by Dianna Taylor and Karen Vintges. Chicago: University of Illinois Press.
Barker, Ernest, translator. 1958. *The Politics of Aristotle.* New York: Oxford University Press.
Bartalos, Michael K., ed. 2009. *Speaking of Death: America's New Sense of Mortality.* Westport: Praeger.
Basting, Anne Davis. 2009. *Forget Memory: Creating Better Lives for People with Dementia.* Baltimore: Johns Hopkins University Press.
Beauvoir, Simone de. 1984. *Adieux: A Farewell to Sartre.* Translated by Patrick O'Brian. New York: Pantheon.
Bender, John and David E. Wellbery. 1991. Introduction to *Chronotypes: The Construction of Time*, edited by John Bender and David E. Wellbery. Stanford: Stanford University Press.
Bettelheim, Bruno. 1989. "Transformations: The Fantasy of the Wicked Stepmother." In *Folk Groups and Folklore Genres: A Reader.* Edited by Elliott Oring. Logan: Utah State University Press.
Binstock, Robert H. 2005. "The Contemporary Politics of Old Age Policies." In *The New Politics of Old Age Policy.* Edited by Robert B. Hudson. Baltimore: Johns Hopkins University Press.
Bliezner, Rosemary. 2007. Challenges and Resilience Among Later-Life Couples. *Generations* 31, no. 3: 6–9.

Bibliography

Bordo, Susan. 2004. "The Body and the Reproduction of Femininity." In *The Gendered Society Reader*. Edited by Michael S. Kimmel. New York: Oxford University Press.
Brennan, Teresa. 1999. "Social Physics: Inertia, Energy, and Aging." In *Figuring Age*. Edited by Kathleen M. Woodward. Indianapolis: Indiana University Press.
Brooks, David. 2010. "The Geezer's Crusade." *The New York Times*, 2 February.
Butler, Judith. 1993. *Bodies That Matter*. New York: Routledge.
_____. 1995. "Melancholy Gender/Refused Identification." In *Constructing Masculinity*. Edited by Maurice Berger, et al. New York: Routledge.
_____. 1997. *Excitable Speech*. New York: Routledge.
_____. 1999. *Gender Trouble*. New York: Routledge.
_____. 2003. "Performative Acts and Gender Constitution." In *The Feminist Theory Reader*. Edited by Carole R. McCann and Seung-Kyung Kim. New York: Routledge.
_____. 2006. *Precarious Life*. New York: Verso.
Butler, Robert. 1975. *Why Survive? Being Old in America*. New York: Harper and Row.
Bytheway, Bill. 1995. *Ageism*. Bristol: Open University Press.
_____. 2005. "Ageism and Age Categorization." *Journal of Social Issues* 61, no. 2: 361–374.
Calasanti, Toni M., and K. Jill Kiecolt. 2007. "Diversity Among Late-Life Couples." *Generations* 31, no. 3: 10–17.
Calasanti, Toni M., and Kathleen F. Slevin, eds. 2006. *Age Matters: Realigning Feminist Thinking*. New York: Routledge.
Carson, Diane. 1994. "To Be Seen but Not Heard." In *Multiple Voices in Feminist Film Criticism*. Edited by Diane Carson, Linda Dittmar, et al. Minneapolis: University of Minnesota Press.
Chomsky, Noam, and Michel Foucault. 2006. *The Chomsky-Foucault Debate on Human Nature*. New York: New Press.
Clarke, Laura Hurd. 2011. *Facing Age*. Lanham: Rowman and Littlefield Publishers, Inc.
Clough, Patricia, and Craig Willse. 2011. "Human Security/National Security." In *Beyond Biopolitics: Essays on the Governance of Life and Death*. Durham: Duke University Press.
Cohen, Gene. 2005. *The Mature Mind: The Positive Power of the Aging Brain*. New York: Basic Books.
Cohen, Lawrence. 1998. *No Aging In India*. Berkeley: University of California Press.
Cohen-Shalev, Amir. 2012. *Visions of Aging: Images of the Elderly in Film*. Portland, OR: Sussex Academic Press.
Cole, Thomas R. 1993. *The Journey of Life: A Cultural History Of Aging in America*. New York: Cambridge University Press.
Comfort, Alex. 1977. *A Good Age*. London: Mitchell Beazley.
Connids, Ingrid. 2006. "Intimate Relationships: Learning from Later Life Experience." In *Age Matters*. Edited by Toni M. Calasanti and Kathleen F. Slevin. New York: Routledge.
Cruikshank, Margaret. 2003. *Learning to Be Old*. New York: Rowman & Littlefield.
Deleuze, Gilles. 1986. *Cinema I: the Movement-Image*. Translated by Hugh Tomlinson and Barbara Habergen. Minneapolis: University of Minnesota Press.
_____. 1989. *Cinema 2: The Time-Image*. Translated by Hugh Tomlinson and Robert Galeta. London: Althone Press.

Bibliography

Derrida, Jacques. 1976. *Of Grammatology*. Translated by Gayatri Chakravorty Spivak. Baltimore: Johns Hopkins University Press.

———. 1995. *The Gift of Death*. Chicago: The University of Chicago Press.

De Vries, Brian, and John Blando. 2003. "The Study of Gay and Lesbian Aging: Lessons for Social Gerontology." In *Gay and Lesbian Aging: Research and Future Directions*. Edited by Gilbert H. Herdt and B. De Vries. New York: Springer.

Dittmar, Linda. 1994. "The Articulating Self." In *Multiple Voices in Feminist Film Criticism*. Edited by Diane Carson, Linda Dittmar, et al. Minneapolis: University of Minnesota Press.

Docter, Pete. 2009. "An Animated Chat with "Up" Director Pete Docter." Interview by Terry Gross. *National Public Radio*, 29 November.

Dumit, Joseph. 2004. *Picturing Personhood*. Princeton: Princeton University Press.

Erikson, Erik. 1997. *The Life Cycle Completed*. New York: W.W. Norton.

Fiore, Robin N. 1999. "Caring for Ourselves." In *Mother Time*. Edited by Margaret Urban Walker. Lanhan: Rowman and Littlefield.

Foucault, Michel. 1995. *Discipline and Punish*. Translated by Alan Sheridan. New York: Vintage Books.

———. 1997a. *Society Must Be Defended*. Translated by David Macey. New York: Picador.

———. 1997b. "The Masked Philosopher." In *Michel Foucault: Ethics, Subjectivity and Truth*. New York: New Press.

Freuh, Joanna. 1999. "Monster/Beauty." In *Figuring Age*. Edited by Kathleen M. Woodward. Bloomington: Indiana University Press.

Friedan, Betty. 1993. *The Fountain of Age*. New York: Simon and Schuster Paperbacks.

Gatens, Moira. 1996. *Imaginary Bodies: Ethics, Power and Corporeality*. New York: Routledge.

George, Daniel, Susan Williams and Dean Southern. 2011. "Humanizing "Alzheimer's" at the Opera." *Journal of Aging, Humanities, and the Arts* 4, no. 4 (October-December): 340–351.

Gilligan, Carol. 1997. "Woman's Place in Man's Life Cycle." In *The Second Wave*. Edited by Linda Nicholson. New York: Routledge.

Graham, Janice E. 2010. " 'Them' are 'Us': Building Appropriate Policies from Fieldwork to Practice." In *Contesting Aging and Loss*. Edited by Janice Graham and Peter H. Stephenson. Toronto: University of Toronto Press.

———, and Peter H. Stephenson, eds. 2010. *Contesting Aging and Loss*. Toronto: University of Toronto Press.

Grosz, Elizabeth. 1994. "Sexual Difference and the Problem of Essentialism." In *The Essential difference*. Edited by Naomi Schor and Elizabeth Weed. Bloomington: Indiana University Press.

———. 1995a. *Space, Time, and Perversion*. New York: Routledge.

———. 1995b. *Jacques Lacan: A Feminist Introduction*. New York: Routledge.

———. 2005. *Time Travels: Feminism, Nature, Power*. Durham: Duke University Press.

———. 2011. *Becoming Undone: Darwinian Reflections on Life, Politics, and Art*. Durham: Duke University Press.

Gullette, Margaret. 1997. *Declining to Decline: Cultural Combat and the Politics of Midlife*. Charlottesville: University Press of Virginia.

———. 2004. *Aged by Culture*. Chicago: University of Chicago Press.

———. 2009. "Our Best and Longest Running Story." In *Narratives of Life: Mediating*

Bibliography

Age. Edited by Heike Hartung and Roberta Maierhofer. New Brunswick: Transaction Publishers.

_____. 2011. *Agewise: Fighting the New Ageism in America*. Chicago: The University of Chicago Press.

Hacking, Ian. 1999. *The Social Construction of What?* Cambridge: Harvard University Press.

Hall, Stuart. 1985. "Signification, Representation, Ideology: Althusser and the Post-Structuralist Debates." *Critical Studies in Mass Communication* 2, no. 2: 91–114.

Haraway, Donna J. 1991a. "A Cyborg Manifesto." In *Simians, Cyborgs, and Women*. Edited by Donna J. Haraway. New York: Rutgers University Press.

_____. 1991b. "Situated Knowledges." In *Simians, Cyborgs, and Women*. Edited by Donna J. Haraway. New York: Rutgers University Press.

_____. 2008. *When Species Meet*. Minneapolis: University of Minnesota Press.

Harrell, Eben. 2010. "Remains of the Day." In *Time*, 11 October: 44–51.

Herdt, Gilbert, and Brian De Vries. 2003. "Introduction." In *Gay and Lesbian Aging: Research and Future Directions*. New York: Springer.

Hochman, David. 2010. "10 Who Inspire." *AARP The Magazine*, January-February, 32, 62.

Holstein, Martha B. 1999. "Home Care, Women and Aging." In *Mother Time*. Edited by Margaret Urban Walker. Lanham: Rowman & Littlefield.

_____. 2005. "A Normative Defense of Age-Based Public Policy." In *The New Politics of Old Age Policy*. Edited by Robert B. Hudson. Baltimore: Johns Hopkins University Press.

Hudson, Robert B. 2005. "Contemporary Challenges to Age-Based Public Policy." In *The New Politics of Old Age Policy*. Edited by Robert B. Hudson. Baltimore: Johns Hopkins University Press.

Irigaray, Luce. 1993. *The Ethics of Sexual Difference*. Ithaca, NY: Cornell University Press.

Jacoby, Susan. 2011. *Never Say Die*. New York: Pantheon Books.

Kakalios, Jim. 2011. "The Physics of Invisibility." *Future*, 9 March.

Kaplan, Ann. 2012. "The Unconscious of Age: Performances in Psychoanalysis, Film, and Popular Culture." In *Aging, Performance, and Stardom: Doing Age on the Stage of Consumerist Culture*. Edited by Aagje Swinnen and John A. Stotesbury. Zurich: Lit Verlag.

Katz, Stephen. 1996. *Disciplining Old Age: The Formation of Gerontological Knowledge*. Charlottesville: University Press of Virginia.

_____. 2005. *Cultural Aging: Life Course, Lifestyle, and Senior Worlds*. Ontario: Broadview Press.

Kertzner, Robert, Ilan Meyer and Curtis Dolezal. 2003. "Psychological Well-Being in Midlife and Older Gay Men." In *Gay and Lesbian Aging: Research and Future Directions*. Edited by Gilbert H. Herdt and B. De Vries. New York: Springer.

Kessler-Harris, Alice. 2001. *In Pursuit of Equity*. New York: Oxford University Press.

Kimel v. Florida Board of Regents. Wikipedia, the free encyclopedia. http://en.wikipedia.org/wiki/Kimel_v_Florida_Board_of_Regents (accessed: January 17, 2008)

Kirby, Vicki. 2011. *Quantum Anthropologies: Life at Large*. Durham: Duke University Press.

Kivnick, Helen Q. 2010. "Dancing Vital Involvement: A Creative Old Age." *Journal of Aging, Humanities, and the Arts* 4, no. 4 (October-December): 421–430.

Bibliography

LeGoff, Jacques. 1992. *History and Memory.* Translated by Steven Randall and Elizabeth Chaman. New York: Columbia University Press.
Leibing, Annette. 2006. "Divided Gazes." In *Thinking About Dementia.* Edited by Annette Leibing and Lawrence Cohen. New Jersey: Rutgers University Press.
Lyotard, Jean-François. 1993. "Prescription." In *Toward the Postmodern.* London: Humanities Press.
Makus, Anne. 1990. "Stuart Hall's Theory of Ideology: A Frame for Rhetorical Criticism." *Western Journal of Communication* 54, no. 4: 495–514.
Mangum, Teresa. 1999. "Little Women." In *Figuring Age.* Edited by Kathleen M. Woodward. Bloominton: Indiana University Press.
Marshall, Barbara, and Stephen Katz. 2005. "Forever Functional: Sexual Fitness and the Aging Male Body." In *Cultural Aging: Life Course, Lifestyle, and Senior Worlds.* Ontario: Broadview Press.
_____ and _____. 2006. "From Androgyny to Androgens." In *Age Matters.* Edited by Toni M. Calasanti and Kathleen F. Slevin. New York: Routledge.
McLean, Athena Helen. 2006. "Coherence Without Facticity in Dementia." In *Thinking About Dementia.* Edited by Annette Leibing and Lawrence Cohen. New Jersey: Rutgers University Press.
Meadows, Robert and Kate Davidson. 2006. "Maintaining Manliness in Later Life." In In *Age Matters.* Edited by Toni M. Calasanti and Kathleen F. Slevin. New York: Routledge.
Meigs, Mary. 1991. *In the Company of Strangers.* Vancouver: Talonbooks.
Mellencamp, Patricia. 1999. "From Anxiety to Equanimity: Crisis and Generational Continuity on TV, at the Moves, in Life, in Death." In *Figuring Age.* Edited by Kathleen M. Woodward. Bloomington: Indiana University Press.
Merleau-Ponty, Maurice. 1968. *The Visible and the Invisible.* Evanston, IL: Northwestern University Press.
Mitchell, Timothy. 2002. *Rule of Experts: Egypt, Techno-Politics, Modernity.* Berkeley: University of California Press.
Mueller, Gabriele. 2009. "The Aged Traveler: Cinematic Representations of Post-Retirement Masculinity." In *Narratives of Life: Mediating Age.* Edited by Heike Hartung and Roberta Maierhofer. New Brunswick: Transaction Publishers.
Mullins, Amy. 2010. "The Opportunity of Adversity." *Talks/TED Partner Series.* Accessed January 2, 2012. http://www.ted.com/talks/aimee_mullins_the_opportunity_of_adversity.html
Nelson, Hilde Lindemann. 1999. "Stories of My Old Age." In *Mother Time.* Edited by Margaret Urban Walker. Lanham: Rowman & Littlefield.
Nelson, James Lindemann. 1999. "Death's Gender." In *Mother Time.* Edited by Margaret Urban Walker. Lanham: Rowman & Littlefield.
Nelson, Todd. 2005. "Ageism: Prejudice Against Our Feared Future Self." *Journal of Social Issues* 61, no. 2 (June): 207–221.
Noe, Alva. 2009a. *Out of Our Heads: Why You Are not Your Brain, and Other Lessons from the Biology of Consciousness.* New York: Hill and Wang.
_____. 2009b. "Back Talk." Interview by Christine Smallwood. *The Nation*, 16 March, 29.
_____. 2009c. "You Are Not Your Brain: Interview With Alva Noe, PhD." By Deepak Chopra. Sirius XM Radio, 25 April.

Bibliography

Nussbaum, Martha C. 2002. "Women's Capabilities and Social Justice." In *Gender Justice, Development, and Rights*. Edited by Maxine Molyneux and Shahra Razavi. New York: Oxford University Press.

_____. 2010. "Representative Women." *The Nation*, 25 October, 27–31.

_____, and Amartya Sen, eds. 1993. *The Quality of Life*. Oxford: Oxford University Press.

O'Grady, Helen. 2004. "An Ethics of the Self." In *Feminism and the Final Foucault*. Edited by Dianna Taylor and Karen Vintges. Chicago: University of Illinois Press.

Overall, Christine. 2006. "Old age and Ageism, Impairment and Ableism: Exploring the Conceptual and Material Connections." *National Women's Studies Association Journal* 18, no. 1:126–137.

Parisi, Luciana and Steve Goodman. 2011. "Mnemonic Control." In *Beyond Biopolitics: Essays on the Government of Life and Death*. Edited by Patricia Ticineto Clough and Craig Willse. Durham: Duke University Press.

Perlstein, Susan. 2010. "A Visionary Investigation and Dynamic Exchange between Science and Artistic Practice." *Journal of Aging, Humanities, and the Arts* 4, no. 4 (October-December): 251–261.

Pisters, Patricia. 2003. *The Matrix of Visual Culture*. Stanford: Stanford University Press.

Pixar Short. *George and AJ*. You Tube Accessed 2/27/11.

Poster, Mark, ed. 1988. *Jean Baudrillard: Selected Writings*. Stanford: Stanford University Press.

Powell, Jason L. 2006. *Social Theory and Aging*. Lanham: Rowman & Littlefield.

Prado, C. G. 1986. *Rethinking How We Age*. Westport, CT: Greenwood Press.

Puar, Jasbir. 2011. "The Turban Is Not a Hat." In *Beyond Biopolitics: Essays on the Governance of Life and Death*. Edited by Patricia Ticineto Clough and Craig Willse. Durham: Duke University Press.

Rand, Barry A. 2010. "We Champion 50+ Workers." *AARP The Magazine*, September, 30.

Ray, Ruth E. 2008. *Endnotes: An Intimate Look at the End of Life*. New York: Columbia University Press.

Reynolds, Gretchen. 2011. "Super Athletes." *AARP The Magazine*, March-April: 48–50, 80–82.

Rodowick, D. N. 1997. *Gilles Deleuze's Time Machine*. Durham: Duke University Press.

Rose, Nikolas. 1999. *Powers of Freedom*. Cambridge: University of Cambridge Press.

_____. 2007. *The Politics of Life Itself*. Princeton: Princeton University Press.

Sacks, Oliver. 1996. "Island of the Colour-Blind." Sydney: Picador.

Schacter, Daniel. 2002. *The Seven Sins of Memory: How the Mind Forgets and Remembers*. New York: Houghton Mifflin.

Schonpflug, Karin. 2008. *Feminism, Economics and Utopia*. New York: Routledge.

Scott, A. O. 2005. "Where the Wild Things Are: The Miyazaki Menagerie." *The New York Times*. 12 June.

Scott, Joan W. 2003. "Deconstructing Equality-Versus Difference." In *The Feminist Theory Reader*. Edited by Carole R. McCann and Seung-Kyung Kim. New York: Routledge.

Sharot, Tali. 2011. "The Optimism Bias." *Time*, 6 June, 40–46.

Sharples, Tiffany. 2009. "Can Language Skills Ward Off Alzheimer's?" *Time*, 9 July.

Shildrick, Margrit. 2002. *Embodying the Monster*. Thousand Oaks: Sage Publications.

Shulman, Alix Kates. 2008. *To Love What Is*. New York: Farrar, Straus and Giroux.

Bibliography

Small, Helen. 2007. *The Long Life*. New York: Oxford University Press.
Smethurst, Paul. 2000. *The Postmodern Chronotype: Reading Space and Time in Contemporary Fiction*. Atlanta: Rodopi.
Smith, Paul. 1995. "Eastwood Bound." In *Constructing Masculinity*. Edited by Maurice Berger, Brian Wallis, et al. New York: Routledge.
Swinnen, Aagje. 2009a. "'One Nice Thing About Getting Old Is That Nothing Frightens You': From Page to Screen: Rethinking Women's Old Age in Howl's Moving Castle." In *Narratives of Life: Mediating Age*. Edited by Heike Hartung and Roberta Maierhofer. New Brunswick: Transaction.
_____. 2009b. "The Orchard Walls are High ... and the Place Death." Paper read at meeting on Aging and Film, 29 October, at the University of New Mexico, Albuquerque, New Mexico.
_____. 2012a. "*Benidorm Bastards*, or the Do's and Don't's of Aging." In *Aging, Performance, and Stardom: Doing Age on the Stage of Consumerist Culture*. Edited by Aagje Swinnen and John A. Stotesbury. Zurich: Lit Verlag.
_____. 2012b. "To Pin Up or Pin Down Women of Age? The Representation of Aging Women's Bodies in the Photographs of Erwin Olaf." In *Aging, Performance, and Stardom: Doing Age on the Stage of Consumerist Culture*. Edited by Aagje Swinnen and John A. Stotesbury. Zurich: Lit Verlag.
Taylor, Charles. 1994. "The Politics of Recognition" In *Multiculturalism: Examining the Politics of Recognition*. Edited by Charles Taylor and Amy Gutmann. Princeton: Princeton University Press.
Van Fraassen, Bastiaan. 1991. "Time in Physical and Narrative Structure." In *Chronotypes: the Construction of Time*. Edited by John B. Bender, and David E. Wellbery. Stanford: Stanford University Press.
Walker, Barbara. 1985. *The Crone: Women of Age, Wisdom, and Power*. San Francisco: Harper and Row.
Walker, Margaret Urban. 1999. "Getting Out of Line." In *Mother Time*. Edited by Margaret Urban Walker. Lanham: Rowman & Littlefield Publishers.
Wilson, Elizabeth. 2004. *Psychosomatic*. Durham: Duke University Press.
Wolf, Naomi. 1991. *The Beauty Myth*. Toronto: Vintage Books.
Woodward, Kathleen. 1991. *Aging and Its Discontents: Freud and Other Fictions*. Bloomington: Indiana University Press.
_____. 1999. Introduction to *Figuring Age*, edited by Kathleen Woodward. Bloomington: Indiana University Press.
Young, Iris Marion. 1990. *Justice and the Politics of Difference*. Princeton: Princeton University Press.
Zimbardo, Philip. 2011. "'Evil Scientist' Wants to Teach People to Do Good." Interview with Amy Standen. NPR Morning Edition, 4 July.

Filmography

Away from Her. 2007. Produced by Daniel Iron, Simone Urdl, and Jennifer Weiss. Directed by Sarah Polley. The Film Farm/Foundry Films/Pulling Focus Pictures Inc.
Beginners. 2010. Produced by Leslie Urdang and Laris Knudsen. Directed by Mike Mills. Olympus Pictures/Focus Features.

Bibliography

The Best Exotic Marigold Hotel. Produced by Graham Broadbent and Peter Czernin. Directed by John Madden. Fox Searchlight.
Calendar Girls. 2003. Produced by Mick Barton. Directed by Nigel Cole. Buena Vista International and Touchstone Pictures.
The Forgetting: A Portrait of Alzheimer's. 2003. Produced and directed by Elizabeth Arledge. Twin Cities Public Television.
Gran Torino. 2009. Produced and directed by Clint Eastwood. Warner Bros. Pictures.
Howl's Moving Castle. 2004. Produced by Toshio Suzuki. Directed by Hayao Miyazaki. Studio Ghibli.
Iris. 2001. Produced by Robert Fox and Scott Rudin. Directed by Richard Eyre. Miramar Films.
The Mother. 2003. Produced by Kevin Loader. Directed by Roger Michell. Sony Pictures Classics.
Saving Grace. 2000. Produced by Mark Crowdy. Directed by Nigel Cole. Fine Line Features.
Something's Gotta Give. 2003. Produced and directed by Nancy Meyers. Columbia Pictures.
Still Doing It. Produced by Jan Rofekamp and Diana Holtzberg. Directed by Diedre Fishel. New Day Films.
The Straight Story. 1999. Produced by Mary Sweeney. Directed by David Lynch. Alliance Films.
Strangers in Good Company. 1990. Produced by David Wilson. Directed by Cynthia Scott. The National Film Board of Canada.
Up. 2009. Produced by Jonas Rivera. Directed by Pete Docter. Walt Disney Pictures.
Wellkamm to Verona. 2005. Produced by Thomas Lydholm and Ulf Ahlberg. Directed by Suzanne Osten. Metronome Productions.
The World's Fastest Indian. 2005. Produced by Roger Donaldson and Gary Hannam. Directed by Roger Donaldson.

Index

About Schmidt 63, 68
Achenbaum, Andrew 48
Activities of Daily Living (ADL) 35, 187*ch*1*n*4
activity theory 23
affect 110–11, 120, 129
Agamben, Giorgio 153
age: as becoming 2, 8–9, 12, 49, 113, 159, 162, 169, 170, 181, 182, 183–186; chronological 12, 27, 34, 38, 59, 79, 97, 182; definition 11; discrimination 24, 42, 55, 89, 118; relations 24, 40; as sliding 179, 183; undisciplining 34
Age Discrimination in Employment Act 24
agential realism 31–32, 34, 165
aging: abnormal or pathological 132, 136, 138–139, 140, 141, 144, 151; normal 26, 136, 138, 139; productive 30–31, 179; stereotypes 5, 6, 19, 20, 37, 59, 62, 65, 68, 69, 91, 92, 98, 101, 107, 108, 118, 120, 124, 125, 132, 133, 134, 135, 136, 158, 185; successful 30–31, 63
Alcoff, Linda 89
Al-Khalili, Jim 31, 187*ch*1*n*3
almshouse 50–51
Alzheimer, Alois 136, 140, 144
Alzheimer's disease 8, 13, 131–157, 190*n*1; *see also* dementia; senility
ambiguity 1, 4, 8, 13–14, 20, 32, 34, 62, 103, 121, 132, 149, 158, 174–175, 181
andropause 100, 189*n*2
anti-aging 82, 84
Aristotle 22–23, 72–73, 136
articulation 17
atavism 151
Aurora Borealis 133
Away from Her 8, 13, 133, 134, 144–148

Bahktin, Makhail 179–180
Ballenger, Jesse 132, 135, 137, 138, 139

Barad, Karen 31–32, 33–34, 163, 165, 167, 168, 169, 174, 175, 183, 185
Barber, Stephen M. 80
Bartalos, Michael 58
Basting, Anne Davis 15, 123, 134, 138, 140, 144, 145, 146, 147, 148, 152, 156
Baudrillard, Jean 82
Beard, George Miller 42, 135
Beauvoir, Simone de 48–49, 187*ch*2*n*3
Beginners 7, 13, 116–121, 125, 126, 127
Bender, John 179, 180
Bergson, Henri 174
The Best Exotic Marigold Hotel 7, 121–126, 128
Bettelheim, Bruno 87, 90; *see also* fairy tale
binary 72, 88–89, 92, 151, 162, 165, 175, 182; normal/pathological 135–139
Binstock, Robert 29
biomedicalization 23, 30, 150, 152, 153, 154, 164, 172, 176, 182
Blando, John 118
Blethyn, Brenda 69, 189*n*9
Blum, Harold 107
Bohr, Niels 32, 192*n*7
Bordo, Susan 80
Bourdieu, Pierre 16
brain 168; brainset 141–142; scan 8, 140–143, 144, 148, 153; type 140, 142, 143
Brennan, Teresa 164, 191*n*2
Brooks, David 60
Butler, Judith 15, 42, 88, 89, 117–118, 147
Butler, Robert 10, 34, 39, 138
Bytheway, Bill 12, 21, 27, 38–39, 57

Calasanti, Toni 16, 31, 35, 40, 52, 127
Calendar Girls 6, 13, 69–93, 189*n*8
capabilities approach 75, 90
caregiving 61, 71, 74, 117, 152, 153; commonality 151–154; person-centered 8, 152, 153, 154; as reciprocity 61, 154

201

Index

Carson, Diane 69, 90–91
Cartesian *see* Descartes
category 25, 27, 28–29, 33–34, 36, 38–40, 89–90, 97, 107, 111, 112, 132, 141, 150, 155, 157, 182, 183
Charcot, Jean-Martin 84, 135–136, 138
Chomsky, Noam 24–25
chronotope 179–180
chronotype 180, 181, 182, 183–184
citizenship: economic 74, 117; sexual 117
Clarke, Laura Hurd 67, 79, 80, 82, 86
climacteric 99, 100, 135, 136
Clough, Patricia 111
Cohen, Gene 48, 77
Cohen, Lawrence 131, 132, 134, 135, 136, 137, 138, 139, 144, 156–157
Cohen-Shalev, Amir 98, 104, 119, 120, 126, 128
Cole, Thomas 19, 42, 44, 50
Comfort, Alex 39–40
Connids, Ingrid 83, 95, 129
consciousness 27, 62, 126, 133, 156, 168, 174, 191n3; camera 161, 162, 163
counterstory 5, 6, 54–56, 57, 58, 61, 62, 64, 67, 91, 121, 153
creativity 6, 13, 34, 48, 50, 85, 118, 124, 158, 164, 166, 170, 172, 173
crone 178
Cruikshank, Margaret 20, 29–30, 38, 41, 44, 60, 65, 67, 71, 73, 119, 123, 173
cumulative advantage/disadvantage approach (CAD) 31, 187ch1n2

Darwin, Charles 174
Davidson, Kate 59, 60, 98
death 57–58, 65, 69, 175, 185; by invisibility 67
decoherence 185
Deleuze, Gilles 160–169, 173, 174, 176, 181, 186
dementia 8, 13, 129, 136, 137, 138, 139, 140, 148, 153, 154, 156, 157; *see also* Alzheimer's disease; senility
Dench, Judi 124
depression 57
Derrida, Jacques 25, 56–57, 147, 150, 151, 190ch5n6
Descartes 27, 163, 164, 169
Deter, Auguste 136, 140
De Vries, Brian 117, 118
disability 173
discourse 12–13, 17–18, 25, 100, 107, 159, 180; of sexual dysfunction 83, 101; of split subject 81

disengagement theory 23
Dittmar, Linda 66
Do You Remember Love? 155
Docter, Pete 39–40, 66
dualism 19, 139; *see also* binary
Dumit, Joseph 140, 141, 142, 143

Eastwood, Clint 40, 52, 53
economics 6, 9, 40, 51, 52, 58, 67, 70–76, 91, 123, 188n3
economy of touch 112–115, 120; *see also* frame
encore 48
Enlightenment 26, 72
entanglement 10, 31–33, 35, 36, 171, 174, 175, 185
Erikson, Erik 44, 45, 48, 107, 187ch2n1, 188ch2n5
Erikson, Joan 44, 45
essentialism 4, 5, 21–24, 36, 158, 165; *see also* strategic essentialism

fairy tale 68, 87–90, 158, 178
femininity 69, 79, 103; emphasized 98, 102
Finding Nemo 156
Fiore, Robin 61
firewall 55, 56, 61, 62
forgetting 147, 156
The Forgetting 8, 133, 134–139, 140, 145, 152, 155
Foucault, Michel 17, 20, 24–25, 35, 43, 46, 47, 55, 76, 80, 99, 101, 111, 148, 187ch2n2
frame 7, 73, 74, 89, 90, 107, 108, 109–113, 121, 129; haptic 112; tactile 112, 113, 114; visual 110, 112, 113
Freud, Sigmund 91–92, 107
Friedan, Betty 34
Frueh, Joanna 66, 83
functionalist theory 23

Gard, Robert 139
Gatens, Moira 72
gaze: of the camera 110; disembodied 112; of others 30; of youth 79
gendered imagination 72
generativity 60, 114, 115, 124, 188ch2n5
"George and AJ" 46–47
geriatrics 43, 84, 136
gerontology 7, 25–26, 42, 43, 83, 132, 137; critical 4–5, 27; feminist 34–35; narrative 34–35; spatial 122–123
Get Low 63, 68
Gilligan, Carol 61

202

Index

Goodman, Steve 175
Graham, Janice E. 122, 158, 172, 173, 183, 184
Gran Torino 5, 13, 37–64, 172
Grandma Alice 3, 10
Grosz, Elizabeth 22, 80–81, 90, 159, 166, 167, 168, 174, 175, 181, 184, 186
Groundhog Day 156
Gullette, Margaret 18, 23, 34, 48, 49, 55, 57, 79, 82, 83, 96, 103, 104, 128

habitus 16
Hacking, Ian 27–30, 49, 79, 111, 132, 137, 141, 142
Hall, Stuart 14, 17, 126
Haraway, Donna 32, 33, 110, 112, 151
Harold and Maude 184
Harrell, Eben 154
Heidigger 25
Herdt, Gilbert 117, 118
hierarchy 16
Hmong 45–46, 47, 54, 56
Hochman, David 40, 52
Holstein, Martha 71, 75
Howl's Moving Castle 8–9, 13, 159, 177–183
Hume, David 31

identity 9, 16, 26, 27, 38, 39, 40, 44, 54, 55, 58, 79, 92, 94, 99, 101, 116, 118, 120, 154, 156, 161, 162, 164, 165, 166; categories 14, 17, 36
image of time: direct 165–168, 169, 170, 173; indirect 162–165, 169
images, virtual and actual 162, 167, 170, 173, 176, 183
immanent tradition 165, 166
Imrie, Celia 125
indeterminacy 32
Innocence 68
interactive kinds 28
intra-action 9, 32, 33, 169; *see also* Barad, Karen
Irigaray, Luce 113
Iris 8, 13, 133, 139–144, 152
The Iron Lady 129

Jacoby, Susan 71–72, 77, 102

Kahalios, Jim 181
Kaplan, Ann 106, 107, 108, 110, 112, 114, 115, 128
Katz, Stephen 18, 19, 20, 21, 25–26, 30, 34, 35, 36, 42, 43–44, 50–51, 84, 97, 99 100, 101, 103–104, 122, 123, 135, 136

Keaton, Diane 103
Kessler-Harris, Alice 72–75, 88
Kiecolt, Jill 127
Kimel vs. Florida Board of Regents 23–24
King, Pearl 107–108
Kirby, Vicky 182, 183
Kivnick, Helen 49–50
knowledge, disciplinary 25, 35, 42; *see also* Foucault, Michel
Kraepelin, Emil 136–137, 144

Lacan, Jacques 163, 164, 165
Ladies in Lavender 129
Le Goff, Jacques 146
Le Guin, Ursula 178
Leibing, Annette 138, 152, 153, 154
Levy, Becca 29, 59, 185, 187*ch1n1*
life course 10, 12, 18, 19–20, 27, 48–49, 50–54, 79, 180, 181
life, embodied 32, 99, 110, 178; boundaries 9, 15, 20, 32, 33–34, 84, 112, 151, 174–175
liminality 151–152
linearity 9, 11, 12, 23, 27, 34, 35, 149, 150, 151, 163, 164, 165, 175, 190*ch5n6*; *see also* non-linearity
logocentrism 150–151
looping effect 29, 44, 141; *see also* Hacking, Ian
Lyotard, Jean-François 113

MacIntyre, Alsadair 145, 154
magic 160, 169, 170, 177
Make Way for Tomorrow 70–71
Makus, Anne 14, 17, 18
Mangum, Teresa 87
manliness 59
mapping 12, 17, 26, 50–54, 140; *see also* Mitchell, Timothy
masculinity 37–64; alternative 59; hegemonic 59, 61, 98, 104, 126, 172
matter 9, 22, 32, 33, 161, 165, 167, 168, 169, 171, 173, 174–177, 180, 181, 183, 185–186, 191*n6*
McLean, Athena Helen 153–154
Meadows, Robert 59, 60, 98
meanings, shared 14–15, 62, 98, 133
medicalization *see* biomedicalization
Medicare 29
Mellencamp, Patricia 92, 93
Memento 156
memory 144–148, 150, 153, 155, 170, 175; loss of 144, 156–157, 167
Merleau-Ponty, Maurice 113

203

Index

metamaterials 181
Metchnikoff, Ellie 136
Miegs, Mary 11, 159, 160, 169, 170
Mirren, Helen 69, 80, 189n9
Mitchell, Timothy 51–52
A Month by the Lake 129
morality 19, 61, 99, 112–115
The Mother 7, 105–116, 125, 126, 128
Mueller, Gabrielle 52–53
Mullins, Aimee 173, 175
myth 13, 18, 19, 20, 62, 68, 82, 92, 120, 159

narrative 3, 18–21, 30, 126, 145, 154, 159; of decline 13, 20, 23, 33–34, 36, 37, 41, 54, 60–61, 63, 98, 104, 134, 163, 164, 172, 176, 184; of progress 6, 18, 19, 35, 48–49, 135; turn 153–154
Nascher, Leo 136, 138
National Institute on Aging (NIA) 138
Nelson, Hilde Lindemann 54–56
Nelson, James Lindemann 76
Nelson, Todd D. 40
Nevelson, Louise 85
Newton, Isaac 163, 164, 169, 180
Nietzsche, Friedrich 25
Nighy, Bill 124
Noe, Alva 33, 168, 185, 191n3
non-linearity 147, 162, 166, 169, 179, 180, 181, 185
normal 15–16, 18, 21, 25, 43, 55, 57, 73, 85, 132, 134, 140–142, 144; *see also* aging, normal
The Notebook 133, 155
Nussbaum, Martha 15–16, 75, 77, 87

O'Grady, Helen 81, 90
Olaf, Erwin 114
Osler, William 41
outsourcing 123–124
Overall, Christine 26–27

Parisi, Luciana 175
passionate scholarship 35
performance 31; age as 9, 10, 15–16, 182
performativity, gender 15, 35, 147
Perlstein, Susan 49
personhood 10, 18, 36, 40, 117–118, 132, 134, 152, 155, 158; wars 154
Pickup, Ronald 125
Pisters, Patricia 161, 162, 163, 165, 166, 167
Pittsburgh compound 140
plane of immanence 168, 191n1
Plato 22, 28, 148

Plummer, Christopher 118
political economy of old age 27
positron emission tomography (PET) 141, 142; *see also* brain scan
poverty in old age 71–72, 83, 123, 128, 176
Powell, Jason 23, 27, 30, 34
Prado, C.G. 126
prejudice 38, 39, 40, 44, 45, 92
progress narrative *see* narrative, progress
prosthetic 9, 146, 174–175, 176
Protagoras 24
psychoanalysis 107–108
Puar, Jasbir 110–111, 112

quantum theory 31, 32, 185, 191n6; quantum world 182

Ralph 3–4, 10
rationality 8, 24, 33, 36, 136
Ray, Ruth 35
the real 149
reason 72, 134, 157
Red 63
representationalism 162–165, 166
retirement 5, 42, 44, 46, 47, 50–54, 57, 58, 73, 107, 121, 123, 134
Reynolds, Gretchen 60, 61
rhizomatics *see* immanent tradition
road movie 52–53
Rodowick, D.N. 158, 161, 163, 164, 165, 166, 167, 168, 169
Romeo and Juliet 149–150
Rose, Nikolas 30, 84, 143
Rosselon, Rina 67–68, 188n1
Russ, Joanna 76

Sacks, Oliver 151
Sartre, Jean-Paul 48–50, 54, 64
The Savages 133, 155
Saving Grace 6, 13, 69–93
Schacter, Daniel 147
Schonpflug, Karin 76–77
science fiction 76–77, 169, 171, 177
Scott, A.O. 178
Scott, Joan W. 15
Secondhand Lions 63
sedimentation 16, 42; *see also* Butler, Judith
self 48, 81, 145, 147–151, 154, 155, 156–157, 158, 161; split self *see* split subject
semiotic subject 150
Sen, Amartya 75
senescam 154
senescence 17–18, 41, 100

Index

senility 132, 134–135, 136, 137, 138; *see also* Alzheimer's disease; dementia
seriatim selves 76
service role 60, 62
sex 7, 79, 83, 86, 94, 95, 99–105, 106, 114, 115, 125, 127, 128, 129
sexual orientation 116–121, 125, 126, 184, 190*ch*4*n*5
sexuality 7, 35, 79, 83, 84, 97, 99–102, 106, 109, 111, 118, 121, 127–129, 188*ch*3*n*5
Sharot, Tali 76
Sharples, Tiffany 142
Shenk, David 134
Shildrick, Margrit 112, 113, 152
Shulman, Alix Kates 151
"Un Siècle" 34
Simmons, Leo 137
Slevin, Kathleen 16, 31, 35, 40, 52
Small, Helen 23, 145, 156
Smethurst, Paul 181
Smith, Maggie 123
Smith, Paul 53–54
social construction 4, 5, 24–27, 158; and essentialism 27–36
social inertia 163–164
Social Security 29, 51, 71, 73, 189*n*7
Something's Gotta Give 7, 13, 95, 96–105, 125, 126, 128
split subject 80–81, 88–90, 92, 103, 113
stages of life 18, 43–44, 51–52, 163; *see also* Erikson, Erik
Stephenson, Peter H. 122, 172, 173, 183, 184
stigma 132–134
Still Doing It 7, 94, 95, 103, 105, 115, 116–117, 124, 125, 126, 128
The Straight Story 8–9, 13, 158, 171–175, 176, 183, 184
Strangers in Good Company 8–9, 13, 158, 159–170, 171, 173, 176, 177, 183, 184, 191*n*4
strategic essentialism 52, 187–188, 187*ch*2*n*4
success 173

suicide 57–58
Sunset Story 155–156
Swinnen, Aagje 95, 114, 150, 153, 178, 179, 182

Taylor, Charles 153
time 9, 158, 160–170, 173, 174, 179–181, 182, 183; nonlinear 166, 175, 179, 181; relational theory 180–181
touch, economy of 105–115, 124
Trollope, Anthony 42

uglification industry 82–83
universe, metacinematic 161, 162
Up 5, 13, 37–64, 66, 172
utopia 75–78, 85–86, 91

validation 153, 191*n*7
Van Fraassen, Bastiaan 180, 192*n*8
Viagra 99, 100, 101, 125
La Vieillesse 48, 187*ch*2*n*3
vital involvement 49–50, 54
voice 66–67, 85, 134, 150–151, 154

Walker, Barbara 68–69, 90
Walker, Margaret Urban 52
Wellbery, David E. 179, 180
Wellkamm to Verona 8, 13, 133, 134, 148–151, 153, 155
Western culture 9, 18, 27, 36, 88, 105, 112, 122–123, 146, 150, 181, 182
Wilkinson, Tom 125
Willse, Craig 111
Wilson, Elizabeth 151
Wolf, Naomi 82–83
A Woman's Tale 119–120
Woodward, Kathleen 67, 84, 85, 92
The World's Fastest Indian 8–9, 13, 97, 159, 175–177, 183, 184

Young, Iris Marion 183
Young @ Heart 184

Zimbardo, Philip 92, 189*n*10

www.ingramcontent.com/pod-product-compliance
Lightning Source LLC
Chambersburg PA
CBHW032057300426
44116CB00007B/779